Social Theory

This textbook offers a new approach to understanding social theory. Framed around paired theoretical perspectives on a series of sociological problems, the book shows how distinctive viewpoints shed light on different facets of social phenomena. The book includes sociology's "founding fathers", major 20th-century thinkers and recent voices such as Butler and Žižek. Philosophically grounded and focused on interpretation and analysis, the book provides a clear understanding of theory's scope while developing students' skills in evaluating, applying and comparing theories.

Carsten Bagge Laustsen is Associate Professor at the Department of Political Science, Aarhus University.

Lars Thorup Larsen is Associate Professor at the Department of Political Science, Aarhus University.

Mathias Wullum Nielsen is a postdoctoral fellow at the Department of History, Stanford University.

Tine Ravn is a doctoral fellow at the Danish Centre for Studies in Research and Research Policy, Department of Political Science, Aarhus University.

Mads P. Sørensen is Senior Researcher at the Danish Centre for Studies in Research and Research Policy, Department of Political Science, Aarhus University.

"Students often experience social theory as intimidating. The braver ones sometimes question its point: why do we have to learn about Durkheim? This welcome new text should go some way towards answering that question, while also encouraging students to see theory as a 'necessary good' rather than an 'unnecessary evil'. Some of their teachers may also breathe a sigh of relief. An impressive achievement."

– Professor Emeritus Richard Jenkins,
University of Sheffield

Social Theory
A Textbook

Carsten Bagge Laustsen, Lars Thorup Larsen, Mathias Wullum Nielsen, Tine Ravn and Mads P. Sørensen

LONDON AND NEW YORK

First published 2017
by Routledge
2 Park Square, Milton Park, Abingdon, Oxon OX14 4RN

and by Routledge
711 Third Avenue, New York, NY 10017

Routledge is an imprint of the Taylor & Francis Group, an informa business

© 2017 Carsten Bagge Laustsen, Lars Thorup Larsen, Mathias Wullum Nielsen, Tine Ravn and Mads P. Sørensen

The right of Carsten Bagge Laustsen, Lars Thorup Larsen, Mathias Wullum Nielsen, Tine Ravn and Mads P. Sørensen to be identified as authors of this work has been asserted by them in accordance with sections 77 and 78 of the Copyright, Designs and Patents Act 1988.

All rights reserved. No part of this book may be reprinted or reproduced or utilised in any form or by any electronic, mechanical, or other means, now known or hereafter invented, including photocopying and recording, or in any information storage or retrieval system, without permission in writing from the publishers.

Trademark notice: Product or corporate names may be trademarks or registered trademarks, and are used only for identification and explanation without intent to infringe.

British Library Cataloguing-in-Publication Data
A catalogue record for this book is available from the British Library

Library of Congress Cataloging-in-Publication Data
A catalog record for this book has been requested

ISBN: 978-1-138-99994-7 (hbk)
ISBN: 978-1-138-99995-4 (pbk)
ISBN: 978-1-315-65799-8 (ebk)

Typeset in Times New Roman
by Apex CoVantage, LLC

Printed and bound by CPI Group (UK) Ltd, Croydon, CR0 4YY

Contents

Preface	*vii*
1 What is sociology?	1
2 Capitalism and alienation: Marx and Weber	14
3 Recognition and anomie: Durkheim and Honneth	35
4 Social interaction and marginalisation: Simmel and the Chicago School	54
5 Power and stratification: Foucault and Bourdieu	72
6 System and differentiation: Luhmann and Habermas	91
7 State and market: Althusser and Boltanski & Chiapello	108
8 Uncertainty and risk: Bauman and Beck	127
9 The reflective self: Goffman and Giddens	144
10 Family and work: Sennett and Hochschild	161
11 Gender, body and identity: Butler and Haraway	179

12 Factish and fetish: Latour and Žižek   **197**

13 Sociology as an analytic praxis   **220**

References   *246*
Index   *259*

Preface

"Sociology" comes from Latin and Greek; "socius", meaning confederate, and "logos", meaning thought or reason. Etymologically, sociology means something in the direction of reasonable thoughts about what is shared. French philosopher Auguste Comte (1798–1857) was the first to use the term in his establishment of a new discipline that would conduct scientific investigation of "the common". What was "reasonable" about sociology was how it distanced itself from the speculative or religious conceptions of the day; as such, the discipline did not take people's conceptions of the common at face value.

Sociology is a relatively young discipline, and its development in the 19th century should be understood in the context of a number of significant changes in society, all of which undermined the traditional and religious perceptions of the world. The first worth mentioning is the dramatic industrialisation, which accelerated in England in the 18th century and later spread to the European continent. Industrialisation led to urbanisation: People moved from country to town, abandoning the traditional forms of rural peasant life to become workers. A new class of workers emerged, which would later prove to have great political significance. The prelude to the class struggles was the French Revolution, which broke with the conceptions of the "natural" privileges of the upper class. All these changes challenged established forms of life and hierarchies and created an understanding that social conditions could be changed; that social conditions were created by mankind, not by God. This sensibility is also fundamental to sociology.

We have already hinted at the analytic strategy of sociology. Pointing out a number of structural conditions behind a given phenomenon – here, the emergence of sociology – is inherently "sociological". It was no coincidence that sociology emerged in the beginning of the 19th century, as a number of structural changes in society in this period made it possible to think in this manner. Generally speaking, sociology assumes that there is always something behind a given occurrence or phenomenon. An individual's actions, identity, understanding of the world, lifestyle, culture and so forth can be explained or understood with reference to something that is precisely not individual in nature but instead *societal*. In its most fundamental form, sociology is interested in the interpersonal – in that which emerges in the meeting between two or more individuals and in that which set the conditions for this meeting.

Sociology is a science informed by history. Many disciplines are interested in what lies behind or conditions action. However, sociology distinguishes itself from the natural sciences and parts of psychology in finding societal explanations rather than pointing out natural or individual explanations. One of the most important characteristics regarding the social dimension is that it consists of actions, relations and institutions that are all based on human activity and therefore could have been different. The social dimension sets conditions and defines underlying social strata, which can be reproduced or changed by our practices. The social dimension is changeable and must be studied as such.

This book introduces key theories in classic and contemporary sociology. Each chapter will be structured around a discussion between two (or more) sociological thinkers about a central theme in the sociological literature. It is our hope that these discussions will deepen the reader's understanding of what sociology is, and how its concepts and theories can help us understand the social world around us.

Chapter 1 introduces sociology as a particular way of viewing and analysing society; it discusses the status of sociology as a discipline; it briefly presents the difference between sociological theory, social theory and social diagnosis; and finally, it discusses whether the social is withering away.

Chapter 2 focuses on two of the greatest classics of the discipline, Karl Marx and Max Weber. The two theorists' oeuvres and core theories are introduced, and their different views on capitalism are examined: Marx's critique of political economy and Weber's descriptions of the relationship between capitalism and Calvinism.

With the key concepts of anomie and recognition as the starting point, Chapter 3 introduces Emile Durkheim's and Axel Honneth's different views on individualisation, morality and social cohesion. Their strands of thought are connected in a comparative discussion of the possible explanations and solutions to the prevalent experiences of inadequacy, malaise and loss of meaning that characterise many people's lives in contemporary society.

Chapter 4 brings together key sociological contributions from Georg Simmel and the Chicago School tradition. The chapter includes a discussion of the theorists' analyses of both negative and positive aspects of life in early modern societies characterized by increased urbanisation, industrialisation and immigration. With a specific view to the analytical duality of distance and closeness, Simmel's theories are compared to those of the Chicago school, in particular the writings of Robert Ezra Park.

After discussing some of the key consequences of modernity, Chapter 5 looks at the concept of power, particularly the execution of power between people and groups. After a general introduction to the sociological conceptualisation of power with focus on Michel Foucault's power analytics and how it differs from a conventional understanding, two aspects of Foucault's authorship are illuminated: his famous analysis of the Panopticon and the emergence of the disciplinary power and his theorising of biopolitics and sexuality. The chapter moves on to Pierre Bourdieu's theories of reproduction, symbolic violence and class. Finally, the two sociologists are compared in a discussion of the difference between a sociological focus on centre or margin.

Chapter 6 draws on two of German sociology's key contributions to social systems thinking, to clarify and discuss society's division into sectors, systems and spheres, or what is called functional differentiation: Niklas Luhmann's perception of societal systems as each other's surroundings as well as the condensation of communication within these through symbolically generalisable media, and Jürgen Habermas' criticism of systemic characteristics in the societal spheres, where communication should, in his opinion, be coordinated on the basis of a common life world.

Chapter 7 continues the discussion of the social system but adopts a more holistic perspective. The starting point is the claim that our society today is capitalistic in a basic sense, which gives rise to a number of questions, including: What is the relationship between state and market, and how are people motivated to work in an absurd system where others reap the profits of their work? These questions led Louis Althusser, Luc Boltanski and Ève Chiapello to reflect on the meaning of ideology in modern societies. Althusser develops a critical sociology and views ideology as repression, whereas Boltanski focuses on criticism as empirically occurring critical competences that can both challenge and consolidate capitalism.

Chapter 8 introduces two of the most prominent sociologists today, Zygmunt Bauman and Ulrich Beck, with focus on their diagnoses of our times. Bauman calls our age liquid modernity whereas Beck describes a paradigmatic shift from modernity to second modernity and introduces

preface

the idea of the risk society. The reappearance of insecurity is central to the diagnoses of both authors. Chapter 8 compares their conceptions of insecurity and risk and discusses how they inform their understanding of present modernity.

After this look at how society and its citizens cope with insecurity and risks, Chapter 9 examines how individuals relate to the same problem based on the theories of Erving Goffman and Anthony Giddens. Erving Goffman's sociology focuses on the microstrategies we use to create order in our interactions with other individuals. This concerns our attempts to control impressions, categorise the behaviour of others and present ourselves in certain ways. Anthony Giddens focuses on the conditions of self-formation; particularly on how individuals in late modernity are expected to create their own self without recourse to tradition and common practice. As the chapter shows, Giddens's analysis of self-formation also informs his conception of late modernity, which puts the sociological analysis of selfhood into a broader context.

With Arlie Hochschild's and Richard Sennett's sociological studies as the starting point, Chapter 10 examines the radical changes to work and family life in the wake of so-called flexible capitalism. In their respective writings, Hochschild and Sennett have tried to pinpoint the societal and individual consequences of the last 20–30 years' intensification and flexibilisation of work – both inside and outside the workplace. The chapter provides an introduction to the authors' different yet often complementary perspectives on these consequences, with a special focus on the implications for family life under flexible capitalism.

Chapter 11 brings together Judith Butler's and Donna Haraway's leading theories in gender research. The first part of the chapter presents Butler's postmodern, anti-essentialist theory of gender as a social construct and her view of gender as something "one does" rather than something "one is". This is followed by a presentation of Haraway's highly influential cyborg figuration and her theoretical notion of "situated knowledge". Finally, we juxtapose Butler's social constructivism with Haraway's transgression of it.

Feminist theory raises a fundamental question about the relationship between the objective, the body, and the subjective and actively created; our identity. Chapter 12 draws this question into a discussion of Bruno Latour's and Slavoj Žižek's sociologies. Latour's central claim is that a pure sociality does not exist and that our being is always mediated and shaped in the interplay with other actants, such as things. Žižek also claims that the social never exists in a pure form. We always meet social reality through a distorted view. Our world is coloured by the basic fantasies that control our observations and actions. In other words, the relationship between subjectivity and conscience on the one side and objectivity and materiality on the other will be the central discussion in this chapter.

The final chapter, Chapter 13, has two purposes. It focuses on a number of challenges for contemporary sociology and discusses what it means to analyse sociologically. As for the critical perspective, it focuses on the critique of the diagnostic trend in contemporary sociology and the danger of overinterpreting today's characteristics as signs of the coming of a new type of society. In addition, the critiques raised against sociology for reducing individuals to their social characteristics are discussed. As for the analytical perspective, Chapter 13 provides a list of basic suggestions for students on how to get started with their own sociological analyses. All students within the field of sociology will at some point face this challenge. But how is this done? Connecting insights from the preceding chapters with more general reflections on how to analyse sociologically, the final chapter provides practical examples of how to use sociological theories and concepts as prisms for gaining new insights on a given social phenomenon.

Finally, we hope that our readers will find this book an interesting read that enhances their curiosity, their sociological imagination and their analytic abilities. We also want to express our gratitude to those who have helped us process the manuscript. A special thanks to Helle Merete Haahr Bundgaard, Frederikke Kaal Laustsen, Lene Kamuk, Annette Andersen, Katherine Wetzel, Jon Jay Neufeld, Benjamin Dalton and Alyson Claffey. The book is a partial translation of a Danish book, *Sociologisk teori – en grundbog*.

Aarhus and Stanford, August 2016

Carsten Bagge Laustsen, Lars Thorup Larsen,
Mathias Wullum Nielsen, Tine Ravn and
Mads P. Sørensen

preface

chapter 1

What is sociology?

As with any other discipline, the subject and methods of sociology are disputed. What is sociology? What is it not? The typical answer is that the subject of sociology is "the social"; or, somewhat less tautologically, "society" and that its method consists of reducing phenomena to a societal root. Saying it in this manner might leave a bit of a bad taste in your mouth, but as sociologists we actually do believe that it is "society's fault". We will qualify this statement later; until then, allow this to serve as the point of departure for our identification of the social and sociology.

Whatever sociology does, it represents a departure from the notion of the autonomous and solipsistic individual. Basically, the social is that which exists between people, between individuals; that is, their interaction, communication and (moving up a level) the rules, roles, norms and values tying them together in communities of different types and sizes. In everyday speech, when we refer to humans as "social", we are saying something about how they are able to create relations to other human beings. And when we criticise others for being asocial, we are saying something about how they do not contribute to or participate in the community.

Humans are social individuals: not just *homo sapiens*, but also *homo socius*. If we do not have others with whom to speak or act in relation to, we go insane. It is natural for us to engage in interpersonal relations, communicate with one another and act together with others. When the communist regimes in Eastern Europe collapsed after the fall of the Berlin Wall in 1989, the world witnessed the horrific images of the understimulated

what is sociology?

children in Romanian orphanages who had spent most of their lives in a crib without intimacy and proper contact with others. Many of these children were ultimately given up for adoption, and a large number of them proved to have suffered serious injury. Or to draw on an example from the world of film, think of the *Robinson Crusoe*-like *Cast Away*, where Chuck Noland (played by Tom Hanks) is stranded on a deserted island together with a number of FedEx packages. One of the packages contains a Wilson volleyball. Chuck puts his dirty hand on it, creating a palm print that resembles a face. He gives the ball some hair, and suddenly Chuck has his "Friday" – unsurprisingly, he named him Wilson. Like Chuck, we all need a "Friday". This is so obvious that we practically need a trip to a deserted island to discover this to be so.

Often, our sociality is so ingrained and implicit that we do not even notice that the social is at stake. We are born into communities and in everything that thus follows; and we are therefore hardly able to imagine living in a different manner. Even when we try to imagine the zero point of our culture, as is the case with Robinson Crusoe-like tales such as the aforementioned *Cast Away*, the sociological sequence of numbers starts with the number 2. The story – at least the sociological – only begins when at minimum a twosome has been established. If we momentarily try to disregard the Romanian orphans, we might say that we are weaned on the social. Just as we hardly think about grammar on a daily basis and yet speak in grammatically correct sentences, "the social" becomes second nature. The social is something we draw upon but not necessarily something we reflect upon.

Sociology does not necessarily contradict our intuitive notions of community life; rather, it sharpens and enriches the knowledge we already possess. Sociology is therefore occasionally accused of producing platitudes. If only it was possible to juggle advanced formulae that demand years of education to understand! The knowledge produced by sociology may occasionally appear somewhat banal, but this only occurs when we become fully aware of that which we already "know". That said, as the professional observer of the social, sociology obviously also contributes with new insights; often in competition with lay knowledge.

In other words, we have an inclination to not think sociologically. For example, a central insight in the sociology of religions is that religion is socialised. The religious convictions of children usually follow those of their parents, the explanation being that they are raised in a certain religious tradition. But reducing religion to something learned means disregarding any talk of actual faith and revelation. It gets worse yet, of course, if you insist, like Karl Marx, that religion is the "opium of the people". This unmasking ambition necessarily means that sociology finds itself in conflict with a number of authorities and therefore occasionally in a bad light.

When we claim that the subject of sociology is "society", reference is being made to the existence of a supra-individual level. In the early years of sociology, reference was made to communities, but that concept quickly became too narrow. The term society is considerably more capacious, as it also makes it possible to conceive of the social as conflict. The aggregated level can then be fleshed out so as to be made up of institutions, organisations, groups, masses or even states – and of course, the relations between these entities. The series can almost be continued indefinitely, and considerable creativity has also been exercised in the attempts at conceptualising that which is "above" the individuals.

Especially in the early years of sociology, there has been a tendency to understand the social as something "soft" and therefore difficult to define, in contrast to more tangible phenomena. Sociology has therefore been more interested in informal control than formalised rules; in culturally given values rather than laws; in masses rather than associations; and in "gossip" rather than official "truths" or formal self-presentations. Sociology is constantly on the hunt after that which is neither said nor written anywhere but nevertheless is absolutely essential to making common life work.

But the societal is also "over" the individual in another sense. As mentioned, we are born into the social, which means that considerable limitations are placed on our actions. As French author Bernard Le Bovier de Fontenelle (1657–1757) wrote, the power of the dead is often greater than that of the living. When we as teachers step into the lecture hall, our behaviour is not only conditioned by the spatial framework but also by the expectations sticking to the conceptions about a university, ideas which are based on centuries of academic practice. When they meet in the courtroom, judges and lawyers are obligated to respect a lengthy number of institutional norms that they can hardly even budge. And finally, examples of less formalised institutions include something as simple as how you are supposed to act on a bus; you don't burp, you wear clothing, you don't stare at the other passengers, and you avoid physical contact. The social might well be some kind of "soft entity", but should you violate the codex for correct behaviour, you will experience sanctions. Just try getting naked on a bus and learn this the hard way.

Further along these lines, the contribution of sociology is to analyse or even construct this level "above" the individuals. In the field of sociology, there is talk of how the social has emerging properties; that is, properties that cannot be reduced to a lower or more fundamental level, usually to the level of the actions of individuals. Sociology distinguishes itself from many other disciplines by constructing its own object of study. The social is not readily observable in the same manner as literary

what is sociology?

works are for a student of literature or verdicts are for a lawyer. In Durkheim's work with the rules for social methods, he argues that sociology ought to analyse social facts (1938). In addition to emphasising how the social is something undeniable and solid, the intention behind this use of terms was that the social is something that cannot be reduced to the level of the individual and which sociology must therefore determine the existence of.

And finally, the third element – how sociology reduces individual behaviour to a societal or social root: Sociology is seeking that which lies behind a given phenomenon. What does it mean? As we will see in the following pages, it can mean very different things. At minimum, it means viewing the social or the societal as something that conditions the behaviour of the individual. To borrow a couple of terms from statistics, the individual is our dependent variable (that which is to be explained) and the independent variable (that which explains) is the social or society. One can focus on the conditions for individual action as being conditioned or perhaps actually something that unequivocally forces us to act in specific ways. Sociologists have attempted to establish regularities and laws, but many – in fact more – prefer to talk about probabilities or a complex network of conditioning factors.

This can be placed in the perspective of the so-called contract argument, which often serves as the basis of liberalism and which sociology fiercely opposes (see e.g. Mead 1977: 242). In the writings of political philosopher Thomas Hobbes, the contract argument is interpreted, when read from a liberal perspective, as the story of how individuals come together in a community. Weary of war, they realise that it would be better to surrender the use of weaponry to a state power which, in exchange, guarantees their security. The point of departure for this liberalistic reading is that the individuals and their interests are primary and that it is therefore necessary to understand the aggregated level – here, the state – as a product of a deliberate action; that is, an epiphenomenon.

Sociology turns this on its head. We cannot start with the individuals and then construct the relations, as in the form of a contract. It is the reverse. The relations, such as the role as citizen, come before the individual. The individual is not the *basis* of society but rather its *product*. Society is something into which we are born. Sociologists therefore start with society and analyse the extent to which society makes it possible for individuals to enter into relationships with one another – for example, as citizens.

We have now introduced three central metaphors. Sociology is occupied with what is "between", "over" and "behind" the individuals – with relations, social facts and that which can explain the individuals and their behaviour. Before we continue, let us mention the most renowned example in the history of ideas of a sociological explanation: Durkheim's analysis of suicide (1951). To begin with, one might believe that suicide is the most individual action of all – as it is about an existential choice. Durkheim does not contest that suicide is often understood as such by the unhappy souls who resort to it. His point is, however, that from a sociological perspective, suicide must be understood and analysed as a "social fact". Suicide is conditioned by a social framework and it is as such a patterned phenomenon that opens itself towards a sociological explanation. One can thus consider suicide both from the perspective of the individual and from an aggregated and supra-individual perspective, which is that of sociology. Sociology often understands our behaviour in an entirely different manner than we do; and it is not necessarily because we are mistaken but because it raises a number of entirely different questions than we (i.e. laymen) normally do.

Durkheim, in his study of suicide, found a number of differences that called for a sociological explanation. First, he found that Catholic countries had lower suicide rates than Protestant countries. The explanation was not religious dogma as Catholicism and Protestantism alike prohibit suicide. An obvious explanation was that Protestantism places the individual before God, whereas in Catholicism this relationship is mediated to a higher degree by a number of authorities, the priest being the most important. The key issue here was individualism versus collectivism in the form of the individual's degree of integration in a given community. Other results would appear to support this assumption. For example, unmarried persons have higher suicide rates than married persons; and suicide rates are inversely proportionate to the number of children a person has. Finally, Durkheim found that suicide rates decline in times of crisis, which could be explained by how communities are strengthened in such periods.

Durkheim used the degree of individualism and collectivism to explain what he referred to as *egoistic suicide*. Another form of suicide, *anomic suicide*, peaks in periods with weak moral regulation where individuals struggle to stay oriented. Finally, *altruistic suicide* is primarily observed in so-called traditional societies in which honour and prestige are central and where death is sometimes preferable to a life in shame or dishonour.

In Durkheim's analysis, we see our three metaphors in use. First, the social is about relations between individuals. Strong relations (as in Catholicism) mean fewer suicides than weak relations (as in Protestantism). If the social glue is strong, as in periods with strong moral values, there should be fewer suicides than in transition periods in which established societal values are under pressure. We also see clearly that Durkheim understands the social as an aggregate level. He made use of suicide

what is sociology?

statistics and knowledge about culture, religion and other macrophenomena. The social is thus above the individuals. Finally, Durkheim is not interested in people's own explanations but rather in the conditions in play behind the backs of the actors. That which is central is the culture (i.e. morals, religion) that they are born into and which conditions their actions.

Sociology as discipline

If we begin with the aforementioned description of what sociology is, one hardly finds a discipline within the social sciences that does not make use of a sociological method. In that sense, political science can be understood as a subgroup within the sociological field of investigation: as political sociology. Anthropology also makes widespread use of a sociological approach. And why not also the historical sciences? In our attempt to define sociology, we must emphasise that sociology is not merely defined by a subject and a method – our three metaphors only take us so far – but it is also shaped by theoreticians and debates. There is a "royal line" of theoreticians, the fathers of the discipline and everyone who relates to them and discusses the questions they raised can be said to practice sociology.

The easiest way to recognise a sociologist is, thus, that he or she makes frequent references to Marx, Weber or Durkheim; or to Bourdieu, Habermas or Foucault, to name some more recent sociologists. This fondness for the sociological classics can find release in journals and book series. As the Polish-British sociologist Zygmunt Bauman writes, it is simply possible to understand sociology as the books that are categorised in the library under the term "sociology" (Bauman and May 2014). In other words, sociology is a specific academic tradition, and that statement alone actually says a lot. Naturally, sociology can be conceptualised sociologically. The discipline is to be understood as a field in which battles are fought over what constitutes sociology. And the result – well, you can see that when you look at the sociology shelf. Some works and authors are categorised as sociology, others not.

Perhaps the most tangible definition of sociology is to identify the sociological as that which at any given point in time is carried out by those who are educated at a sociological department. A lawyer has studied the law; a doctor has studied medicine; and so on. However, the title "sociologist" is not restricted or protected (unlike the titles "doctor and "lawyer"). Moreover – and just as important – a considerable number of the great sociologists were not actually educated within the discipline. Philosophy, among other disciplines, has had a great impact on the development of sociological thinking. Again, we can attempt to forward a sociological explanation: Those employed at sociological departments and institutes attempt to take a patent on all things sociological. Like all others, they are fighting for their legitimacy and to show that they are able to do something that others can only achieve with great difficulty or not at all. Fortunately, they do not win every time.

A further difficulty is that sociology thrives among other academic traditions; for example, the sociology of religions is studied at faculties of theology, political sociologists can be found at departments of political science, and the sociology of law is studied at faculties of law. Finally, many researchers practice the sociological perspective as one among many.

The fourth definition is the most open and inclusive (and a trifle naïve): A sociologist is someone who wishes to contribute to a sociological milieu and to an academic discussion about issues pertaining to sociology. When we call it naïve, it is because those who are already established decide who is granted admission and who is kept out. Ideally, sociology will become a more open discipline over time and the establishment within the field more tolerant in their academic demarcations.

In the 1970s, sociology was practically the dominant discipline in some countries due to the status of Marxism, and sociologists delivered the hard-hitting arguments and enjoyed political attention. Later, it found itself in a somewhat more humble position in the social sciences, as economists took the spotlight. Throughout the 1990s, however, sociology again established itself in departments of sociology, among researchers and students, in textbooks and attracted renewed media attention.

As far as international differences, American sociology is often more empirical, whereas continental sociology is more theoretical. The great, canonised sociological theoreticians are thus almost all from the European continent. The postwar generation of sociologists is heavily influenced by the experiences with Nazism and the Holocaust, whereas the American-dominated consumer society and its consequences have a more central position among more recent theoreticians.

It makes sense to draw a distinction between what is often referred to as general social theory and so-called hyphenated sociology (*Bindestrich-Soziologie*). As the term indicates, social theory offers a more theoretical approach to the social, often characterised by general soundings with respect to the society in which we find ourselves. Many have surely heard terms such as risk society, knowledge society, the society of control and reflexive modernity. An important task for social theory is to critically discuss contemporary diagnoses such as these and attempt to provide a holistic characterisation of contemporary society and contrast this with social formations of the past. German sociologist and philosopher Theodor W. Adorno (1903–1969) claims that sociology is the only discipline with an eye for society as a whole – in its totality (2000: 110). Not everyone goes that far, but it is correct that social theory is very inclusive.

In order to be so inclusive, social theory must be relatively abstract and general, meaning that it often leans on other disciplines, such as philosophy. However, social theory is marked by far stronger empirical foundations. Philosophy is typically interested in whether or not arguments are good and logically rigorous; social theory is more about the applicability of concepts in a diagnosis of specific societies and social forms. Social theory is empirically grounded, although the empirical matter can vary, including examples, paradigmatic illustrations and the like. Hyphenated sociology is the term for all specialised disciplines ending with sociology. Here, sociological method is associated with a demarcated field, such as sociology of the law, family sociology, sociology of work or urban sociology. The empirical dimension is in focus, whereas the concepts often only function within the given field.

Allow us to conclude this rather institutional determination of what sociology is with the fact that sociology is not only an academic field. It is also present and active in society. Works of sociologists are read by politicians, administrators and laypersons. There is nothing virginal about the empirical material that sociologists get under their nails. Sociology offers interpretations of social phenomena; but these phenomena often already consist of interpretations. Just as when a person goes to a psychoanalyst and complains about Freudian or Lacanian symptoms, we are often faced by clients and citizens who speak as though they were social workers themselves; or interview persons who already are quite convinced of how this or that is "society's fault". Sociology is not merely an academic discipline. It offers knowledge that everyone, regardless of education or occupation, is able to acquire and act upon.

Sociology as diagnosis of the times

We have now attempted to identify sociology in two ways: by outlining the method and object of sociology and by outlining sociology as an institutionalised practice. In addition to account of sociology in terms of its substance and philosophy of science, we will now describe sociology as a science about the modern society. As stated in the preface, sociology was born in the emergence of modernity. In its early years, sociology was heavily accented by reflection on the extent to which modernity was undermining traditional ways of life. Allow us to dwell a bit on this particularly sociological approach.

As mentioned, a fundamental feature of sociological thought is that the field of study is not merely social processes, seen in isolation, but that concrete phenomena are also studied in relation to society as a whole. Even microsociological theories include a conception of society, although it is often implicit. Examples of how the form of society was identified are Karl Marx's characterisation of capitalistic society and Luhmann's notion of the functionally differentiated society. In addition to comprehensive theories about society's fundamental functionings, these terms are similarly marked by an element of a "diagnosis of the times" (*Zeitdiagnose*); that is, an attempt at articulating the predominant characteristics of the age and relating them to an earlier period.

In this context, it is worth mentioning Michel Foucault, whose concepts regarding power and knowledge we will return to in Chapter 5. In addition to his analysis of power, he formulated a concept regarding "the history of the present"; that is, a kind of writing of history whereby in order to understand the issues addressed in contemporary society one must relate historically to the formation of the concepts currently being questioned (Foucault 1969). When the state came under heavy attack towards the end of the 1970s for having violated the freedom of the individual, Foucault turned the question on its head, asking instead how it had ever come about that the state is regarded as a dynamo for leading society and questioning the background for understanding freedom as a societal problem (Foucault 2004; 2007).

In Foucault's eyes, diagnoses of the times do not represent a distinct sociological discipline. Such studies have been with us since the Enlightenment, when German philosopher Immanuel Kant suddenly stopped in the middle of an article he was writing to a newspaper and seized the opportunity to summarise contemporary changes. What is unique in this context is not so much the answer Kant arrives at in the text "What is Enlightenment?", but rather the very reflection that lies in the question as to what characterises the present and distinguishes it from a period in the past (Kant 2010; cf. Foucault 2008).

Diagnoses of the times do not necessarily aim at a representative description of a given society. They are more about capturing the new tendencies that are in the process of making themselves felt and have the potential to become dominant. In this connection, it is useful to dwell on the concept of diagnosis. The diagnosis concept is used in the medical sciences, among other places, where, on the background of one or more symptoms, it is about drawing conclusions regarding the existence of a given illness. Sociology does not necessarily focus exclusively on pathological phenomena to analyse states of social illness, but also to identify phenomena that are either regarded as typical of the age or possibly embryonic manifestations of future mass phenomena.

In the world of art, for example, the period from around 1880 to 1910 is often described as the impressionist period, even though many more

what is sociology?

paintings of deer in pastoral settings were produced in this period. It was not as though everyone was wearing tie-dyed clothing, getting in on free sex and smoking pot in 1968. The vast majority of people continued to live rather bourgeois lives. Nevertheless, it is the hippies who represent this period. And to provide a very current example, Danish sociologist Henning Bech (1999) claims that homosexuals constitute a kind of *avant-garde*, the incarnation of the *zeitgeist*, which Bech describes as a focus on pleasure and recreation. The phenomenon of the metrosexual male may be an indication that there is something to this claim.

Diagnoses of the times often become "hits", possibly because they capture a particular cultural tone that marks the age. An example is Ulrich Beck's renowned *Risk Society: Towards a New Modernity* (Beck 1992). It was published the same year as the Chernobyl nuclear disaster and thereby put a name on the fear of technology, which the accident suddenly rendered rather acute. Presumably, not even Beck would claim that everything in contemporary society is about risks; but rather that many sociological issues must be reconsidered in the light of the risk society.

Diagnoses of the times are thus about characterising a number of dominant features concerning the development characterising society at this very moment. Even if this development is only about a limited part of modern society, the analysis can be entirely relevant. At the same time, the diagnosis of the times must be carried out with a certain measure of self-criticism because it is a balancing act between prophecy and analysis.

Regardless of how many threads can be traced back through the history of ideas, there is general consensus that classic sociology was established in the 19th century. Before considering more concrete ideas drawn from classic sociology in the coming chapters, it is worth noting how its emergence relates to the formation of modern society. This process is notoriously difficult to pinpoint in time, as it stretches throughout the so-called long 19th century, spanning from the French Revolution in 1789 to the outbreak of the First World War in 1914. In other words, what we are referring to here as classic sociology largely consists of attempts at formulating a general theory about this society, its formation, and how it is distinguished from traditional society, which preceded it.

This classic fundamental theme about the transition from traditional to modern society is often referred to as "the social question". As the Danish historian of ideas and philosopher Lars-Henrik Schmidt writes, nobody can remember any more what traditional society was (Schmidt 1999b: 209). The point of this cryptic phrasing is not only that the transition is difficult to pinpoint in time on the grounds that this has obviously been a gradual process – which furthermore varies from place to place. Schmidt's message is, to the contrary, that it is experience with change – not the exact description of the two periods – that is the central aspect of the social question.

We find a classic formulation of the social question in *Manifesto of the Communist Party* (first published in 1848), where Karl Marx and Friedrich Engels characterised modern society as the place where "all that is solid melts into air, all that is holy is profaned" (Marx and Engels 1969). Modern society entails, in other words, a social revolution because traditional norms and values fall apart and are replaced by new ones.

Regardless of whether one subscribes to Marx and Engels' concrete analysis, it is important to be aware of the rhetorical figure in the social question. We observe how what was taken for granted in the past is now in the process of disintegration, after which we search for a new principle capable of uniting the separated parts. The experience from modernity was formulated by Marx and Engels in 1848 and was repeated throughout the history of social theory, not least in the formulation of a diagnosis of the times, as discussed earlier.

Finally, we will look at the perception of change as a societal phenomenon. In this period, people began to add the prefix "social-" or "societal" to a long range of phenomena as they for the first time started placing more isolated issues in connection with the form of society, such as conflicts between various groups of people.

> The rise of sociology can be better understood if it is borne in mind that social conflicts and disputes themselves underwent a peculiar depersonalisation during the period of industrialisation in the nineteenth and twentieth centuries. There was an increasing tendency for social disputes to be conducted not so much in the name of particular people as in the name of certain impersonal principles and articles of belief. This seems obvious to us, so we often do not realize how strange and unique it was when people in these centuries came to be fighting no longer in the name of ruling princes and their generals, nor in the name of religion, but chiefly in the name of fixed impersonal principles like "conservatism" and "communism", "socialism" and "capitalism".
>
> (Elias 1978: 62)

What is central to this quotation is not which specific "isms" Elias is referring to but rather the fact that conflicts as relations and processes are elevated to a higher level and reconsidered in relation to society.

After the social

Sociology is, then, the science of the social, which in general terms can be described as that which is found between, over and behind individuals. At the same time, sociology was born as a science about the modern society. As Elias touches upon in the preceding quotation, a comprehensive social development can be traced to the roots of the sociological perspective, as it requires that a vast array of issues are lifted out of their concrete, local contexts and are scrutinised on the societal level instead. The understanding of problems at the societal level also has a political dimension, as it makes it possible to deal with or solve the social problems and conflicts that sociology has traditionally described.

The following chapters address in greater detail how this classic perception was later challenged and portrayed in a more subtle manner in more recent sociology. Because the book as a whole is based on contemporary society, it is important to note here that the chapters on classic sociology do not merely have historical interest. The question regarding society and the social is still up for debate within and outside of the discipline of sociology, as illustrated by a couple of brief examples from the debate on the transition from the modern to the postmodern.

The perception of the social as a central focal point for both society and sociology has been criticised by, among others, French sociologist and philosopher Jean Baudrillard (1929–2007). In *À l'ombre des majorités silencieuses ou la fin du social (In the Shadow of the Silent Majorities: Or, the End of the Social and Other Essays)* from 1978 (Baudrillard 1982), he claims that social classes and other groupings have lost their integrative function and been replaced by the masses, who prefer the spectacular over the meaningful. Social theory has thus lost its purpose. The social has disappeared. This also means that the social can no longer serve as the centre for political mobilisation in the welfare state.

Although Baudrillard's claim is not widely accepted in sociology, there is little doubt that the concept regarding the social has been challenged in recent decades; also politically, in the form of neoliberal criticism of the welfare state. Merely consider former British Prime Minister Margaret Thatcher's harsh statement, "There is no such thing as society. There are individual men and women" (Thatcher 1987). This coupling between the political and changes in the social is also captured by Bauman, who describes it as being part of a so-called liquid modernity:

> Ours is, as a result, an individualized, privatized version of modernity, with the burden of pattern-weaving and the responsibility for failure falling primarily on the individual's shoulders. It is the patterns of dependency and interaction whose turn to be liquefied has now come.

They are now malleable to an extent unexperienced by and unimaginable for, past generations; but like all fluids they do not keep their shape for long.

(Bauman 2000: 7–8)

In this diagnosis of the times, Bauman claims that the shift towards considering problems on the societal level, as described earlier, has now come to an end. Social problems, as they are typically formulated and worked with within the framework of the welfare state, are instead articulated as problems on the individual level – the individual's own problems.

Liquid modernity thus replaces an earlier phase, which Bauman conversely refers to as "solid modernity". Perhaps somewhat paradoxically, solid modernity served as a melting pot, attempting to break down what was previously considered stable and solid; that is, tradition and the premodern social structures (cf. Marx and Engels' expression, "all that is solid melts into air"). The intention was to "discover or invent solids of – for a change – lasting solidity, a solidity which one could trust and rely upon and which would make the world predictable and therefore manageable" (Bauman 2000: 3).

The melting pot that has been used in modern society to dissolve and replace traditions with new social structures is now used to dissolve the social – without anything to replace it. According to Bauman, we are now facing liquid modernity, where the stable has been replaced by the liquid, the mobile and the flexible.

We will return to how these shifts in society are unfolding, including new concepts used in sociology to analyse this development. Are we witnessing the demise of the social? Or do the liquid, mobile and flexible social structures make a new form of societal integration possible?

chapter 2

Capitalism and alienation

Marx and Weber

What is capitalism? And how does living in capitalist societies affect people's lives? These questions have been central in social theory right from the beginning. Already the classic sociologists Karl Marx (1818–1883) and Max Weber (1864–1920) were preoccupied with these issues – and capitalism remains a central theme in sociology. In Chapter 10, we discuss Richard Sennett's (1943–) ideas about how capitalism currently develops into a so-called flexible capitalism that places new demands on how we organise our lives both within and outside of the workplace, and in Chapter 7 we will discuss Luc Boltanski (1940–) and Ève Chiapello's (1965–) inquiry into a possible new spirit of capitalism.

We begin this chapter by looking at Marx's and Weber's theories of capitalism. Both are engaged in understanding capitalism as an economic system that characterises and dominates the society they live in. They see capitalism as a historically developed economic system, but find the roots of capitalism in different places. Weber claims that capitalism has religious roots, whereas Marx understands it in relation to a general theory of historical development, known as historical materialism. Weber links the rise of capitalism to the spread of Protestantism, more specifically Calvinism. He shows how capitalism first became established in the Calvinist-Protestant countries and explains this as an offshoot of the ideas about predestination found in Calvinism. God has already decided who is saved, but we do not know whether we are among them. According to Calvinism, worldly success, for example as a manufacturer or businessman, can be interpreted as a sign that one is among the chosen. According to Weber, the desire to know if one is among the selected is the fuel that drives capitalism and creates the so-called Protestant work ethic.

Marx is also interested in the rise of capitalism, but is equally concerned with understanding the law of motion of capitalism, which, according to him, permeates most activities in capitalist societies. Marx claims that life in any society will be characterised by the economic system of that society and that the capitalist mode of production is a structure that influences society and assigns people specific roles. In societies dominated by the capitalist mode of production, work is turned into wage labour, and workers are forced to sell their labour for wages to the capitalists to survive.

In the following, we will first look at the main focal points of Marx's writings: alienation, historical materialism and economic critique. Then we turn to Weber's writings and especially his theory of the rise of capitalism. The chapter concludes with a discussion of their theories of capitalism.

Marx: alienation, historical materialism and economic critique

When Marx was buried at Highgate Cemetery in London on 17 March 1883, his good friend Friedrich Engels (1820–1895) gave a speech that praised him and tried to summarise his contributions to the social sciences (Engels 1975). Engels compared Marx with Darwin and said that Darwin had discovered the law of development of organic nature, and Marx had discovered the law of development of human history. According to Engels, this law could be boiled down to the simple fact that people in all societies at all times must first of all eat, drink, have shelter and clothing, before they can pursue politics, science, art, religion, etc. The historical law of development that Engels is talking about has since been given the name historical materialism, and Engels sums up the theory by pointing out that:

> The production of the immediate material means, and consequently the degree of economic development attained by a given people or during a given epoch, form the foundation upon which the state institutions, the legal conceptions, art, and even the ideas on religion, of the people concerned have been evolved, and in the light of which they must, therefore, be explained, instead of vice versa, as had hitherto been the case.
>
> (Engels 1975: 16–17)

capitalism and alienation 15

Engels, who had been involved in many of the writings, where historical materialism was developed and presented – not least *The German Ideology* written in 1845–1846 and *Manifesto of the Communist Party* from 1848 – also claimed that Marx with his new understanding of surplus value had revealed the law of motion of the capitalist economic system and thus of bourgeois society.

Before Marx arrived at his theory of history, he was primarily concerned with the phenomenon of alienation in connection to modern wage labour. His early writings – until 1845 – focused, among other things, on the alienation that wage workers experience when they are forced to sell themselves to the capital owners and with their labour produce products that do not belong to them, but to the capitalists who buy their labour. He describes this wage labour as "labor of self-sacrifice, of mortification" and in this kind of labour the worker experiences a "loss of his self" (Marx 1959a). The total sum of products and wealth in society is in fact the product of the workers' labour. But the workers do not see this. They only see the small part of the production, of which they are a part.

In his critique of the alienating character of wage labour, Marx is inspired by Ludwig Feuerbach (1804–1872) and other so-called Left or Young Hegelians' critique of religion. Feuerbach, among others, argued in his book *The Essence of Christianity* from 1841 that critique of religion had to be carried out as anthropology. Instead of understanding mankind as something God has created, Feuerbach reverses the perspective and claims that God is man's product. With a concept taken from the German philosopher Hegel (1770–1831), who inspired Feuerbach as well as Marx, he understands God as man's negation. God is truly good, forgiving, just, knowledgeable, etc., whereas we humans always are full of errors and omissions. According to Feuerbach, we have created God as a picture of everything that we are not. To eliminate the alienation between people and religion, we therefore have to negate the negation, and in this way get back to humans and see things in their proper perspective.

In other words, Feuerbach wants us to see the true relationship between God and man; that man created God and not vice versa. He also warns us against letting ourselves be ruled by a God that we ourselves have created. Similarly, Marx points out that mankind in bourgeois society is blind to how things really are. The workers do not see that in reality they have created all the values that exist in society. Wealth is in other words accumulated via exploitation of them.

The historical materialism

For Marx, the road from the problem of alienation to historical materialism goes via a confrontation with Feuerbach. In the "Theses on

Feuerbach", written by Marx in 1845, he dissociates himself from Feuerbach because his critique did not go far enough. Admittedly, as Marx writes in the sixth thesis (Marx 1969), Feuerbach resolves the religious essence into the human essence. But Marx does not see man as a pre-given, ahistorical being. Instead, he believes that we have to understand human beings in relation to the society that they live in. Marx argues in favour of a historical-materialist understanding of humanity. Social conditions change throughout history, and the individual will to some extent always reflect the society that he or she lives in.

In his understanding of individual societies, Marx distinguishes between an economic structure of society and a legal and political superstructure. In the Preface to *A Contribution to the Critique of Political Economy* he writes:

> The totality of these relations of production constitutes the economic structure of society, the real foundation, on which arises a legal and political superstructure and to which correspond definite forms of social consciousness.
>
> (Marx 1977)

How to understand this model has been a hotly debated issue. After Marx's death, Engels had to clarify the model in his so-called old age letters (1890–1895). In a letter to Walther Borgius, he explains that he and Marx find that the economic conditions ultimately determine historical development, but adds that political, legal, philosophical, religious, literary and artistic matters also influence each other as well as the economic structure. He speaks of an interaction between the different parts of the superstructure and between the superstructure and the economic foundation. Ultimately, it is the economic structure that is essential (Engels 1988).

The economic system thus has great influence on other matters in a society. To understand a society, one therefore needs to study its economic structure closely. In particular, Marx focuses on what he calls the productive forces – a concept for the combined human knowledge and technology that can be found in a society. The forces of production tell us something about how much it is possible to produce in a given society. With reference to Adam Smith (1723–1790), who was the first to truly understand the importance of this, Marx further points to the degree of division of labour and specialisation as crucial in determining the productive forces of a society.

Smith writes in 1776 in *The Wealth of Nations* that the work of one man in primitive societies often is carried out by several men in more advanced societies and that the source of the wealth of nations can be found in this division of labour. His arguments are partly based on the observations he made when he visited a small pin factory (Smith 1937: 5). Ten people worked together to produce pins; they produced 12 pounds per day, equivalent to 4,800 pins per person per day. If one man had to perform all the functions in making a pin and produce the pins all by himself, he would only be able to make between 1 and 20 pins per day, according to Smith. But because this factory had divided the production of pins into 18 partial functions, they were able to reach this high number, because it allowed them to start using machines. The division of labour and specialisation – splitting up the production into many simple subfunctions that machines could carry out – was also a prerequisite for industrialisation.

According to Marx, historical development is about the development of the productive forces. As we have already touched upon, humans have at all times and in all types of societies first and foremost had to think about providing clothing, a roof over their head, and enough to eat and drink. The primitive humans had to spend almost all their lives and waking hours on this work, but as a result of the increased productive forces that develop through history – an increase that really accelerates in bourgeois, capitalist society where the division of labour and specialisation enable increased use of machinery – this is no longer necessary.

Marx therefore hopes that we can organise society in such a way that we can achieve more free time. In the third volume of *Capital* he distinguishes between a realm of necessity and a realm of freedom (Marx 1959b: 820). The realm of necessity encompasses all the necessary work we have to carry out in order to provide food, clothes and a roof over our heads. We will never completely get rid of this realm but with the increase in the productive forces, one day it will be possible to spend less time in this realm and more time in the realm of freedom, where, as Marx writes, true individuality can flourish. Marx imagines that we can only really give space to the realm of freedom, when we reach a communist society, i.e. a classless society based on common property. However, we cannot skip the bourgeois, capitalist societies. Capitalism's historical role is to improve the productive forces to a level that makes it possible to perform the necessary work in a very short time and thus provide maximum conditions for the realm of freedom.

But how do we reach the classless society which for Marx is the end goal of history? According to historical materialism, history moves from stage to stage towards a still higher degree of development of the productive forces. The shift from one stage to the next takes place when a society's property relations no longer match the development of the productive forces taking place in society. When the tensions between the economic system and the political and legal system become sufficiently intense, an era of social revolution will begin.

For example, feudal societies in the late 1700s and especially in the first half of the 1800s faced growing problems with the existing distribution of power and privileges. The bourgeoisie increasingly demanded political and legal rights that corresponded to their actual economic role in society. They obtained these rights through the so-called bourgeois revolutions that began with the French Revolution in 1789 and culminated in the mid-1800s with 1848 as the great Year of Revolution. The bourgeoisie established itself as the new ruling class at the expense of especially the nobility and its privileges. According to the historical materialism, all previous societies – except some primitive societies based on common property – have been class societies characterised by class struggles. The opening line in the first chapter of the *Manifesto of the Communist Party* reads: "The history of all hitherto existing society is the history of class struggles" (Marx and Engels 1969). They continue:

> Freeman and slave, patrician and plebeian, lord and serf, guild-master and journeyman, in a word, oppressor and oppressed, stood in constant opposition to one another, carried on an uninterrupted, now hidden, now open fight, a fight that each time ended, either in a revolutionary reconstitution of society at large, or in the common ruin of the contending classes.
>
> (Marx and Engels 1969)

According to Marx and Engels, the modern bourgeois society that arose when the feudal societies collapsed has not abolished the class struggle, but slimmed it down to two main classes: the bourgeoisie (the capitalists) and the proletariat (the workers).

The bourgeoisie established itself as the new ruling class through the bourgeois revolutions. But according to historical materialism, this new ruling class will eventually perish too – as has been the case with all previous ruling classes. Marx's prophecy is that the proletariat in the future will join forces to resist the exploitation they are subjected to in bourgeois society. At some point they will rise up, revolt and seize power – and then introduce a new, classless society based on common rather than private property.

The reason why it is essential for Marx to replace private property with common property is because private property makes it possible for capitalists to exploit the proletariat. In Marx's writings, the capitalists are a concept for the social class that owns the means of production, but the proletariat's only property is their labour. Workers are forced to sell their labour to the capitalists in order to survive. The problem with this system is that when the capitalists honestly have purchased the item labour in the labour market at an agreed price for a specified period, they also as an effect of private property have the right to use this product in full. This means that if the worker is paid for a full day's work but is able to produce a value that corresponds to the amount the capitalist has paid for his or her labour in the course of half a day, the value of the last half-day's work accrues to the capitalist.

Marx calls the value created above and beyond the worker's wages surplus value. Because of the private property rights in bourgeois, capitalist society, the surplus value does not accrue to the worker who created it through his work, but to the capitalist. Marx's point is not that the surplus value arises because of individual cheating, for example because the worker does not get the payment he should. By contrast, Marx is trying to show that there is a fundamental structural discrepancy between the mode of production on the one hand, where the division of labour and specialisation mean that more and more people are involved in the production of even the simplest products, and the private property rights on the other hand, which means that only a few people get a part of the surplus value. Marx shows how this imbalance is constantly maintained and reinforced in the capitalist system because of private property rights. For Marx it therefore becomes vital to replace the principle of private property with common property rights to ensure that the legal superstructure corresponds to the economic structure; i.e. to the high degree of specialisation and division of labour in advanced capitalist societies.

Capital's law of motion

To understand how the capitalist production system works in detail, Marx initiates a comprehensive study of capitalism in the 1850s. Until his death in 1883, he works on his analysis of capitalism, at the British Museum's library and other places. He studies classical economics, production statistics, and much more. The analyses are published in a number of works, of which *Capital* is the most famous. The first volume of *Capital* was published in 1867, and it was the only volume Marx lived to see published. The second and third volumes were published by Engels after Marx's death, in 1885 and 1894.

Capital is not an empirical examination of the state of affairs in capitalist societies in the latter half of the 1800s. There are of course plenty of empirical examples from mainly England in the work, but it is first and foremost an analysis of the concept of capital. He imagines that he will reach a deeper understanding of the core of the capitalist societies through a conceptual clarification; that such an analysis will uncover the inner law of motion of capitalism, which ultimately governs the development in the existing bourgeois, capitalist society.

Marx opens his analysis by stating that the wealth of the capitalist society is revealed in "an immense accumulation of commodities" (Marx 1887: 27). He begins by taking a closer look at the commodity, continues with an analysis of money before he arrives at the concept of capital. He defines capital as "value constantly expanding, constantly multiplying itself" (Marx 1887: 217). It is capital's nature to constantly try to transcend itself and become more than it was. And it is this logic that asserts itself as a general law of motion in capitalism and comes to dominate life in capitalist society. The capital will therefore try to fit and subordinate everything under it in an attempt to increase its own value. More and more elements of bourgeois society will eventually become instruments for the capital in its attempt to create more surplus value.

This will first and foremost affect the organisation of production and work. Surplus value can only be created through work. A basic assumption in Marx's analysis is that work and only work creates value. Surplus value emerges in the production via the workers' labour. It can be accomplished by making the working day longer to get more hours worked beyond the equivalence point for the workers' wages, or by shortening the time it takes to create a value that corresponds to the wage bill. Marx calls the first form of surplus-value production the production of absolute surplus value, and the other form the production of relative surplus-value (Marx 1887: 126–357). Empirically he can show that working hours have increased over time. Working hours rose significantly in England until 1830–1840 when the first laws limited the work day to 12 hours.

Marx further shows that the introduction of these laws did not impede growth and surplus value creation, but rather catalysed it. When surplus value creation cannot be increased by extending the work day or by hiring more workers in the production, it is necessary to find new, more efficient ways to produce, so that fewer hours are needed to produce a value that corresponds to the costs of the salaries. The subordination of production to capital leads to a continuous development and improvement of production processes, methods and technology, or in other words: to innovation and improved productive forces.

This process intensifies competition between the capitalists. If you are not able to produce your goods in an efficient way, you will lose market shares and eventually be outperformed. This means that while production keeps growing – i.e. there is a constant accumulation of values in capitalism – the number of capitalists shrinks, but those who survive will own ever greater values. In Marx's words, a centralisation and concentration of the means of production and values takes place and the mismatch

capitalism and alienation

between the widespread division of labour (the societal character of work) and the legal framework (private property) stands out more clearly. Towards the end of the first volume of *Capital*, Marx writes:

> Along with the constantly diminishing number of the magnates of capital, who usurp and monopolise all advantages of this process of transformation, grows the mass of misery, oppression, slavery, degradation, exploitation; but with this too grows the revolt of the working class.
>
> (Marx 1887: 542)

Thus capitalism carries with it an unprecedented production of wealth and improvement of the productive forces, both of which are necessary to make room for the realm of freedom besides the realm of necessity in the classless society. But, says Marx, capitalism also leads to its own downfall.

Weber: an understanding sociology of capitalism

Like Marx, Weber has had excessive influence on modern sociology and its neighbouring disciplines, including political science, religious studies, economics and organisational studies. In the following, we will discuss how Weber's sociology differs from Marx's, and introduce his influential analysis of the rise and character of modern society, especially the rise of the spirit of capitalism in the West.

Contrary to Marx, Weber does not believe that sociology should uncover general societal regularities with natural science as the model. Weber is inspired by historical methods and is therefore critical of the general macrotheoretical models provided by positivist sociology. To document empirically the structural patterns operating behind society's individuals, as Durkheim did in his analysis of suicide, is not enough. On the contrary, Weber argues that sociology should seek to develop "explanatory understandings" that provide insights into individuals' motives and conceptions (Weber 1978a: 8). To understand a social phenomenon such as capitalism, sociologists must understand and explain why some individuals act in accordance with the capitalistic model and what meaning they ascribe to their actions.

Compared to Marx's more holistic approach, Weber's sociology is best described as a form of methodological individualism. While Marx is interested in the actual formation of society – in capitalism and its laws – and its current stage of development (cf. historical materialism), Weber emphasises the role played by individuals in the emergence of the capitalist system.

However, the difference between Weber's individualism and Marx's holism is often exaggerated and translated into problematic distinctions between structure and agency or micro and macro. If we use capitalism as an example, Weber's point is that the legitimacy of this order is not necessarily justified by economic categories such as productivity and wealth. At its starting point, capitalism derived its energy from individuals, who translated their work into religious categories (more on this later in the chapter). In this sense, Weber's individualism is methodological. He does not claim that collective and aggregated phenomena should be understood as the mere sum of individuals' wills and actions. Like Marx, he sees individuals as products of the culture and society in which they are embedded. The difference in their approaches does not lie here.

Then, how do we understand the methodological and the individualistic in "methodological individualism"? Simply put, we see it in Weber's assumption that the reproduction of a system such as capitalism requires that the system appears meaningful and valuable to the people operating in it. Methodologically speaking, it is therefore wise to investigate individuals' own reasons and ways of making sense of the world; but the nature of capitalism, of course, cannot be reduced to such reasons and sense-making. This individualism is methodological and nothing more, as it does not involve a claim about capitalism being reducible to individual actions.

Capitalism, which is the most extensive social order in Weber's analysis, is in many ways an absurd system: Why must we give up part of the value we produce to a capitalist? Why must we save up and postpone our consumption? And why invest altogether? To understand capitalism – or any other social order – it can be productive to devote attention to the individuals and their understandings of the world. Of course, this is only a beginning and not necessarily the complete analysis. It is a methodological grip.

Before discussing Weber's analytical strategy in more detail, we will look at another example of how his methodological individualism adds nuance to the more structural and macro-oriented understandings of social phenomena.

Consider in this regard Weber's famous definition of the sovereign state as an organisation given by a legitimate monopoly of violence: "A state is a human community that (successfully) claims the monopoly of the legitimate use of physical force within a given territory" (Weber 1978c: 78). Because we understand the state as legitimate, its actions are perceived as expressions of use of power, not violence; conceptually speaking, power is a legitimate use of violence. Hereby, the "use of violence" executed by the state gains a special character. If individuals do not see themselves as citizens of a state, the state's monopoly of violence cannot be considered legitimate, and the state will quickly degenerate into tyranny.

This does not mean that Weber understands the state as a product of conscious individual choices. Indeed, his rejection of such individualistic interpretations applies to the broader development of society. Like Marx, Weber is inspired by Hegel's notion of the cunning of reason. But while Marx understands this cunning as a systemic logic operating behind the back of the actors, Weber sees it as an unintended and contingent outcome of historical developments that could have taken a different path.

Because sociological theory, according to Weber, must devote attention to the individuals' own understandings, it can be difficult to establish general terms that lump everything together, so to speak. Weber is not a positivist. He acknowledges that theoretical terms are not depictions of the social world *per se*. Nonetheless he believes that it is possible to describe typical examples of social phenomena using ideal types. An ideal type is neither an ideal in a moral sense nor something that exists in reality. Weber describes the point of origin of the ideal type as follows:

> It is obtained by means of a one-sided accentuation of one or a number of viewpoints and through the synthesis of a great many diffuse and discrete individual phenomena (more present in one place, fewer in another, and occasionally completely absent), which are in conformity with those one-sided, accentuated viewpoints, into an internally con-sistent mental image.
>
> (Weber 2012: 125)

In *Economy and Society*, published in 1922, Weber formulates a number of ideal typologies (1978a; 1978b). A famous example is his distinction between traditional, charismatic and legal-rational authority, which rep-resent different ways of legitimising state power (1978a: 212–301). Whereas force can be understood as one individual (a) having authority over another (b), power is about why b obeys a. Once again, we here see an example of Weber's methodologically individualist starting point, and his interest in understanding how individuals ascribe meaning to social phenomena.

More specifically, the ideal type is a heuristic tool that cultivates certain aspects of a phenomenon. It is an interpretive scheme or pre-understanding used to make sense of reality. Ideal types should in other words not be conceived of as *de facto* expressions of the social world. They help us understand the being and inherent rationality of a phenomenon. And in order to reach such an understanding, typical characteristics must be pulled to the foreground.

Rationalisation

Weber is known for his long lists of ideal types, of which three have already been mentioned. His analyses are based on heuristic distinctions between ideal typical forms of action (traditional, affective and purposive rational), legitimacy (traditional, charismatic and purposive rational), and organisation (traditional, charismatic and bureaucratic).

At first glance, these ideal types follow the same principle. The rational aspect is always present as one among other ideal types. Other forms, which may focus on the normative, the emotional or the traditional, are usually not described as rationally purposeful in the conventional sense.

Here, some introductory observations seem appropriate. According to Weber's historical analysis, Western societies are increasingly thinking and organising themselves into rationally purposeful categories, and ideal types can be constructed to describe this rationalisation process over time. However, Weber finds it important to describe this development as a shift from one form of rationality to another, and not as a development from a nonrational to a rational society.

A similar intuition underpins Weber's comparative studies. Weber does not start from a conception of the Western population as being more rationally advanced than people in non-Western societies. In contrast, he seeks to describe how the ideal-typical Western rationality differs from the rationality prevalent in other parts of the world.

When we talk about rationality in the Western world, we typically rely on a binary distinction between rational and nonrational thinking. Purposive rational thinking hereby often becomes taken-for-granted as the most advanced form of reasoning. Weber, however, refrains from making this type of judgment in his analysis. Instead, his purpose is to illustrate that Western societies have followed a certain path of development, which becomes distinct when compared to other societies.

As we shall see in the following, this rationalisation has brought along various dynamic effects. Before we discuss these, we will introduce Weber's four ideal typical forms of action. We will begin with the purposive rational form of action, which is carried out to achieve or fulfil a certain outcome or purpose. What makes an action purposive rational does not depend on the actual outcome, but the fact that we carefully consider the best way to achieve it. In other words, the individual is aware of what he or she wishes to achieve and behaves in a cool and calculating manner to achieve it using as few resources as possible. As mentioned, Weber's thesis predicts that this coordination of action will become dominant in modern Western societies. The other types of action are traditional, affective and value-rational.

capitalism and alienation

When we act traditionally, our actions are informed by tradition or habit. We act in a certain way because this is how things are usually done. We shake hands, we don't burp during dinner and so on. Or rather: This is how things are done in a specific cultural context, and they may have different meanings in other cultures. For instance, handshakes between men and women are prohibited in strict Muslim environments and a burp during dinner in China could mean that the food is appreciated. The traditional action is, in other words, conditioned by the cultural context.

Affective actions are actions controlled by emotions or affect. We are not necessarily aware of the purpose of this form of action or whether the action is rational in relation to achieving a specific outcome. Instead, we act on the basis of spontaneous feelings of anger, hatred, pleasure, sorrow, and so on.

Finally, value-rational actions are conscious actions made for their own sake without any view to their potential outcomes. This form of action is, in other words, never just means to an end. We act in a certain way regardless of the consequences. Art is often evaluated in this way, and we also relate to actions in this way, when we evaluate them ethically or morally. If a person wishes to make fast money, a purposive rational calculation might summon him to commit burglary (if the risk of being caught is considered minimal – but this is part of the calculation). By contrast, one would abstain from this action on the basis of an ethical and moral calculation, simply because it is considered wrong by a normative standard.

Weber's thesis does not imply that these three last-mentioned types of action disappear with the rationalisation of society, but merely that the purposive rational form will dominate in certain contexts. Specifically, he claims that societies, especially in the Western part of the world, have been disenchanted as part of the rationalisation process. The disenchantment is equivalent to what is usually called secularisation. Religious explanations are no longer privileged as the basic principle of societal organisation, and become replaced by modern mentalities, institutionalised as capitalism, science and bureaucracy.

The rationalisation process, according to Weber, is characterised by a diffusion of instrumental means-ends mentalities. One example concerns the emergence of modern bureaucracy (Weber 1978c: 196–244). Today, the term bureaucracy has a negative connotation. It is frequently used in everyday language to describe ineffective and unnecessarily complicated regulatory systems. But in Weber's terminology this concept refers to a particularly modern way of organising the world in social hierarchies based on a rationalised means-ends mentality. The ideal typical bureaucracy is characterised by a system of general rules applied to concrete cases by public servants, who act in a completely professional and impersonal manner. These public servants are subject to the duties that follow from their place in the organisational hierarchy, which at the same time constitutes their primary career path. The bureaucracy is professional by nature and as such independent of personal interests. It is founded on a clear distinction between politics and administration, and the key responsibility of its members is to loyally administrate the general rules of the organisation.

Weber's rationalisation thesis is formulated most concisely in the preface of *The Protestant Ethic and the Spirit of Capitalism* from 1905 (Weber 1991: 13–27). The rationalisation process, so he argues, constitutes an important premise for the development of the modern society. As already mentioned, the modern bureaucracy constitutes an illustrative manifestation of this rationalisation process. Modern Western science is another concise expression of great significance to the development of capitalism, primarily via mathematics and experimental method. Politically, the rationalisation process is seen in the development of positive law (see Weber's sociology of law (1978b: 809–814)). Weber also highlights the changing role of the citizen in modern society and developments in cultural life, as key examples. For instance, he argues that Western music expresses a particular form of rationality that cannot be found in other cultures: harmony, chromatics, accompaniment, concerts with string instruments, symphonies, and so on. The Gothic arches also express this rationality, as they do not merely serve as decorations but are designed to hold together monumental constructions.

In general, Weber considers the means-ends mentality to be connected to major societal progress. For instance, the extension of bureaucracy is a great gain for society, because it guarantees a general sense of calculability and professionalism. At the same time, he is critical of the individual consequences of this development. As purposive-rationalism becomes the leading principle in several parts of society, it inevitably leads to a stronger rationalisation of the lifestyle of the individual. See, for instance, this classic passage from the concluding pages of *The Protestant Ethic* (1991):

> The Puritan wanted to work in a calling; we are forced to do so. For when asceticism was carried out of monastic cells into everyday life, and began to dominate worldly morality, it did its part in building the tremendous cosmos of the modern economic order. This order is now bound to the technical and economic conditions of machine production which today determine the lives of all the individuals who

are born into this mechanism, not only those directly concerned with economic acquisition, with irresistible force. Perhaps it will so determine them until the last ton of fossilized coal is burnt. In Baxter's view the care for eternal goods should only lie on the shoulders of the "saint like a light cloak, which can be thrown aside at any moment." But fate decreed that the cloak should become an iron cage.

(Weber 1991: 181)

Weber can be argued to leave his methodical individualistic foundation for a moment in this passage. Indeed, his gloomy description of the individual consequences of capitalism might just as well have been written by Marx. He seems to believe that purposive-rationalism and especially capitalism may involve negative consequences for the individual in the form of meaninglessness and alienation.

Weber's conception of the iron cage of rationality has since inspired others to develop more sophisticated criticisms of the continuous diffusion of instrumental rationality in modern society, including *Dialectic of Enlightenment* (1996) by the German social philosophers Max Horkheimer (1895–1973) and Theodor W. Adorno, and Jürgen Habermas' (1929–) theory about system and life world (see Chapter 6).

The spirit of capitalism

The Protestant Ethic and the Spirit of Capitalism is Weber's most famous analysis. Although he agrees with several basic points in Marx's theory of capitalism, including that capitalism is a profit-oriented system, his aim is to criticise Marx. As opposed to Marx, Weber seeks to explain macro phenomena such as capitalism on the basis of individual actors' motivation; i.e. why some people at some point in time start living, thinking and acting in a capitalistic manner. According to Weber's description, the ideal typical capitalist does not wallow in material pleasure, but often lives a rather modest life and considers profit and economic growth as an end in itself. Weber refers to this as the spirit of capitalism. But how does he understand capitalism? Not surprisingly, in an ideal typical manner:

We will define a capitalistic economic action as one which rests on the expectation of profit by the utilization of opportunities for exchange, that is on (formally) peaceful chances of profit. Acquisition by force (formally and actually) follows its own particular laws, and it is not expedient, however little one can forbid this, to place it in the same category with action which is in the last analysis, oriented to profit from exchange. Where capitalistic acquisition is rationally pursued, the corresponding action is adjusted to calculations in terms of capital.

(Weber 1991: 17–18)

Note that Weber refers to rational capitalism in this quote. He finds it important to separate the rational underpinnings of modern capitalism from mere pursuit of wealth and consumption. Capitalism, he says, has nothing to do with greed – rather the opposite. The capitalist shows moderation as he or she seeks profit and reinvests this profit to make even more profit. We are dealing with a rational calculation in which the individual constantly seeks to multiply its capital, and therefore book-keeping is a central aspect of rational capitalism; balancing and calculating each element; estimating expenses in relation to income; optimising and distributing the workforce allocated via a labour market; standardising and streamlining the work process; weighing investments against each other, and so on. Besides being driven by profit, rational capitalism distinguishes between the household and the factory/company. Capitalism is not concerned with private consumption.

Marx and Weber both see capitalism as given in relation to pursuit of profit. They both conceive of it as a relatively recent phenomenon, which cannot be reduced to the exchange of products with money as a medium. But while Marx emphasises the ownership of means of production, Weber emphasises the process of rationalisation, which is both the premise and driving force of capitalism. Marx points out how different modes of production may coexist, while each historical period is dominated by only one mode of production. Once again, Weber agrees. Rational capitalism is an ideal type which does not necessarily exist in a pure form and may coexist with other types.

Rational capitalism has replaced what Weber describes as adventure capitalism:

This kind of entrepreneur, the capitalistic adventurer, has existed everywhere. With the exception of trade and credit and banking transactions, their activities were predominantly of an irrational and speculative character, or directed to acquisition by force, above all the acquisition of booty, whether directly in war or in the form of continuous fiscal booty by exploitation of subjects. ... The capitalism of promoters, large-scale speculators concession hunters, and much modern financial capitalism even in peace time, but, above all, the capitalism especially concerned with exploiting wars, bears this stamp even in modern Western countries, and some, are closely related to it, today as always.

(Weber 1991: 20–21)

capitalism and alienation

Modern, rational capitalism is dynamic and characterised by innovation, whereas adventure capitalism is epitomised by stagnation. Modern, rational capitalism operates in large markets characterised by frequent transactions that each create a small profit. In comparison, markets in adventure capitalism are small: The frequency of exchange is low, the profit of each transaction is large. Adventure capitalism mainly focuses on production of luxury goods; rational capitalism primarily focuses on production of everyday goods. Adventure capitalism is driven forward by consumption, whereas rational capitalism advances through investments and the wish to increase profit in the long term. A final difference is that the production units primarily aim at self-sufficiency in traditional capitalism, whereas they are given by a division of work in rational capitalism.

Weber is interested in explaining the shift from adventure capitalism to rational capitalism. As mentioned, he looks to changes in religious orientations and seeks explanations outside the capital structure. However, Weber only offers a partial explanation for the outbreak of rational capitalism in *The Protestant Ethic and the Spirit of Capitalism*. The book suggests that a historical shift in religious doctrines has accompanied and influenced the coming of the spirit of capitalism. But what is this spirit? It is the way in which capitalism is legitimated and rendered meaningful to individuals. This is close to Marx's conception of ideology. An important difference is that Weber sees ideas as a driving force in historical development, whereas Marx gives analytical priority to the development of the productive forces. Marx sees ideology as an instrument of repression, but according to Weber, the spirit of capitalism is an expression of rationalisation which contributes to the wealth of all. The spirit hides nothing, and those who subscribe to it do not suffer from false consciousness.

So what are the central elements of the spirit of capitalism? Once again, Weber uses ideal types to articulate the spirit in its purest form. Specifically, he draws on the writings of the famous US intellectual Benjamin Franklin (1706–1790), which he sees as the grammarian of this spirit. Franklin notes:

> Remember, that time is money. He that can earn ten shillings a day by his labour, and goes abroad, or sits idle, one half of that day, though he spends but sixpence during his diversion or idleness, ought not to reckon that the only expense; he has really spent, or rather thrown away, five shillings besides. ... Remember, that credit is money. If a man lets his money lie in my hands after it is due, he gives me the interest, or so much as I can make of it during that time. This

amounts to a considerable sum where a man has good and large credit, and makes good use of it ... Remember, that money is of the prolific, generating nature. Money can beget money, and its offspring can beget more, and so on. Five shillings turned is six, turned again it is seven and three pence, and so on, till it becomes a hundred pounds. The more there is of it, the more it produces every turning, so that the profits rise quicker and quicker. He that kills a breeding-sow, destroys all her offspring to the thousandth generation. He that murders a crown, destroys all that it might have produced, even scores of pounds.

(Franklin as quoted in Weber 1991: 48–49)

Whereas Weber's ideal typical description of rational capitalism offers insight into the character of modern capitalism, his identification of its spirit helps us understand what renders capitalism meaningful for the modern individual. The importance of the postponement of consumption, central to Weber's distinction between adventure capitalism and rational capitalism, is clearly illustrated in Franklin's ideas. We see the praise of work, the moderation and the orientation towards the future. And above all, we see the rational attitude: We must deal with our means in a sensible and rational way, in which each transaction is carefully considered and optimised. This is the spirit of capitalism, whose roots Weber seeks to identify.

He finds these roots in the historical development of Protestantism. Specifically, he examines different Protestant movements. In some of them he finds a combination of two key elements: a strict work ethic and an ascetic lifestyle.

The most influential Protestant movement is Calvinism (others are Baptism, Pietism and Methodism). The conception that God's will cannot be known is quintessential to this branch of Protestantism. God does not exist for mankind; mankind exists for God. God is not tied to any law and we therefore do not know what his plan for us might be (Weber 1991: 101–104). Of particular importance is the thesis of predestination. God has already decided who shall be redeemed, but we cannot know whether we are among the chosen ones. Good actions, absolution and similar religious deeds do not bring redemption closer.

The rejection of redemption through the church and sacraments separates Protestantism from Catholicism. Roughly speaking, the Catholic can sin and seek absolution, which provides a basis for *stop-and-go-luxury living*. At Weber's time of writing, great differences existed between the economically prosperous Protestant Northern Germany and the poorer Catholic Southern Germany. The explanation appears so obvious to Weber

capitalism and alienation

31

that he only cares to mention it sporadically. This is what he writes about the Protestant ethic:

> Thus, however useless good works might be as a means of attaining salvation, for even the elect remain beings of the flesh, and everything they do falls infinitely short of divine standards, nevertheless, they are indispensable as a sign of election. They are the technical means, not of purchasing salvation, but of getting rid of the fear of damnation. In this sense they are occasionally referred to as directly necessary for salvation or the possession salutis is made conditional on them ... In practice this means that God helps those who help themselves. Thus the Calvinist, as it is sometimes put, himself creates his own salvation, or, as would be more correct, the conviction of it. But this creation cannot, as in Catholicism, consist in a gradual accumulation of individual good works to one's credit, but rather in a systematic self-control which at every moment stands before the inexorable alternative, chosen or damned.
>
> (Weber 1991: 115)

We must face God completely on our own. According to Weber, this causes a form of existential anxiety that the Calvinists try to mitigate by being successful in their work activities. Secular success is not a guarantee of redemption in the afterlife, but some Calvinists interpret it as a sign of being among the chosen. Calvinism is radically individualistic, but it also draws on the conception that our actions must be *ad majorem Dei gloriam*: to the greater glory of God. This conception encourages systematic behaviour, and the calling of Calvinism is no longer about living ascetically in abbeys or the like.

In the absence of a religious promise of redemption, the Protestant ethic becomes a question of working hard and accumulating profits in our earthly lives. Weber's explanation does not resemble a causal logic, as he neither claims that Protestantism has created capitalism nor that it is necessary for its further existence. But there has been a so-called elective affinity, an unintentional connection, between this individualistic form of asceticism and the establishment of capitalism as a new, economic form of production.

Ideas and matter

The distinction between methodological individualism and holism and between the historical-materialistic and ideal typical method has occasionally led to unproductive oppositions between Marx and Weber. Basically, they both want the same thing: to explain historical *longues durées* and understand the emergence of modern society through complex explanations. Marx is mainly concerned with historical changes in how production is organised, whereas Weber sees modernisation as the result of an ongoing rationalisation process.

The differences between Marx's and Weber's analyses of capitalism are often represented in terms of a difference between ideas and matter. Is history driven by ideas or by technological development and change in the conditions of production? As we have attempted to illustrate, this difference should not be exaggerated. Like Weber, Marx is interested in ideas as an element in what he describes as the superstructure of society, but he does not conceive of such ideas as being part of "the engine" of history. Weber understands the development of capitalism as an ambiguous process, where the emergence of new ideas interacts with many other components to form new patterns. But like Marx, his descriptions of the different forms of capitalism also emphasise material developments, for instance in bookkeeping, technology and science.

Both authors begin with the premise that capitalism is an absurd system that requires justification for those who work within it. Both see capitalism as a source of incredible economic growth that also causes alienation. According to Marx, the capitalistic production process alienates the worker by distancing him or her from the product he or she is producing. Weber thematises alienation as the iron cage of rationality, where means-ends calculations make us blind to other forms of rationality. We shall return to this discussion in Chapters 6 and 8.

According to Marx, another downside of capitalism concerns the exploitation of workers. This perspective remains largely unaddressed in the writings of Weber, who primarily focuses on the role played by independent tradesmen in the emergence of the spirit of capitalism. Indeed, Weber is more interested in the fact that more Protestants than Catholics own means of production. For him the capitalists' ownership of private property is not the explanation, but that which has to be explained.

As for the theme of social classes, Weber makes an overall distinction between class, status and party. He defines a class in the economic sense as a social group with the same life chances. This resembles Marx's definition, but for Weber status is not merely a question of being a worker or capitalist. He supplements his understanding of class with a conception of status that includes more subjective factors such as lifestyle, consumption and education. As we will see in Chapter 5, French sociologist Pierre Bourdieu inherits this conception.

Later in this book, we will discuss two additional questions adding new dimensions to the ideas of Marx and Weber. First, is contemporary capitalism especially flexible, and if so, how does it affect the social? This question will be addressed in our discussion of Richard Sennett's sociology in Chapter 9. Second, how can we understand the current spirit of capitalism? Weber considered the religious legitimation of capitalism central during a start-up phase, after which he imagined rationalisation (and secularisation) to come through. However, the question is whether capitalism still needs a spirit to appear meaningful. This question will be raised in continuation of Boltanski's and Chiapello's work on the new spirit of capitalism outlined in Chapter 7.

chapter 3

Recognition and anomie

Durkheim and Honneth

The Chronicle of Higher Education (2015) recently published a special report, "Today's anguished students", addressing the mental health condition of American college students. Eighty-four per cent of college counselling centres had experienced noteworthy increases in students with clinical depressions, and 58 per cent had seen increments in students with anxiety disorders.

A recent survey questionnaire conducted by the American College Health Association (2014) confirms this tendency. Of the approximately 93,000 college students participating in the study, 48 per cent reported having experienced severe feelings of hopelessness within the last twelve months, 82 per cent had felt mentally exhausted and 86 per cent had felt overwhelmed by all they had to do. Further, 59 per cent had felt very lonely, 57 per cent had experienced overwhelming feelings of anxiety, and more than one-third had been so depressed that it was difficult for them to function. Finally, 6 per cent reported having intentionally hurt or injured themselves physically, 8 per cent had seriously considered suicide and just over 1 per cent had, at some point in life, attempted suicide. Indeed, besides road accidents, suicide is the most frequent cause of death among American college students, and the proportion taking their own life has tripled since the 1950s (Iarovici 2015).

The *New York Times* recently focused attention on the problem. Under the headline "Suicide on Campus and the Pressure of Perfection", their story paints a picture of an American performance and comparison culture creating strong feelings of inadequacy, emptiness and declining self-esteem among college students. Indeed, such feelings seem to be reinforced by a perfection-driven social media culture that filters out the difficult and mundane facets of student life and distorts the students' notions of what it means to be young, and what it takes to gain recognition and respect among peers (Scelfo 2015).

The social factors creating these disquieting patterns are many and complex, and we should be careful not to ascribe too much weight to the anecdotal explanations suggested in the *New York Times*. Nevertheless, the article contains an important sociological point relating to our discussion of suicide in Chapter 1: Although mental problems are experienced and dealt with individually, we can also think of them as social problems. They gain existence through social interaction, when individuals meet society.

Whereas psychological methods and theories can help us identify and comprehend the individual prerequisites for the development of such dysfunctions, sociology offers useful analytical tools for carving out the underlying social circumstances and societal factors involved.

In Chapter 2, we introduced the classic sociological themes of capitalism and alienation. In this chapter, we will maintain the focus on early sociological ideas in a discussion of the pathological aspects of modernity. With a particular emphasis on the theoretical concepts of anomie and recognition, we introduce the works of Émile Durkheim and the contemporary German social-philosopher Axel Honneth and their perspectives on individualisation, morality and social cohesion. We will connect their strands of thought in a comparative discussion of the possible explanations and solutions to the prevalent experiences of inadequacy, malaise and loss of meaning that characterise many people's lives in contemporary society.

Durkheim and Honneth are both interested in understanding society's integrative structures, i.e. the ties or "societal glue" ensuring and maintaining a social cohesion. They also share an ambition for sociology to offer suggestions and practical solutions on how to overcome central societal challenges and create better, more solidary societies.

However, the two authors also diverge on a number of issues. Durkheim's theoretical foundation is anchored in a value-free, empiricist scientific ideal, whereas Honneth's sociology adopts a more abstract normative moral-philosophical starting point. Durkheim seeks to empirically map the moral and social prerequisites for social cohesion in both traditional and modern society, whereas Honneth starts from a theoretical, philosophical standpoint with an ambition to draw up the moral grammar of social recognition and hereby identify the basic conditions for "the good life". Likewise, the two thinkers operate on separate analytical levels. Durkheim's research program is oriented towards the development of a macrosociological theory about society as a collective reality. Honneth limits his focus to the intersubjective processes of social life and the interpersonal relations forming the basis for human self-realisation and recognition.

Émile Durkheim: sociology as a theory of society

In the few available biographical descriptions of Durkheim's life and legacy, he is often depicted as a "time-traveller" between the old and the new world. Durkheim came from an orthodox Jewish family and grew up under modest conditions in Épinal, a small French village far from the urban life of Paris, which later became the context of his adult life and sociological endeavours. Durkheim, in other words, personally experienced the societal transition from traditional to modern society, and this experience gave him an in-depth understanding of the comprehensive social changes in 19th-century France (Østerberg 2002: 1–23). This is illustrated quite well in the following excerpt from his first great work *The Division of Labour in Society* published in 1893:

> As we advance in the evolutionary scale, the ties which bind the individual to his family, to his native soil, to traditions which the past has given to him, to collective group usages, become loose. More mobile, he changes his environment more easily, leaves his people to go elsewhere to live a more autonomous experience, to a greater extent form his own ideas and sentiments.
>
> (Durkheim 1964: 400–401)

This excerpt is interesting for several reasons. First, Durkheim identifies two core sociological themes that guide his writings: individualisation and social differentiation. Second, the excerpt is a telling example of Durkheim's own life biography and break with his orthodox Jewish family and its more traditional lifestyle. Last but not least, the excerpt contains an almost prophetic description of the modernisation process exceeding Durkheim's own lifetime. Durkheim's description of the societal evolvement does not merely crystallise the 19th century's movement towards a new and more individualistic organisation of society; his ideas about mobility and the loosening of social ties have also proven crucial to many of the 20th century's most dominant sociological theorisations about modernity and late modernity (see especially Chapter 8 and 9).

As mentioned in the preface, the notion of sociology dates back to the writings of the French social philosopher Auguste Comte (1798–1857), but Durkheim has played a central role in establishing sociology as a

recognition and anomie

37

separate academic discipline in its own right. He became the first professor of sociology, and he was the leading force behind the first academic sociological journal, *L'Année Sociologique*. Durkheim was also the first academic to write a methodological book on sociology, *Rules of Sociological Methods* (1938), originally published in 1895. This book is often referred to as establishing a positivist position for sociology, i.e. a social science approach that, inspired by the natural sciences, seeks to acquire objective and general knowledge about the laws and mechanisms of social life. It is, however, debatable whether Durkheim's own writings are positivist or more interpretive in nature (we will return to this). In any case, he defines the sociological subject matter as the study of social facts.

Unlike Marx, Durkheim does not intend to go below the surface to identify deeper-lying ideological structures circumscribing the human consciousness. Nor does he seek to acquire interpretive understandings that expand our insights into the actors' individual motives and dispositions like Weber. Rather, his objective is to observe and describe social facts and develop more general sociological explanations based on statistical material, religious writings or law books. As he remarks in *Rules of Sociological Methods*, social facts are external to individuals and determine their actions. More specifically, he considers social facts as "collective representations" of society's moral consciousness, and the central task of the sociologist, according to Durkheim, is to observe and describe this consciousness via thorough and systematic scientific analysis.

Durkheim distinguishes between material and nonmaterial social facts. Material social facts refer to the social structures, patterns and forms of interaction that have crystallised into material objects over time and have become available for empirical observation. They include societal infrastructure, architecture, technology, law books, money systems and population statistics. Nonmaterial social facts refer to society's less explicit realm of moral forces, including unwritten norms, rules, values and ideas, which are inaccessible for direct empirical observation but still influence human conduct and behaviour. According to Durkheim, sociology should start with the material social facts but only to obtain a deeper understanding of the implicit nonmaterial level. The material level, so he argues, represents our only empirical access to the implicit realm of nonmaterial moral forces. Society's nonmaterial facts should therefore be approached through studies of their material manifestations, e.g. in law books, religious writings or statistics.

This approach implies an ontological idea of social reality as something unique and something of its own kind that cannot be derived from its parts. Durkheim refers to this idea as studying social reality "sui generis".

38   recognition and anomie

The basic assumption is that the aggregated social patterns and structures of society represent something more than the mere sum of individuals' actions and motives. In this sense, Durkheim subscribes to the idea of methodological holism. As he puts it, "the determining cause of a social fact should be sought among the social facts preceding it and not among the states of the individual consciousness" (Durkheim 1938: 110). This implies that individual social phenomena should always be explained with a view to the larger social system. Society is beyond the individual and determines its intensions and dispositions through both material and nonmaterial social facts.

Durkheim also seeks to expand the repertoire of sociological forms of explanation. In addition to scientific causal explanations, he emphasises the importance of functional explanations, where a phenomenon is understood and explained with a view to its role and function in the larger social system. Consider, for instance, the idea of social trust: A functional explanation could be that social trust represents a necessary condition for society's social cohesion, whereas a causal explanation could focus on the causal link between this and other social phenomena, e.g. that trustfulness is instilled through socialisation. According to Durkheim, sociologists need to rely on both forms of explanation; but due to his particular interest in the functional aspects of social facts, he is often considered the founding father of functional sociology.

In *The Division of Labour in Society*, Durkheim presents his analysis of the advent and evolvement of modern society. The book's main argument is that society, with the gradual urbanisation and increased levels of population density, has evolved towards higher levels of occupational separation and specialisation, or what he coins "the social division of labour". This gradual transition has entailed a more socially differentiated society. Durkheim's book is also about the implications of this development for society's social integration. More specifically, he seeks to identify and understand the collective consciousness ensuring social integration and moral order in a period where the traditional collective ties binding individuals to their family, geographical origin and biography have loosened.

Durkheim conceives collective consciousness as the moral superstructure of society. In negative terms, this superstructure constrains the conduct and actions of human beings through generally accepted norms and rules. In positive terms, it represents a basic prerequisite for maintaining social order, because moral rules and norms chart the basic directions and goals for appropriate human conduct and ensure social integration through positive interpersonal relations.

Durkheim introduces a core distinction between two forms of social integration: mechanic solidarity and organic solidarity. Solidarity here refers to the shared values, norms and processes tying individuals to a larger whole – a society representing its own reality, sui generis. The basic idea is that premodern, segmental societies with low degrees of work differentiation, and modern industrial societies with high degrees of work differentiation, contrast in their general mode of social integration. Premodern (or traditional) societies are characterised by high levels of equality – not necessarily economic equality, but equality and homogeneity in people's norms and values. Because of these similarities, people feel intuitively connected with one another. Durkheim therefore depicts this form of solidarity as the relationship between molecules in nonorganic bodies; they lack any movement of their own and therefore move together (Durkheim 1964: 100). In societies characterised by mechanical solidarity, the collective consciousness will almost automatically be strong; partly due to the limited variation in norms and values, and partly because any breach of society's rules entails severe punishment. Indeed, Durkheim argues that the strictness of a country's penal law system represents a useful proxy for its level of mechanical solidarity.

Modern societies are characterised by a more complex, *organic* form of solidarity. Basically, the increased population density and the highly specialised work functions render the traditional similarity-based forms of social integration impossible. The notion "organic" may sound misleading, but picture modern society's many specialised functions as integrated parts in a living organism. Consider the human physiology as a concrete example: Each body part and organ plays an important role in the general maintenance and function of the body. However, some body functions are more important and vital than others. Thus, unlike Marx, Durkheim conceives a certain degree of social inequality as a basic prerequisite for society's continuance. Some occupations and work functions, so the argument goes, will be particularly crucial to society's perpetuation, and should, with a view to the common good, be rewarded accordingly.

Although the organism metaphor represents a relic of the past, Durkheim's general theory of social integration remains powerful. Bear in mind that most 19th-century theories of modernity had a tendency to describe society's evolvement as a form of disintegration. Many writers feared that society, due to comprehensive technological and sociodemographic changes, would dissolve into conflict. In that light, Durkheim's theory stands out as slightly more sophisticated. Rather than dwelling on what is lost, he develops a more complex model for social integration seeing individual ideas, sentiments and preferences as integrated into a differentiated, yet mutually dependent whole.

Indeed, some aspects of Durkheim's theory appear almost too modern, even today. He predicted that the use of repressive penal sanctions would be inversely proportional with society's degree of organic solidarity.

Breaking the law in modern society would, in other words, not involve the same forms of repressive punishment as in traditional society. Rather than enforcing "collective revenge" on the offender, the main purpose of the modern legal system would be to restore social order through rightful compensation. However, violent crimes still evoke strong feelings of collective revenge, even among people who are not directly affected by the crime. This suggests that mechanical and organic solidarity coexist as different principles of social integration: one that integrates through equality and similarity and another that integrates through differentiation and mutual dependence.

From solidarity to anomie

Despite general optimism, Durkheim also had an eye for the potential downsides of modernity. Social differentiation, he argued, involved a serious risk of deregulating society's normative structure by detaching individual behaviour from the collective consciousness. He describes it thus:

> Profound changes have been produced in the structure of our societies in a very short time; they have been freed from the segmental type with a rapidity and in proportions such as never before been seen in history. Accordingly, the morality which corresponds to this social type has regressed, but without another developing quickly enough to fill the ground that the first left vacant in our consciences.
>
> (Durkheim 1964: 408)

As given in the quote, modernity's rapid social differentiation has weakened society's collective consciousness. The nonmaterial realm of shared rules, values and ideas tying individuals together as part of a larger whole is no longer fully "up to date", and this creates severe feelings of hopelessness, distraction and confusion in the population. Durkheim summarises these conditions with the term "anomie". Anomic trends, he observes, will be most prevalent in periods characterised by comprehensive social changes, where new role patterns emerge and the norms and values that tie people together become pluralised.

In *The Division of Labour in Society*, Durkheim mainly focuses on the collective downsides of these anomic trends. For example, he emphasises the 19th century's frequent financial fluctuations and the rising unemployment rates and social inequality as indications of society's deregulation and weakened social integration. Yet, despite these signs of danger, Durkheim maintains an optimistic view on the many individual opportunities provided by modernity and the organic form of solidarity.

recognition and anomie

In *Suicide* from 1897, Durkheim presents a more pessimistic analysis of modernity and its consequences. As touched upon in Chapter 1, *Suicide* represents, for the time being, a new way of thinking about the apparently individual act of taking one's own life. As in *The Division of Labour in Society*, Durkheim adopts a holistic methodological perspective on suicide, seeing it as a social phenomenon. He moves from whole to parts and seeks to understand the social structures and trends explaining this pathological phenomenon. More specifically, he interprets the historical developments in suicide trends as conditioned by society's level of social regulation and integration. Suicide rates have doubled over a 30-year period, and he argues that broader social conditions and trends may play an important role in this development. Suicide frequencies, in this sense, become a proxy for society's level of dysfunction and disintegration. Indeed, the two conceptual distinctions regulation/integration and collectivism/individualism, as touched upon in Chapter 1, represent the main theoretical contribution in *Suicide*.

In accordance with the methodological premises put forth in *Rules of Sociological Methods*, Durkheim begins with the material social facts – in this case, available statistics concerning the European countries' financial fluctuations, family status, religious affiliations and suicide rates – but only to obtain a deeper understanding of modern society's equilibrium state, i.e. its capacity to maintain balance and stability through social integration and normative regulation.

As mentioned earlier, Durkheim identifies three forms of suicide: *the altruistic suicide*, which is most prevalent in premodern societies epitomised by strong collective norms and the embodiment of shared ideas and values; *the egoistic suicide*, which is most prevalent in individualised societies lacking social integration; and *the anomic suicide*, which typically peaks during periods of significant societal change, high levels of social differentiation and weak normative regulation.

It is difficult to draw an unequivocal distinction between egoistic and anomic suicide on the basis of Durkheim's own examples. Indeed, one may contend that these "ideal types" have certain overlaps. As shown in *The Division of Labour in Society*, both social integration and regulation are conditioned by society's immaterial realm of moral forces. Thus, though conceptually separated, egoistic and anomic suicide does not necessarily occur separately. Experiences of loneliness, hopelessness and powerlessness, as illustrated in the first pages of this chapter, are all relatively common emotional conditions among US college students. This indicates that both the individual's embeddedness in the collective (the social integration) and the moral rules and norms guiding its behaviour (the normative regulation) may be insufficient. Durkheim is most detailed in his descriptions of societal conditions causing anomic suicides, which according to him have become an almost normal feature of the socially differentiated society:

> The state of crisis and anomy is constant and, so to speak, normal. From top to bottom of the ladder, greed is aroused without knowing where to find ultimate foothold. Nothing can calm it, since its goal is far beyond all it can attain. Reality seems valueless by comparison with the dreams of fevered imaginations.
>
> (Durkheim 1951: 256)

The societal state of equilibrium always requires some level of normative regulation. The human desire is a "bottomless pit", Durkheim asserts, and in the absence of collective rules and guidelines, our insatiable pursuit of personal needs and desires will lead to despair, loss of meaning and, in the worst instance, social chaos. Durkheim's main concern is that the modern pursuit of happiness, as a result of society's pluralised moral values, ideals and goals, will be marked by heightened levels of coincidence, selectivity and subjectivity (Jensen 2011). Human desires, wants and ambitions are therefore no longer proportionate with their available opportunities of fulfilment. Society has, in other words, become unable to make its will prevail over the individual, through generally accepted standards, norms and practices.

To briefly summarise, anomie represents a societal state of crisis which, in addition to causing inexpedient financial fluctuations, growing unemployment rates and social inequality, also manifests itself as personal feelings of hopelessness, depression, apathy, exhaustion and, in the extreme case, suicide.

Meursault, the apathetic protagonist in Albert Camus' classic novel *The Stranger* (2016) from 1942 is a telling example. In absence of clear and meaningful existential and social conditions, Meursault struggles in vain to find value and purpose in life. His emotional detachment and anomic state of being is probably best illustrated in the novel's frequently quoted opening lines: "Mother died today. Or maybe yesterday, I don't know" (Camus 2016: 1). Another famous literary character facing the anomic tendencies of modern society is Holden Caulfield in J.D. Salinger's 1951 American classic *Catcher in the Rye* (1991). Salinger's book intensely captures the malaise and despair of the fictional teenage narrator. According to Caulfield, everyone and everything is "phony", and very few things in life really seem to make sense to him. A third and more topical example is how the prevailing performance and comparison culture among US college students causes feelings of inadequacy, emptiness and declining self-esteem (cf. the earlier mentioned story from the *New York Times*). In view of Durkheim's theories, it seems plausible to interpret these tendencies as expressions of anomic discrepancies between the needs, ambitions and expectations of many college students and their chances of fulfilling them.

Over the course of the 20th century, Durkheim's concept of anomie has been taken up by several other sociologists; most often to describe situations where society's reproduction of shared norms and values is weakened and a destructive form of individualism takes its place. One of the most famous revitalisations is Jürgen Habermas's discussion of communicative action and the system's colonialisation of the life world (see Chapter 6). In the following, we will look more closely at Habermas's successor at the Frankfurt School, Axel Honneth, who like his predecessor – if not directly then indirectly – draws on Durkheim in his own theoretical writings.

Axel Honneth: sociology as a theory of recognition

Honneth is the leading third-generation representative of the Frankfurt School, a German school of critical theoretical social research and philosophy dating back to the early 1930s. The first generation of Frankfurt scholars, including Max Horkheimer and Theodor Adorno, introduced immanent critique, a particular form of social critique inspired by Marxist materialism (see Chapter 2).

The basic principle of immanent critique is that progressive critical theoretical thinking, rather than resorting to idealistic philosophical speculation, should take the practical world as its starting point. Critical theory should focus on society's existing social practices and based on these identify emancipatory potentials challenging oppressive power structures and ideological underpinnings.

However, as Honneth (1994) observes, Adorno and Horkheimer never really fulfilled this ambition. Their pessimistic critiques of society's instrumentally rationalised forms of organisation and manipulative cultural machinery devoted little attention to the question of how to create more authentic and just conditions for human development. Put differently, the first generation of Frankfurt scholars were good at detecting societal problems and ideological power structures but less good at providing suggestions on how to overcome these power structures.

The second generation of Frankfurt theorists, in particular Habermas from the 1960s and onwards, gradually sowed the seeds for a more optimistic and pragmatic analysis of modernity's hidden potentials and opportunities. Habermas found a new basis for immanent social critique and emancipatory thinking in the human language. His basic idea was that human communication, under the right conditions, can create positive societal change. Our language, so he argues, represents an innate function as medium for intersubjective understanding (Nielsen 2010: 14). Identifying the normative conditions of language can therefore help us establish the basis for an "ideal speech situation", leading to more fair and open human interaction.

Honneth's work can be viewed as an extension of this theoretical project. In accordance with Habermas, Honneth sees the analytical effort to identify the normative foundations of the good society as a prerequisite for conducting fertile social critique. Indeed, one could contend that Habermas, and especially Honneth, are turning Horkheimer's and Adorno's pessimistic analyses upside down. If we want to understand which practices and relationships impede human actualisation and development, Honneth asserts, the first analytical step is to distil out the basic normative conditions of "the good life".

Honneth's theory of recognition thus represents a social philosophical exploration of the normative premises for "the good life". His main ambition is to develop a general theory that is formal enough to accommodate the diversity of life forms, ethics and values at play in modern society (Carleheden 1998: 66). Whereas Durkheim investigated the social implications of society's moral conditions, Honneth is interested in identifying the normative minimum conditions of this moral. Scholars have therefore also referred to Honneth's position as an "ethical turn" in critical theory.

In his magnum opus, *Struggle for Recognition* (1995), Honneth draws heavily on the early writings of the German philosopher Wilhelm Friedrich Hegel (1770–1831). Inspired by Hegel, he develops an idea of human self-realisation as a stepwise process conditioned by experiences of recognition in three analytically distinct spheres: love, rights and solidarity. Each sphere can (in a Durkheimian sense) be viewed as basic "integrative components" that condition social cohesion (Honneth 1996: 369–370; Willig 2003: 17). However, unlike Durkheim's top-down approach to social integration, Hegel and Honneth comprehend these integrative components as intersubjective processes. They emerge as a result of interpersonal human relations and form the basis of our social coexistence.

Honneth considers Hegel's original ideas about recognition too fragmented and abstract to form the singular basis of a contemporary critical normative theory. To develop a more consistent and material theory of recognition, anchored in the practical world, he reconstructs (or updates) Hegel's original writings through a (re)reading of American social psychologist George Herbert Mead's (1863–1931) more empirically driven work.

Mead comprehends human thinking and identity construction as a dynamic, intersubjective process. When we think, we imagine that we are facing someone. Sometimes we imagine standing in front of a real person, but in principle our thinking is informed by the attitudes of the

recognition and anomie

"generalised other". The generalised other represents the incarnation of role expectations shared by an organised community or social group (Mead 1977: 34). Our thinking, in other words, involves a cognitive reflection of how our behaviour and actions will be conceived by others. As Mead puts it, we adopt the role of the generalised other.

This idea plays an important part in Honneth's fine-tuning of Hegel's early writings about recognition. The human striving for recognition, Honneth asserts, requires an orientation towards the generalised other. But this orientation is not always without complications. Consider in this regard that Mead conceives identity construction as an ongoing dialogue between the "Me" and the "I", i.e. between the role expectations of the generalised other, which are integrated into the "Me", and the ways in which we respond to these expectations on the basis of individual impulses and prior experiences (the "I"). Honneth describes the potential complications related to this dialogical process as follows:

> Because subjects are forced, under pressure from their I, to constantly loosen the constraints on the norms embodied in the "generalized other", they are to a certain extent, psychologically required to do what they can to expand ... recognition relations. The social praxis resulting from the collective effort to "enrich the community" in this way is what can be called, within Mead's social psychology, the "struggle for recognition".
>
> (Honneth 1995: 88)

As illustrated, Mead's ideas do not merely serve as a practical anchoring of Hegel's abstract philosophical ideas. In Mead's thinking, Honneth identifies a conception of society's morally motivated conflicts as "struggles for recognition" tied to the encounter between the "I" and the generalised other (Juul 2013: 88).

Against this backdrop, we can now indulge more deeply in Honneth's synthesisation and refinement of the concept of recognition in *Struggle for Recognition*. As mentioned, Honneth conceives self-realisation as a stepwise process conditioned by experiences of recognition in three spheres of interaction: love, rights and solidarity. Each sphere corresponds to a certain type of self-relation acquired by the individual through processes of interaction and socialisation: self-confidence (acquired in the sphere of love), self-respect (acquired in the sphere of rights) and self-esteem (acquired in the sphere of solidarity). To fully realise ourselves, we must develop a positive self-relation in all three spheres.

Honneth also ascribes a certain form of disrespect to each recognition sphere. To adequately describe the normative conditions of recognition, so he asserts, one must first identify the factors that impede successful self-realisation. Each form of disrespect, in this sense, refers to an array of situations where positive recognition is replaced by infringement and violations damaging the individual's self-relation (Honneth 1995: 131).

The sphere of love comprises the mutual forms of emotional recognition expressed in the family and among close friends. It is through this form of interaction that the child, early in life, meets itself (through the eyes of others) and develops feelings of love, mutual dependence and unconditional support. In this sphere the individual is recognised for its unique value in the world and develops a self-confidence that enables it to engage in meaningful social relations with others (Honneth 1995: 25, 37–42, 95–107).

Self-confidence here refers to the individual's basic ability to express needs and wishes to others, without which its participation in the other spheres of interaction will be impeded (Anderson 1995: xiii). Honneth therefore also describes the sphere of love as the primary arena of recognition. Disrespect in this sphere manifests itself in violations related to the individual's physical integrity. Honneth highlights torture, rape and physical abuse as fundamental, intersubjective forms of disrespect that impede the individual's confidence in itself and its surroundings (Honneth 1995: 132).

In the sphere of rights, the individual is recognised as a citizen with the same constituted rights and opportunities as anyone else. Recognition here implies an ability to take on the perspective of the generalised other and recognise the basic societal rights and opportunities of one's fellow citizens. The sphere of rights in this sense underpins the individual's notion of self-respect through a form of mutual commitment. "Self-respect" is here to be understood as a cognitive experience of universal dignity instigated by the broader community's or society's conception of the individual as a morally responsible, rational human being (Honneth 1995: 107–120).

Occurrences of disrespect in this sphere relate to the exclusion of individuals or social groups from the basic rights and opportunities held by the rest of society. This form of exclusion indirectly implies that a given individual is not considered to be a morally responsible, rational citizen on equal footing with anyone else (Honneth 1995: 132). The historical discrimination of blacks in South Africa and the United States is a concrete example. Among Honneth's own examples are the rapidly expanding groups of socially excluded immigrants and refugees in Europe and North America. They often lack the necessary rights, opportunities and legal security to lead a somewhat bearable life in their new countries of residence (Honneth in Petersen and Willig 2002: 267).

Whereas the sphere of rights (in its ideal form) supports the individual's self-relation by referring to shared rights and opportunities, the sphere of solidarity focuses on abilities and characteristics that separate society's

recognition and anomie

citizens from one another. Honneth's main point is that the recognition of each individual's particular contributions to the common good represents an important premise for successful human self-realisation and social integration (Honneth 1995: 125).

Honneth conceives solidarity as the web of societal interests and values that tie citizens from different backgrounds together and recognise each for their unique contributions and qualities. Modern society is epitomised by a multiplicity of ethics and values, and thus the sphere of solidarity needs to be pluralistic in its foundation. Put differently, society's web of shared values and interests must be inclusive enough for all individuals, irrespective of religious beliefs, cultures, ethnicities and life-forms, to feel recognised for their uniqueness and particular contributions to the common good. Solidarity in this sense supports the individual's self-esteem by affirming the relevance and value of its particular traits and abilities. Honneth formulates it as follows:

> In modern societies ... social relations of symmetrical esteem between individualized (and autonomous) subjects represent a prerequisite for solidarity. In this sense, to esteem one another symmetrically means to view the other in light of values that allow the abilities and traits of the other to appear significant for a shared praxis. Relationships of this sort can be said to be cases of "solidarity", because they inspire not just passive tolerance but felt concern for what is individual and particular about the other person. For only to the degree to which I actively care about the development of the other's characteristics (which seem foreign to me) can our shared goals be realized.
>
> (Honneth 1995: 128–129)

As illustrated by this quotation, Honneth's conception of solidarity shares many similarities with Durkheim's. But while Durkheim conceives solidarity as something external to the individual determining its behaviour, Honneth is primarily interested in solidarity as an intersubjective process integrating a wide array of value orientations through mutual interests and shared understandings.

Disrespect in the sphere of solidarity arises in situations where the individual, or a social group, is not recognised as contributing to the common praxis in any meaningful or beneficial way. Such occurrences can trigger personal experiences of humiliation, demotion and lowered self-esteem (Honneth 1995: 134). Honneth highlights unpaid housework and caregiving as examples. If such activities are not considered worthy of recognition by society at large, homemakers are left with poor chances of acquiring the necessary level of social esteem to establish a positive self-relation (Honneth 1994).

Summing up, it is important to note that the boundaries of recognition in Honneth's theory are by no means static. The breadth and scope of what is considered recognisable is under constant negotiation and changes over time; especially in the spheres of solidarity and rights, we see ongoing social struggles for recognition. Consider, for instance, racial discrimination, which over the last 60 years has resulted in dramatic, morally motivated struggles for recognition with subsequent social changes. Historical developments in the rights of women and sexual minorities are likewise the result of continuous struggles for recognition in the spheres of rights and solidarity. Last but not least, it seems relevant to interpret the recent decades' immigrant riots in Gothenburg, Paris and London as recurring struggles for recognition. More specifically, these riots can be interpreted as social conflicts caused by the inadequate opportunities that young minority men are offered in pursuing their personal conceptions of the good life and acquiring a positive self-relation under society's existing forms of recognition.

From recognition to social pathologies

Based on this introduction to Honneth's ideas about recognition, we can now turn to his writings on social pathologies. As shown, Honneth's most famous work carves out the normative prerequisites for the good life and healthy society. In his later writings, these prerequisites function as cues and enable him to identify and describe the more anomalous and pathological aspects of modernity in clearer ways. Ominous social practices, one could say, stand out more distinctively when investigated in light of positive counterexamples (Jakobsen 2011).

According to Honneth, social pathologies should be understood broadly. They represent the multiplicity of obstacles and forms of disrespect that impede human self-realisation (Honneth 1996: 388). In fact, the social conflicts mentioned earlier are all manifestations of underlying social pathologies. In the following, we limit our focus to a particular form of pathologies prevalent in contemporary society – "the pathologies of individual freedom", also described as "suffering from indeterminacy" (Honneth 2010: 28).

As a result of material, social and spiritual developments over the last 50 years, individual self-realisation has today, according to Honneth, become an almost inescapable institutional requirement. Human beings are confronted with increasing demands for authentic self-actualisation in both their work and private lives; and as we shall return to in a moment, these demands are closely intertwined with the emergence of new pathological symptoms such as inner emptiness, absence of purpose and insufficiency (Honneth 2004).

recognition and anomie   49

As described in the article "Organized Self-Realization: Some Paradoxes of Individualization" (Honneth 2004), two divergent, individualising tendencies have intertwined to establish a particular form of individualisation in today's society. The first relates to the rapid social and economic transformations of Western societies from the 1960s and onwards. As a result of increasing salaries, decreasing work hours and expanding social mobility, the ways of life open to the individual have gradually diversified. Simultaneously, the hippie movement's reorientation towards the romantic ideal and a more authenticity-focused life-form praising aesthetic creativity, sensuous impulsiveness and sexual liberation has opened new modes of self-realisation.

The intertwinement of these structural and cultural developments has paved the way for a new and more qualitative form of individualism: "subjects [now] experiment ... with various forms of existence to realise the core of their own self in the light of their experiences, a core that distinguishes them from all others" (2004: 470).

According to Honneth, this form of individualism has been co-opted by the contemporary capitalist system as leverage to increase human productivity and promote employee engagement. Referring to the work of Luc Boltanski, Ève Chiapello and Richard Sennett (see Chapters 7 and 10), Honneth describes how increasing demands for adaptability, flexibility and mobility have become important prerequisites for maintaining a successful career and life narrative. Today, employees are conceived as innovative cocreators of their own work activities and increasingly take part in the organisation of the firms' production and service processes. As a result, work has become an almost religious "call" and a primary arena for self-realisation. At the same time, the evolvement of electronic media has kept the authentic and creative life narrative alive and well outside the workplace. Indeed, with the increasing use of social media platforms such as Facebook, Twitter and Instagram, this point seems more topical than ever.

Honneth's concern about this development is rooted in what he conceives as the pathological one-sidedness of the modern ideal of self-realisation (Honneth 2010). The pluralisation of moral values and recognition forms implies freedom from something, but not necessarily freedom to do something. His main argument is that the absence of intersubjective commitments places the individual in a false social and self-relation, where individual freedom becomes the central tenet of personal development. In a 2002 interview, he said:

> It is still my belief that the success of the normative integration of societies depends on their potential to create stable structures of social recognition. The situation of our present societies is progressing

towards becoming more and more flexible, and in that sense, liquid. These traits can be described as forms of disintegration even as the dissolution of forms of recognition, thus creating societies which are less and less able to realise normative integration.

(Honneth in Petersen and Willig 2002: 271)

As the observant reader may have noticed, this quotation shares clear similarities with Durkheim's writings on the anomic tendencies of modern society. In accordance with Durkheim, Honneth regards the absence of stable recognition forms (and hereby collectively shared moral values) as a threat to contemporary society's social integration. Further, both authors are tracing the symptoms of this development in pathological traits emerging in the individual: Durkheim highlights the anomic and egoistic forms of suicide, whereas Honneth emphasises the new millennium's increasing prevalence of mental disorders, such as anxiety and depression. More specifically, he conceives the increasing consumption of antidepressants in Western countries as a pathological expression of unstable recognition forms. Contemporary society, so he argues, lacks clear and stable "recognition frameworks" and therefore cannot ensure meaningful and satisfactory self-actualisation (Honneth 2004; 2010). The result is personal exhaustion and lowered self-esteem in individuals; how does the "I" develop a healthy and sustainable self-relation when the generalised other is out of sight?

To clarify this point, let us return to the report on "today's anguished students" described in the first pages of the chapter. Following Honneth's line of argumentation, it is not entirely out of place to interpret the hopelessness, mental exhaustion and anxiety experienced by US college students as pathological effects of distorted demands for individual self-realisation. As he puts it, our individual freedom cannot succeed without at least some level of certainty about the value of our own abilities. In the absence of stable structures of social recognition, feelings of indeterminacy and unrealistic self-expectations are therefore likely to burgeon. The lack of a shared framework of external norms and values in society becomes re-embedded in the individual as an absence of inner inhibitions (Honneth 2010); and this absence may help explain the pathological consequences of the prevalent performance and comparison culture at US college campuses described in the *New York Times*.

Modernity and its downsides

Starting with the concepts of anomie and recognition, this chapter has given two theoretical accounts of the classic sociological questions: "By what means is social integration possible?" and "How can we understand

and explain the pathological downsides of modernity?" This concluding section summarises the core similarities and differences characterising these accounts and points to caveats and limitations in their scope of argumentation.

As we have shown, Durkheim and Honneth both seek to carve out the basic conditions for social integration in modern society. Likewise, they share a practical ambition to develop theoretical accounts that offer concrete suggestions on how to diagnose and counter the pathological downsides of modernity. The authors also diverge on a number of issues. As a declared positivist, Durkheim aspires to a value-free, empiricist science, but when we delve into his writings it becomes clear that this scientific ideal does not always correspond with his actual analytical approach. Indeed, Durkheim moves from the material to the nonmaterial social facts in his investigations, but most of his conclusions are based on interpretations that refer only indirectly to the empirical foundations of his work. In this sense, one could contend that Durkheim's analytical approach has more similarities with Weber's interpretive sociology than what he describes in his methodological writings (Østerberg 2002). Further, despite his explicit ascription to the ideal of value-free objectivity, Durkheim's analyses often resort to implicit normative presumptions about what the "healthy" and "just" society looks like. These points illustrate the dynamic and relative nature of social science terminology. What was conceived as an "empiricist" and "value-free" alternative to the dominant strand of abstract social philosophical writings in the 19th century, today stands in a different light.

Honneth is more explicit about his normative stance. Yet, like Durkheim, he also tends to break with his own methodological principles. Despite a declared ambition of conducting immanent social critique with a practical anchoring in "real-world problems", Honneth's theoretical arguments often lack concrete empirical examples to test and clarify the range and applicability of his theory. Critics have raised concerns about the validity of his writings as a universal "grammar" for the good life. The idea that the normative boundaries of recognition should be identified in individual experiences of disrespect, for instance, has been a matter of some contestation. Two pertinent questions arise in this regard: Do individual experiences of disrespect always represent a relevant proxy for unjust societal practices? And, are individuals always aware of their suppression? By default, the answer to both questions must be no, and Honneth has therefore also revised his view on the scope and range of his arguments in *Struggle for Recognition* since its original publication in 1992 (Honneth and Boltanski 2009; cf. Jakobsen 2011).

Finally, it seems relevant to briefly highlight Durkheim's and Honneth's diverging conceptions of the structure-agency relationship. Durkheim, as mentioned, conceives society as a supra-individual reality determining the behaviour of its citizens. In his thinking, individual actors do not possess any noteworthy analytical status as cocreators of institutions and their own lives, and critics therefore problematise an "agency-deficit" in his theories. By devoting analytical attention to the intersubjective processes underpinning society's social structures and change processes, Honneth partly overcomes this "agency deficit". As we describe in the following, other sociologists such as Goffman, Giddens and Beck offer far more systematised conceptualisations of how individual actors create and make sense of their lives in modern society.

chapter 4

Social interaction and marginalisation

Simmel and the Chicago School

> The urbanization of the world, which is one of the most impressive facts of modern times, has wrought profound changes in virtually every phase of social life.
>
> (Wirth 1938: 1)

Georg Simmel (1858–1918), like Weber, Marx and Durkheim, was concerned with the profound societal changes that characterised the second half of the 19th century. The dynamic and progressive transition from a feudal and traditional society to the rise of a modern society prompted the need for new understandings of how (modern) societies emerge and develop. Although their "diagnosis of the times" (Zeitdiagnose) varies and they focus on different characteristics and consequences of the processes of modernisation (see also Chapters 2 and 3), they were all preoccupied with determining the facts relevant for sociological analysis in developing a "science about society" (Park in Jørgensen 2005: 40; Tonboe 2009).

In this chapter we address the work of Simmel and the Chicago School, whose different strands were highly influenced by Simmel's sociology. Marx theorised modernity in terms of capitalism, Durkheim theorised it in terms of differentiation and Weber theorised it in terms of rationalisation.

Simmel saw modernity as particularly related to urbanisation and the money economy that followed the growth of the metropolis. He – and later the Chicago School sociologists – perceived the city as the place to study modernity in its most wide-ranging and comprehensive form, and he perceived society in terms of social relations and human interaction rather than individuals or institutions. This line of thought is carried on in the Chicago School but in a modified and more empirically founded version than in Simmel's work.

With the oft-cited essay "The Stranger" (1908) and "The Metropolis and Mental Life" (1903) as point of departure, the chapter identifies central tenets in Georg Simmel's classic work on social interaction vis-à-vis his analysis of the relations between individuals and the greater society. With a specific view to the analytical duality of distance and closeness, Simmel's theories are compared to the Chicago School's influential theories on marginalisation and the (dis)organisation of society. Like Simmel, the representatives of the Chicago School of sociology were concerned with new ways of life in modern cities, especially their consequences for social life. The introductory epigraph by Louis Wirth (1897–1952), a central figure in the Chicago School, reflect the recurring motif of the consequences of urban life.

Simmel: content and forms of social interaction

Georg Simmel is regarded as one of the four founding fathers of sociology along with Durkheim, Marx and Weber, but he has never obtained their status as a sociological classic. Simmel is often described as brilliant and original. Indeed Hungarian philosopher Georg Lukács (1885–1971) referred to him as the "most significant and interesting figure in the whole of modern philosophy" (Lukács 1991: 145). His work was praised by students and sociological contemporaries, but it was rejected by most colleagues in philosophy and social sciences.

In many ways, he was a "stranger" in academia, and his particular essayistic writing style and somewhat unsystematic and "unscientific" research approach were often criticised. Due to the anti-Semitic climate and the nonestablished position of sociology at the time, Simmel spent much of his career working as an unpaid private docent and later in an unpaid position as extraordinary professor at the University of Berlin. He did not obtain a permanent (nonetheless unsatisfactory) academic position until the age of 56 at the University of Strasbourg. Without a permanent position and formalised relations to students, it was difficult for him to set a fashion like Weber and Durkheim had been able to, due to their more solidified positions in the academic world (Levine 1971; Tonboe

social interaction and marginalisation 55

2009). However, Simmel's ambition was not to set academic fashion, and he often said that he wished for his scientific inheritance to be distributed as one would distribute money – to intellectual heirs who could administrate it at their own discretion.

> Any social phenomenon or process is composed of two elements which in reality are inseparable: on the one hand, an interest, a purpose, a motive; on the other, a form or mode of interaction among individuals trough which, or in the shape of which, that content attains social reality. ... It becomes society only when the vitality of these contents attains the form of reciprocal influence; only when one individual has an effect, immediate or mediate, upon another, is mere spatial aggregation or temporal succession transformed into society. If, therefore, there is to be a science whose subject matter is society and nothing else, it must exclusively investigate these interactions, these kinds and forms of sociation.
>
> (Simmel 1971: 24–25)

This quotation from "The Problem of Sociology", originally from 1908, illustrates four key theoretical issues.

First, Simmel's scientific approach is referred to as "formal sociology". Simmel claimed that different human phenomena – however distinct they may appear – can be understood according to similar formal concepts. For example, interaction in different groups such as gangs, religious communities or families is likely to exhibit identical underlying forms of interaction such as "superiority, subordination, competition, division of labour, formation of parties, representation [and] inner solidarity coupled with exclusiveness towards the outside" (Simmel 1971: 26).

Hence, if we abstract from specific and diverse contents and isolate the specific forms of interaction, we can describe society by way of these structures and study how different behaviours and relations occur and develop. Simmel understands content as each individual's "drive, interest, purpose, inclination, psychic state [and] movement" for interaction (Simmel 1971: 24). Content as such is not social, but it becomes social when "it attains the form of reciprocal influence".

Second, these social forms are not to be understood as fixed or pure as they intersect in various ways according to different social phenomena. The concepts of form and content are thus analytical constructs. In reality, they interlink, but to understand society and establish the subject matter of sociology, we have to expose the notion of society to an abstraction to distil content and form. Unlike Weber (see Chapter 2), Simmel keeps his focus on the notion of interaction, which to him is of key sociological

social interaction and marginalisation

importance, by placing content in brackets and leaving individual agency and individual motives out.

All these interactions can be structured according to different social forms of interaction. According to Simmel, it is precisely these forms that compose the sociological field of research. This leads us to the third and related point: The sociohistorical developments that have shaped the rise of modern society and brought changes in terms of culture, knowledge, economy and industry, among other things, cannot be adequately explained by a few brilliant individuals or by God. Simmel claims that any explanation for the constitution of society must be found in the interactions between individuals. And to properly understand the formation of society (*Vergesellschaftung*), new approaches need to be applied. Society is not a fixed and observable unit – it is dynamic, contextual and changeable due to continuous interactions (Simmel 1998).

Fourth, it is reciprocity of actions (i.e. interactions) that constitute society. In other words, society consists of all the small and large interactions that occur between individuals, and often at the microlevel. The sociological lens must therefore zoom in all on the small interwoven "threads" of interaction (Simmel 1998: 39) that link humans, rather than on the institutional level. This ambition to include the microlevel in studies of society can be described as social microscopy, and Simmel likens his theoretical approach to the medical sciences and the microscope which allows for studying an organism at the level of cells rather than the level of organs. Just as cellular-level knowledge is essential to understanding the formation of the body, knowledge about the smallest relations between people is vital for understanding the formation of society. It is exactly these primary microscopic and bounded interactions that translate into (hypostasise) macroscopic unities and society at large (Simmel 1998).

Though Simmel's approach is an essentially microsociological approach, he maintains a focus on the reciprocity between individuals and society. In general, his work is informed by a dialectical approach that is multidirectional, dismisses clear demarcations between social phenomena and is tuned in on relations, including contradictions and conflicts (Ritzer and Goodman 2003: 156–157). The dialectical approach is particularly evident in his essay "The Metropolis and Mental Life" (see below). Yet, the relationship between the individual and society is also a theme in Simmel's understanding of "How Is Society Possible?"

In this essay from 1908, Simmel stipulates three a priori individual conditions that render society possible: The conditions relate to the premise that you constitute a unity/society with others, and they express that "concrete processes in the individual consciousness are actually processes of sociation" (1971c: 8). First, the uniqueness of each person makes it

social interaction and marginalisation 57

impossible for us to fully realise any other individuals, because for us to do so would mean that we resembled them completely in every regard. Instead, in the meeting with others we generalise and categorise each other according to type or position based on available information.

Second, each individual is both in and outside society, i.e. more than just part of society. For example, the officer, the businessman and the bureaucrat are more than just their "type" in specific interactions. There is also a nonsocial element to each individual and their personality and this second a priori reads that "life is not entirely social" (1971c: 14). Although we are social beings living in a society, we are not absorbed by it; we all have our own personality. This relates to the third a priori; taking part in social life requires a certain harmony between an individual and society in the sense that society provides the individual with a position that is based on the individual's qualities in the specific social milieu, while allowing each individual to maintain its individuality. These three a priori conditions illustrate Simmel's general individual-society dialectic in showing that individuals are both constituted by and constitute society.

The stranger: between closeness and distance

"The stranger" is one of Simmel's most well-known types. Like "the poor", "the adventurer", "the miser", "the spendthrift" and "the nobleman", "the stranger" represents certain behavioural characteristics that constitute typical and observable features in a given time and context. By virtue of the individual's position in different social relations, he or she is assigned certain social roles which contain a societally defined set of expectations that the individual is expected to meet. Like analytical concepts of form and content, a type is a social construct that Simmel applies as an abstraction to study diverse configurations of interaction. In the case of "the stranger", Simmel considers his abstraction to be more than just a type; indeed strangeness translates into a "sociological form" (Simmel 1971a: 143). As we will see later, in Simmel's essay "The Metropolis and Mental Life", the stranger comes to represent modern life in general.

> In case of the stranger, the union of closeness and remoteness involved in every human relationship is patterned in a way that may be succinctly formulated as follows; the distance within this relation indicates that one who is close by is remote, but his strangeness indicates that one who is remote is near. The state of being a stranger is of course a completely positive relation; it is a specific form of relation. ... The stranger is an element of the group itself, not unlike the

poor and sundry "inner enemies" – an element whose membership within the group involves both being outside it and confronting it.

(Simmel 1971a: 143–144)

The first lines emphasise that every social relationship is defined by strangeness, which to Simmel includes the duality of closeness and distance. The stranger is not the wanderer who comes and goes but the "potential wanderer" (Simmel 1971a: 143) who comes and stays with the group but does not originate from it. The stranger should not be confused with the kind of strangeness that precludes membership in a group and results in a nonrelation. Simmel mentions the example of the nonrelation between the Greeks and the barbarians. But unlike those entirely non-related, the stranger in Simmel's terminology is a member of a group. The specific combination of closeness and distance allows the stranger to adopt a specific position in relation to the other group members and enter into a form of interaction that Simmel regards as predominantly positive.

Without kinship and occupational ties to the social group, the stranger remains a mobile and nonorganic group member with a certain degree of objectivity and impartiality that, paradoxically, is likely to make the stranger a confidante to other group members. The lack of specific agendas and interests makes the stranger a well-suited receiver of secrets and confessions. Such an objectivity or "bird's eye view" (Simmel 1971a: 146) unattached from bound anticipations bestows a certain degree of freedom upon the stranger, but also comes with certain risks and dangers; social detachment may make the stranger an easier target for accusations of betrayal and likewise make him or her more likely to be singled out as a scapegoat. Still, Simmel is keener to emphasise the positive aspects of the previously mentioned freedom attached to the greater degree of objectivity of not being confined to common and traditional practices.

Furthermore, the relation between the stranger and the group is more abstract than relations between existing in-group members because the stranger and the group only have the most general of qualities in common. The nature of this relation may draw our attention to differences between the stranger and the group, and it is the specific character of similarities and differences that determines the degree of closeness and distance. For example, if the stranger and the group resemble each other in terms of e.g. nationality, occupation or social position, the group may consider the stranger as close. If the similarities are universal and extend far beyond the scope of the social group, the stranger will become remote. Although a specific "reciprocal tension" (Simmel 1971a: 149) between closeness and distance characterises the relation to the stranger, all types

social interaction and marginalisation 59

and social relations contain both elements. When the exceptionality of a relationship disappears, estrangement is likely to appear. As Tonboe (2009: 276) points out, the ever-present element of strangeness (and potentially estrangement) is relevant to all of us, and this could account for the broad sociological interest in this particular type.

City strangers and the ambiguity of individuality

Simmel has argued that his work mainly has focused on "the limits of individuality in modern society" (Featherstone 1991: 7). This theme is clearly manifested in Simmel's renowned 1903 essay "The Metropolis and Mental Life" in which he analyses modern city life and dissects the limitations and possibilities – the enabling and constraining structures – of increased individuality. The essay forms the basis of later theories on urbanisation and urban sociology and is to this day a highly relevant sociological work.

Metropolitan individuality emerges in the interplay between physical, social and psychological causes. The agglomeration and concentration of individuals within the confines of the city area increases the number of social relations and the number of stimuli encountered by each individual. Consequently, social relations become more fluid and noncommittal, integration decreases and individual freedom of movement grows. The intensification of both internal and external stimuli makes an emotional response to all such impressions impossible, and the individual reacts with "intellectual distance" (Simmel 1971b: 334) to protect itself from the threats of the "profound disruption" (Simmel 1971b: 326) that characterises city life.

> The mutual reserve and indifference, and the intellectual conditions of life in large social units are never more sharply appreciated in their significance for the independence of the individual than in the dense crowds of the metropolis because the bodily closeness and lack of space make intellectual distance readily perceivable for the first time. It is obviously only the obverse of this freedom that, under certain circumstances, one never feels as lonely and deserted as in this metropolitan crush of persons.
>
> (Simmel 1971b: 334)

Unlike the emotional and geographical closeness and togetherness of small-town relations, urban social relations are much more calculated and intellectual, as it is only the human mind (and not human emotions) that allows the individual to adapt fast enough to the city's stimuli. Bodily closeness stands in opposition to intellectual distance, and for the individual this combination manifests itself as a blasé and reserved attitude towards fellow citizens.

This defensive, blasé attitude is the most central characteristic of modern life and it defines the city as a new social form. As discussed earlier, the element of strangeness lies in wait as a likely result of the intellectual distance causing loneliness. Still, individuals are not indifferent towards one another, as the division of labour makes every individual mutually dependent; nonetheless, rather than approaching one another as individuals, each individual is merely seen, and sees others, according to type and function (Simmel 1971b; Tonboe 2009).

For the metropolitan type, the division of labour is a mechanism that characterises the late 19th century and modern life. The transition from life in a hamlet – a self-sufficient unit with limited social division of labour – to city life and a greater concentration of individuals requires more specialised work functions. The social division of labour results in greater differentiation among individuals, but it also makes them mutually dependent.

Another related factor is the growth of a money economy, which thrives under the conditions offered by the metropolis. Unlike in small villages, the producer of goods and the purchaser of these goods do not necessarily know each other. Instead, the money economy is driven by a market logic that relies on rational exchanges, numbers and intellect (not emotions) and "reduces all quality and individuality to a purely quantitative level" (Simmel 1971b: 326). This all happens at the expense of emotional relations and social life. The intellectual distance and the money economy interrelate closely and this reciprocity further promotes the blasé attitude that characterises the metropolitan type.

The rise of urbanisation, differentiation and industrialisation threatens the independence and the individuality of each citizen and necessitates a "resistance of the individual to being levelled, swallowed up in the social-technological mechanism" (Simmel 1971b: 324) that represents societal macro structures and constrains outside forces. In "The Metropolis and Mental Life", Simmel studies the interaction between individual and society – or between subjectivity and objectivity – or to use yet another sociological duality, between agency and social structures. Importantly, Simmel sees subjectivity and objectivity as interrelated rather than antithetical concepts. This is not an easy balance and "the deepest problems of modern life" is to keep "the sovereign powers of society" at bay and assert the individuality and personality of one's own (Simmel 1971b: 324, 336).

Simmel understands modernity according to the concepts of subjective versus objective culture. The sovereign powers just mentioned also refer to how the objective culture dominates the subjective one. Humans may

social interaction and marginalisation 61

be the creators of art, religion, science, law and other cultural elements, but with the social division of labour and increased differentiation, our cultural products detach from their creators, become independent of the subjective culture, and the individual loses its ability to produce, maintain and acquire them. As they crystallise into social structures, the individual "becomes a single cog" (Simmel 1971b: 337) in the societal machine and is at risk of withdrawing from social life. This is at the heart of what Simmel calls the "tragedy of culture", a notion he explores further in his major work *The Philosophy of Money* from 1900. It has been suggested that Simmel's theory is akin to Marx's theory of alienation (see Chapter 2), that he offers a dialectic developmental theory, and against the backdrop of the metropolitan opposites accounts for the developments of modern life (Tonboe 2009).

Despite the dreary picture of the existential conditions of modern life, Simmel is not unequivocally critical or pessimistic in his interpretation. Metropolitan life is in nature cosmopolitan, and it offers an unparalleled degree of freedom and individuality in releasing people from the trammels of tradition. The objective culture also brings with it an unprecedented volume of knowledge, innovation and technology that is conducive to individuals' intellectual mental life. Simmel conducts a detailed and complex analysis of the ambiguity of modernity and individuality, not to condone or complain about social and historical developments, but merely to understand their implications. Nevertheless, he mainly focuses on the dangers of society's iron grip on its citizens.

The Chicago School: urban life and social (dis)organisation

While Simmel's scientific inheritance has been distributed to a wide range of beneficiaries among his contemporaries and later generations, his sociological thoughts and ideas are especially prominent in the collected works of the Chicago School. In its early days of glory, important inheritors within the Chicago School included sociologists like Robert Ezra Park (1864–1944), Albion Small (1854–1926), Louis Wirth (1897–1952), William Isaac Thomas (1863–1947) and many others. The later generation of the Chicago School scholars, also referred to as the "Second Chicago School" (Plummer 1999: 10) included key figures such as Everett Hughes (1897–1983), Erving Goffman (1922–1982, see Chapter 9) and Howard Becker (1928–), who were all strongly influenced by Simmel's theories. In this chapter we will concentrate on the early period of the Chicago School, which dominated the American field of sociology in the first third of the 20th century. This period of approximately 35 years covers a massive body of work from a range of important scholars, and we can only

62   social interaction and marginalisation

include a small selection in this introductory chapter. Thus, though The Chicago School tradition is broad and heterogenetic, we will focus on major and common features that identify it as a "school". After a broad discussion, we will delve into the academic work of Robert Park, the most prominent figure of the early Chicago School.

Professor Albion Small is credited as the founder of the world's first department of sociology at the University of Chicago in 1892. In 1895, he established the still leading *American Journal of Sociology*, and in 1905 he cofounded the American Sociological Society (today the American Sociological Association). These efforts were essential in establishing and solidifying the discipline of sociology in an American context. With Park's article "The City: Suggestions for the Investigation of Human Behaviour in the City Environment" from 1915 and the pioneering five-volume *The Polish Peasant in Europe and America* (1918–1920) by W.I. Thomas and Florian Znaniecki, the Chicago School's leading sociological position was established even though it was not referred to as a unified school until 1930 (Jørgensen 2005).

To understand the sociohistorical context that shaped the Chicago School and provided the empirical foundation for its studies, we need to take a closer look at the drastic developments in the city of Chicago in the late 19th and early 20th century. In 1840, Chicago was a small town with around 4,500 residents. Sixty years later, the city had become the second-largest in the United States with approximately one and a half million citizens, largely due to migration from Ireland, Poland, Sweden, Denmark, Germany, Italy and Croatia, among others. In 1930, the population had reached three million, a quarter of which had been born in a foreign country. For the Chicago sociologists, the rapid transformations that had turned Chicago into a modern city had also made it an evident case for empirical studies of modern city life in all its complexity and paradoxical tensions. The city prospered culturally, intellectually, economically and technologically, but it also experienced severe gang crime, corruption, poverty and a high degree of segregation. Chicago, says Plummer, represented the "pathos of modernity" and the inherent tension of the city, and modern life, became the common denominator for the theoretical work of the Chicago School sociologists (Plummer 1999: 7).

The Chicago School cannot be encapsulated or recapped within a "single paradigm", but Chicago sociologist Andrew Abbott (1999: 6) has pointed to a number of common features that justify its designation as a school of thought. First, the city of Chicago was always the primary subject of studies, whether the object was delinquency (Shaw 1930), homelessness (Anderson 1923), gang crime (Whyte 1943) or any other topic. Second, the studies shared a processual character in their efforts to examine social movements and social change, conflict and accommodation, and

social interaction and marginalisation 63

organisation and disorganisation. Third, Chicago School sociology sees society – as Simmel sees it – through a perspective of interaction and social groups rather than the perspectives of single individuals. Fourth, although the theoretical works and approaches of its members may have differed in terms of empirical, conceptual and theoretical orientation, most studies were empirically grounded and made use of observational methods. However, in the words of Martin Bulmer (1984: 3), it would be wrong simply to characterise the Chicago School's approach to sociology as "unbridled empiricism"; Chicago School sociologists may have taken empirical research as a starting point for their work, but they were always concerned with integrating theory as well.

The preoccupation with concrete and particular social phenomena, human experience and the practical bearings of ideas and conceptions on abstract and metaphysical ideas is well rooted in the pragmatist source of inspiration which guided the Chicago sociologists. American philosophy of pragmatism, as developed and represented by Charles Sanders Pierce (1839–1914), William James (1842–1910), John Dewey (1859–1952) and George Herbert Mead (1863–1931) provided the strongest influence for the Chicago School. Nowhere was this influence more apparent than in the Chicago sociologists' empirical approach to everyday life and social phenomena (focus on concreteness and detail); in the contextual and situated meaning making processes (rejection of a single fixed truth) and in the insistence on dialectic relations such as subject and object (transcendence of philosophical dualisms). For instance, Mead's social psychological notion of the self is an example of the dialectic relation between the individual and the social as incorporated in the concepts of "Me" and "I" (see Chapter 3). "Me" denotes the external and societal "organised set of attitudes" (Mead 1977: 230) and expectations which we internalise and act from; "I" denotes the individual's spontaneous and experiential responses to "the attitude of others" (Mead 1977: 230). In short, Mead's notion of the self is a dialectic relation between individual autonomy and structural influences (Mead 1977: 230; Plummer 1999). Plummer (1999) identifies two sources of inspiration in addition to American pragmatism: a wish for progressive social and political reform and opposition to racism, industrial and human exploitation and non-democratic systems, and the European, especially the German, philosophical and sociological tradition. As mentioned, Simmel was the key inspiration, which will be discussed again in this chapter's closing comparison and discussion.

It has been said that the Chicago School tradition covers four more or less distinct theoretical approaches to sociology. Building on Abbott's (1999) three trajectories, Jørgensen and Schmidt (2009) expand and develop this classification. They propose a model (see the following)

64   social interaction and marginalisation

comprising four approaches: the human ecological trajectory, the trajectory of social (dis)organising, the social psychological trajectory and the trajectory of action research and social work.

The human ecological trajectory interlinks the spatial with the social and biological processes with societal developments. Among its main representatives are Robert Park and Ernest W. Burgess (1886–1966). Park defines human ecology "as an organization that springs up from the competition that is linked to the struggle to survive" (Jørgensen and Schmidt 2009: 62). Competition, says Park, is a foundational form of interaction; just as plants compete for sunlight, human beings compete for values and goods. The symbiotic and ecological order found in the processes through which plant and animal communities develop, says Park, can be compared to that of human communities, and studying the former may tell us something about the social and moral order of the latter. The moral order curbs the inherent condition of competition and mutual struggle via social control and collective actions among individuals (Coser 1971). At its core, this theoretical framework aims to explain the developments of the metropolis and their influence on communities and forms of interaction. Hence, the metropolis has evolved from a more unconscious community based on direct competition between individuals and agents, to an economic, political and moral community based on communication. This evolution has changed the nature of different forms of interaction such as conflict, adjustment and assimilation. It is through these evolutionary stages that the Chicago school sociologists within the human ecological trajectory study the metropolis and its processes of stabilisation, community building and geographical dislocation.

The trajectory of social (dis)organisation focuses on homelessness, delinquency, gang crime, ghetto life, "taxi-dance halls", immigration, urban enclaves and other subjects. Common features include an interest in social problems, norms and social phenomena that occur in the interaction between traditional and modern influences. This trajectory is clearly influenced by the reform thinking described earlier with its indirect request for reform and social change.

Wirth's "Urbanism as a Way of Life", which is heavily inspired by Simmel and is mentioned in the introductory epigraph, is shaped by a social disorganising approach, and Thomas's and Znaniecki's landmark study on Polish peasants can likewise be placed within this trajectory. *The Polish Peasant in Europe and America* (1918–1920) consists of five volumes, and its primary objective is to examine intercultural processes of migration among Polish immigrants in Chicago. Thomas and Znaniecki explore processes of social change through the disorganisation and reorganisation of social life based on a transition from a Polish premodern society to American modern industrial society. Here, social disorganisation

social interaction and marginalisation 65

is understood as the instability that occurs when existing rules lose their unifying and controlling powers, resulting in a "decrease of the influence of existing social rules of behaviour upon individual members of the group" (Thomas 1966: 4). A group may dissolve, but a reorganisation in which new adaptable "schemes of behaviour" are produced is more likely to occur (Thomas 1966: 5).

Though the study includes different types of life story material, it is mainly based on the autobiographical account of a single Polish immigrant, Wladek Wizniewski. It is credited for being the first sociological study to use life histories for the purpose of exploring how macrosociological developments manifest at the level of single individuals. The importance of subjective meanings and individual "definitions of situations" in understanding social processes is famously expressed in the Thomas theorem, "if men define situations as real, they are real in their consequences" (Thomas and Thomas in Coser 1971: 521). The dictum implies that individual actions are shaped by individual interpretations of a given situation and acknowledges that individuals respond differently to different situations and challenges.

The social psychological trajectory is represented by thinkers such as Mead and Dewey. W.I. Thomas also contributed to this line of research, which focused on the "relationship between individual consciousness and the group/society" (Jørgensen and Schmidt 2009: 63), for example attitudes and values in relation to human action and social norms. The last trajectory on action research and social work is tied to the Hull House, a female student settlement established by Jane Addams (1860–1935) and Ellen Gates Star (1859–1940), which mobilised social activism, social work among Chicago's poor and extensive action-related research on social problems and life conditions in the poor areas of Chicago.

While the four trajectories remain analytical constructs, they point to distinct and substantive areas of research as well as to different theoretical foundations and developments. For instance, the more social psychological approach within the Chicago School with Mead in a leading role founded the basis for the theory of symbolic interaction as it was coined by Mead's student Herbert Blumer (1900–1987).

Park: urban sociology and marginality

Robert Park is probably the most prominent scholar of the early Chicago School tradition. He did not follow the standard academic trajectory, but worked as a journalist and press agent for nearly two decades before embarking on an academic career at the age of 50. It is argued that his great journalistic commitment to covering the complexities of urban life as it played out in relation to immigration, corruption, crime, and so on formed his outlook on the city as well as his later research interests. He saw the city as a natural laboratory for studying modern individuals – or the modern type, to use Simmel's terminology – shaped by industrialisation and division of labour. In general, Park was analytically concerned with societal processes that engendered new social forms and disturbed and dispensed with existing adjustments and accommodations in society (Coser 1971). In his celebrated article "The City: Suggestions for the Investigation of Human Behaviour in the City Environment" (1915), he looks at how processes of mobility and segregation create new forms of social interaction and solidarity but also result in greater social distance among groups of individuals.

Specifically, Park outlines four main issues or characteristics that depict the city according to his urban sociology. Based on the theoretical foundation of human ecology, the city is seen as a social organism, a continually developing "psychophysical mechanism" (Park 1915: 578) of processual rather than of structural character. Increased mobility in terms of increased access to transportation served, along with developments in communication technology, to destabilise the sense of neighbourhood intimacy and stability known from smaller rural communities. In the metropolis, the great amount of personal information that characterised these smaller communities is decreased substantively and, says Park, such absence of personal information, is indeed a hallmark of the metropolis (Park 1915: 607). Furthermore, the marked segregation between different groups of individuals – divisions influenced by race and class – shape the social organisation of the city. Park mentions the Chinatowns in New York and San Francisco and the Little Sicily of Chicago as examples of "cities within cities" (Park 1915: 582). This observation led to Park's first main characteristic of the metropolis: The city, he says, develops according to natural processes, patterns and areas in agreement with individual and group preferences, and in this way it is always substantiating area-specific norms, conducts and values (Jørgensen 2001; Park 1915). This segregation results, in Wirth's words, in a geographically dispersed "mosaic of social worlds" (Wirth 1938: 15), which again is the cause of the numerous "cities within cities" that reinforce both the physical and emotional distance of the metropolis. This social distance is a second characteristic of city life. Park writes that the high degree of segregation and social distance in the city,

> ... tends to give to city life a superficial and adventitious character; it tends to complicate social relationships and to produce new and divergent social types. It introduces, at the same time, an element of chance and adventure, which adds to the stimulus of city life and gives it for young and fresh nerves a peculiar attractiveness. ... The

social interaction and marginalisation

attractiveness of the metropolis is due in part, however, to the fact than in the long run every individual finds somewhere among the varied manifestations of city life the sort of environment in which he expands and feels at ease.

(Park 1915: 608)

While the city entails segregation and alienation, it also supports and enables the individual's need to express itself freely, to explore individual interests and to be acknowledged – and not only tolerated – for their personal eccentricities. Like Simmel, Park has an ambiguous view of the city: He applauds its many possibilities and is concerned by the moral and social distance; the city, he says, "shows the good and evil human nature in excess" (Park 1915: 612), and he adds that it is exactly this ambiguity that makes the metropolis a fitting "laboratory" for the study of social processes and developments in human nature. Park encouraged his students to conduct ethnographic fieldwork, including observational methods in the city itself. Of course, members of the Chicago School also worked with quantitative data and method, but its hallmarks are fieldwork, use of qualitative data, life story and mapping techniques.

In addition to the natural processes of segregation and accompanying issues of social distance and marginality, the city is characterised by a money economy that is closely related to the division of labour. In line with Simmel's analysis in "The Metropolis and Mental Life", the money economy increases individualisation, creates distinct vocational types and "depersonalize[s] social relations" (Park 1915: 589) and causes greater mutual dependency between citizens as jobs become increasingly specialised. The final important characteristic relates to the disintegrating effects of city life and the dissolution of a moral order. As primary relations are weakened, the character of familiar institutions such as the family, school and church change. As Park points out, the school fulfils some functions previously reserved for the family. The increase in secondary relations over primary relations also influences the nature of social control in the city. From previously being regulated by existing customs and norms, the conditions and developments characterising the growth of the city (e.g. greater interdependence among individuals) increasingly necessitates a more formalised social control regulated by law and by political and administrative authorities.

According to Park, the social control of collective behaviour and the resulting processes of competition and conflict may be able to reach certain degrees of accommodation but they will never be stable; new groups will always arrive to compete over resources and challenge existing accommodations. Park's notion of the marginal man poses such a challenge to prevailing societal adjustments (Coser 1971), and just like

Simmel's stranger, the marginal man comes to represent modern life in general.

> It is in the mind of the marginal man that the moral turmoil which new cultural contacts occasion manifests itself in the most obvious forms. It is in the mind of the marginal man – where the changes and fusions of culture are going on – that we can best study the processes of civilization and of progress.
>
> (Park 1928: 893)

The marginal man is the representative of a certain personality type, who displays a number of characteristics formed by his (or her) experiences of belonging to "conflicting cultures" (Park 1928: 881) without fully belonging to any of them. The conflict between well-known ways of life and new, not yet adopted cultural norms also constitutes a conflict within the self and one's identity. As opposed to Simmel's stranger, who never fully wishes to settle but is still accepted as a member of the group, the marginal man never quite finds his place due to "racial prejudices". The marginal man is often of "mixed blood", like the "mulatto in the United States or the Eurasian in Asia" (Park 1928: 892–983). According to Park, physical traits are a major barrier to cultural assimilation. Erving Goffman later described this as a tribal stigma (see Chapter 9).

According to Park, all human migration, as a "type of collective action" (Park 1928: 886), shares certain typical features that allow us to study its specific form and its societal effects and, more broadly, modern ways of life. Some elements in the transitional and conflictual processes of immigration, such as "spiritual instability, intensified self-consciousness, restlessness, and malaise" (Park 1928: 893), to a certain extent become a basic condition for all modern individuals, but it is more likely to become a permanent condition for the marginal man. The crystallisation of such characteristics makes the marginal man a distinct personality type. Park offers his marginal man a much less positive position than Simmel offers his stranger, but he does point to a number of positive aspects of the marginal man which mirror those proposed by Simmel: Freedom from previous ties and belonging to different cultures may allow the marginal man a greater degree of objectivity, cosmopolitanism and individual opportunities of expression and lend him an enlightened and rational point of view.

In addition, even though conflicts of culture and identity may be recurrent themes of the human condition, a permanent state of societal disorganisation does not have to be. As Park writes, the transitional phase of becoming familiar with a new culture is often followed by individual reintegration into a novel social order. With a clear reference to the social

social interaction and marginalisation

processes outlined within the human ecological framework, it is possible to assimilate (i.e. it is possible for an individual to achieve adaptation to the prevailing culture). The result is a greater sense of shared community even though processes of conflict and competition will always remain. This relation between states of disruption and states of equilibrium is also theorised in the work of W.I. Thomas in his distinction between social organisation and individual life-organisation. Like Park, he perceives the states of – in his terms – disorganisation and reorganisation as dynamic processes, but he focuses more on the intergroup dynamics between individual aspirations and the social rules and norms of the group in keeping with his social psychological standpoint (Thomas 1966).

The ambiguity of modern city life

Simmel and the Chicago School scholars sought to provide an analysis of the modern ways of life and to understand the profound social changes that followed urbanisation, industrialisation and the division of labour. The emergence and effects of these complex and dynamic changes were the main study objects for both Simmel and the Chicago School representatives, notwithstanding the heterogeneity of the latter.

Simmel's preoccupation with the limits of individuality in modern societies is carried on in the Chicago School tradition. But where Simmel maintains a focus on analytical abstractions in constructing the field of sociology as a distinct science, the Chicago School sociologists are concerned with examining concrete social phenomena and seek theoretical conceptualisations grounded in empirical data. Both share the view that the task of sociology and the sociologist is to attend to human interaction and social relations at the analytical level of groups rather than on the level of institutions or individuals. Both address social processes and social phenomena according to an individual-society dialectic in an effort to avoid forced dualisms. Simmel's analytical focus on forms of interaction and specific personality types is also found among the Chicago sociologists (e.g. Park's marginal man) and so is his focus on contradictions and conflict (e.g. in connection with immigration and disorganisation). The interaction between disruptions and stability is comprised in Simmel's work, and it is resumed and refined in the Chicago School sociology, for example in the contributions from Park and W.I. Thomas.

Levine (1971: lii) argues that Simmel pays little attention to norms and sees them as mere "side effects of social interaction". To Park, for instance, the issue of norms is key to his idea of the normatively unregulated ecological order versus the regulated moral or social order. Social control becomes "the central fact and the central problem of society" (Park and

Burgess in Levine 1971: liii). In general, the issue of change and breach of norms is a key area for the "social psychological trajectory" within the Chicago School tradition.

The ideas in Simmel's analysis of the ambiguity of modernity and individuality in "The Stranger" (1908) and "The Metropolis and Mental Life" (1903), respectively, seem in particular to have left their imprint on the Chicago School tradition. The tension of modern city life and the tension between societal forces and the individual remain an important concern throughout. Whereas Simmel to a greater degree addresses societal developments in understanding modern ways of life, the Chicago sociologists pay more attention to their implications for specific societal groups. In many ways, however, the Chicago sociologists adopt a similar ambiguity towards the modern ways of life: The social distance created among citizens is likely to result in states of marginalisation, alienation and social disorganisation and create a sense of malaise and a blasé attitude towards others. In general, these developments happen at the cost of emotional relations and social life, but they also carry with them new opportunities for individual expression, for intellectual endeavours and for the creation of new forms of solidarity.

Like Durkheim's theoretical contributions (see Chapter 3), Simmel's analysis of modernity and individualisation processes offers a substantial contribution to later individualisation theories that have occupied 20th century sociologists in general and in particular late modern sociologists such as Zygmunt Bauman, Ulrich Beck and Anthony Giddens (see Chapters 8 and 9). Though the influence of the Chicago School on European sociology may have been somewhat sporadic, its impact on American sociology has been profound. Its contributions to urban sociology, to symbolic interaction theory and to interpretative sociology, to mention a few, still make many of the theoretical ideas and conceptualisations of the Chicago School relevant for contemporary sociology.

social interaction and marginalisation

chapter 5

Power and stratification

Foucault and Bourdieu

After the review of the classic sociologists, this and the following chapters introduce a number of dominant positions in sociology after World War II. We start out with two prominent figures in French sociology, Michel Foucault (1926–1984) and Pierre Bourdieu (1930–2002), who both use a modernised power analysis to decipher social relations. Their analytical approaches differ, but they share some key characteristics, which makes it interesting to compare them here.

The concept of power is central to their respective approaches. Both want to analyse power in a way that deviates significantly from its traditional conception in the social sciences as a substantial resource that actors can have or exert upon others. Foucault and Bourdieu understand power as an embedded quality of social relations, which facilitates a more sophisticated power analysis than has previously been the norm in sociology. They both shift focus from material structures of power and physical domination to various forms of symbolic exercise of power. In a symbolic conception of power, social relations and individuals are subject to indirect discursive control through phenomena such as knowledge, language, cultural codes or aesthetic taste.

Foucault engages most directly with the concept of power, whereas Bourdieu undoubtedly addresses the chapter's second thematic, stratification, more explicitly. We introduced Marx's and Weber's theories of class structure in Chapter 2, and though Bourdieu also draws on these works, both he and Foucault aim for a more nuanced analysis of how differences between social groups are created and articulated in society. Foucault never addresses the concept of stratification explicitly but is nonetheless preoccupied with how social order is constituted by dividing practices. These practices separate human beings into two groups based on a distinction between, for instance, normal and deviant or sane and mad. Bourdieu takes his point of departure in a more traditional type of class analysis, but expands the analytical framework with a discursive focus on symbolic distinctions that various groups employ in the struggle over social positions.

In the first half of the chapter, we present Foucault and his analytic integration of knowledge, power and subjects. This involves key examples from his most well-known analyses of power, which are responsible for his impact on contemporary sociology. The second half of the chapter describes key concepts in Bourdieu's theory about forms of capital, social fields, habitus and class.

Foucault's analytics of power

Foucault did not understand himself as a sociologist, philosopher or historian in the traditional sense, although his work has clear affinities with all three disciplines. His chair at the Collège de France was formally dedicated to the study of the "history of systems of thought". That entails a particular type of practical history of ideas that focuses on the historical connections between scientific categories, the political and the social. It is essential to keep this cross-disciplinary perspective in mind, as Foucault himself is often implicit about the broader ambitions of his works. Usually, there is much more at stake than the specific episode in the history of ideas that he describes. This is exemplified in his book *The Birth of the Clinic* from 1963 (Foucault 1973), which details a specific phase in the history of medicine and chronicles the emergence of a particular, scientific "gaze" on the human body with a series of important social and political implications. Foucault thus uses the history of science to demonstrate how we have come to see, talk about and regulate social phenomena in a particular way.

Foucault's analytics of power is very much indebted to this cross-disciplinary approach. He underlines that it is an analytic and not a "theory" of power, which would mistakenly imply that power was a thing in and of itself. It is not, Foucault argues, but rather a certain strategic and tactical way in which to understand social relations (Foucault 1978: 92–93). Consequently, Foucault does not offer a clear-cut definition of power, because a fundamental trait of power is that it may mask itself as freedom, knowledge or other categories seemingly in contrast to power.

power and stratification 73

He instead formulates some rules of thumb for how to study relations of power in specific empirical contexts, be it historical or contemporary. The rules also illustrate how he understands power as a social phenomenon more broadly even if it does not amount to an actual definition. The remaining part of this section focuses on these broader reflections on power followed by sections with examples from Foucault's most well-known analyses of disciplinary and biopolitical power.

First, Foucault seeks to avoid a substantialist conception of power, which in his eyes still dominates the social sciences. The substantialist conception of power originally stems from absolutism, where it designated the king's sovereign power. Foucault sarcastically writes that "in political thought and analysis, we still have not cut off the head of the king" (1978: 88–89). What this means is that we still conceive of power in the same juridical manner as did the absolutist king, i.e. as something you can own, have and centralise (Foucault 1978: 89). If we instead understand power as a web of subtle, tactical relations embedded in all social institutions, it is no longer possible to analyse power simply by adding up the allocation of resources in society. Power must be studied in its exercise rather than as a resource one can possess. In practice, however, it can be difficult to trace the exercise of power across different historical periods, but you can study the technologies, mechanisms and apparatuses that have been applied in each of these historical periods with the aim to organise and rationalise power.

Second, this analytics of power is not particularly interested in individual actors or in formal rules and institutions. Foucault claims that because traditional theories focus on actors, resources and formal institutions, they are unable to see how power is actually exercised and why it works. His alternative is to study the different technologies that have been used over time to make individuals do, think or understand themselves in certain ways. As these technologies of power are continuously developed and rationalised further, power is not necessarily the same phenomenon across time and space.

Third, power does not primarily have a negative, but a positive mode of functioning. This point is sometimes misunderstood as if Foucault understands power as being good in a normative sense. The point is rather that power relations do not function as a limiting or inhibiting structure upon human action. It is a productive force that may induce certain forms of behaviour, certain emotions or facilitate social processes. A key example of power's positive mode of functioning is Foucault's analysis of sexuality where power does not simply function as a limiting force on an otherwise free and uninhibited form of sexuality. Power is to make individuals desire certain objects and perhaps rationalise how they use their desires for certain ends.

Fourth, Foucault conceptualises power relations as being far less centralised and fixed structures than has traditionally been the approach in sociological studies of power. He sees power relations as being mobile and amenable to change, not least because there is a continuous development of resistance to power. In other words, power rarely works as intended. The constant possibility of resistance makes power "tactically polyvalent" as Foucault writes (1978: 100). Resistance may turn the dominant understandings in a given period inside out and thereby constitute a new power relation. He exemplifies this with the historical repression of homosexuality. Although the category may very well have been invented with the aim to pathologise and condemn homosexuals, the same category was later taken over by groups of homosexuals and given a positive meaning (Foucault 1978: 101). Power and resistance are thus intimately related, of which sociological analyses of power should be aware.

Finally, power is closely associated with knowledge and the production of subjects. Knowledge is essential to power, because any exercise of power requires knowledge about its object. More broadly, however, the very production of knowledge and documentation serves to establish new power relations. Not necessarily scientific knowledge, because as illustrated in the discussion of surveillance below, the main thing is to make visible the object that power is trying to affect. Power and knowledge are often connected through forms of subjection, i.e. the ways in which individuals are made into a given type of subjects.

One example of a form of subjection is the "homo oeconomicus", which is the idea of the individual as one that constantly calculates and maximises utility in order to serve its own interests. Most economic theory is built on this type of subject and so are many of the incentive-based governing tools applied in social spheres outside the economy. For tools such as these and for power more generally to actually "work", individuals must act in accordance with the intended form of subjection. Subjectivity and forms of subjection are consequently a necessary element of the analytics of power. Foucault's claim is that the exercise of power in contemporary settings draws on many forms of subjection, because there is an ongoing reflection about and refinement of the techniques applied to construct given types of subjects. In addition to being calculating consumers, we may also be expected to live healthy lives, to be learning children or adults, flexible employees, partners with empathy and responsible citizens towards the community. All these labels are forms of subjection, and Foucault basically claims that the exercise of power is always dependent on these ideas about how power aims to regulate.

Foucault is very hesitant to build a new theory of power, but some general characteristics do seem to apply across all empirical contexts. He

power and stratification

always focuses on the tactical element of power relations as well as the tiny and subtle techniques we often use in everyday life. The analysis of power relations is practically always associated with a keen interest in the impact of knowledge and forms of subjection. However, Foucault also studies more detailed and specific historical episodes in the transformations of power, which are often used as model examples of a Foucauldian approach in sociology. Among these is his analysis of discipline and surveillance.

Discipline and surveillance

Foucault's analysis takes its point of departure in the history of the modern prison, but his study has a broader agenda. The idea is to show how disciplinary power relations spread and become integrated into all the core institutions of a modern society from schools and workplaces to hospitals, urban centres and the military.

Foucault illustrates the contrast between these disciplinary institutions and predisciplinary forms of power with a description of a public execution in 1757. As a brutal manifestation of the king's absolute power, a man condemned to death was pulled to pieces by horses at a public spectacle in a central square in Paris. Foucault then contrasts this type of power with a set of disciplinary regulations used at a French juvenile delinquent facility only a few decades later. Here, there is no brutality, but a minute and calculated regulation of every little individual task from dusk till dawn, all of it designed to educate and improve the souls of the delinquents. In broader terms, the contrast between the two examples illustrates a major change in most European penal codes around the 1800s when disciplinary forms of power become the norm.

There are at least three defining aspects of a disciplinary technology of power. First, the target of discipline is always individual behaviour, often at a very detailed bodily or corporeal level. Even when applied to larger groups of people, disciplinary technologies of power always aim to individualise each singular element from each other. Second, discipline always has a pedagogical objective to improve upon the moral status of its subjects. The objective is to make individuals law-abiding, moral, capable, efficient or productive. Discipline thereby seeks to make itself superfluous, because properly disciplined individuals will always act morally of their own will. In many cases, however, the objective is not necessarily individual perfection, but rather what is considered normal in the given context. Foucault occasionally refers to discipline as a power of normalisation. Third and finally, discipline typically seeks to make its object visible and thereby enable a detailed governing of each individual element. Making an object visible is a question of exposing it to an outside view and not necessarily in a visual sense. It may take the form of documentation, for instance if a public institution implements an advanced system of quality indicators and thereby makes the institution's activities transparent to an external point of observation. The classic way to make individual behaviour transparent according to Foucault is through surveillance, which he analyses on the basis of the Panopticon.

Panopticon was the name of a plan for the ideal prison structure as designed by the British utilitarian philosopher Jeremy Bentham (1748–1832) in 1791. This period sought to develop a modern and enlightened penal system, which in Bentham's eyes would mean to be able to discipline the largest number of prisoners with a minimum of resources and use of violence. The core idea of panopticism as a technology of power is to use a circular architecture with a watchtower in the middle and prison cells along the periphery. This allows light from the outside to pass through each cell and make the silhouettes of all prisoners easily observable from a centralised gaze. The prisoners are individualised, i.e. separated from each other in individual cells, and though they know they might be under surveillance, they can never actually see if anyone is observing them at a given time.

The idea is to gradually make the prisoner take the surveillance upon himself so he "becomes the principle of his own subjection" (Foucault 1977: 202–203). The genius of this architecture is the combination of individualised elements observable from a central point and the inability of subjects to know when they are actually being observed. The architecture creates a rational, but also highly asymmetrical structure of visibility that exposes each individual to a central eye, which makes the subjects take the observing eye upon themselves.

Foucault is interested in the Panopticon – and "panopticism" as he more broadly refers to – because it also clearly illustrates how knowledge, power, and forms of subjection are intimately connected. Transparency exposes an object (knowledge), which through a set of asymmetrical, tactical relations (power) installs automatic self-control among the inmates (subjection). The Panopticon also illustrates some of the other key characteristics of Foucault's power analytics, not least the idea that power relations are productive and "polyvalent". He characterises the Panopticon like this:

> It's a case of "it's easy once you've thought of it" in the political sphere. It can in fact be integrated into any function (education, medical treatment, production, punishment). ... It arranges things in such a way that the exercise of power is not added on from the outside, like a rigid, heavy constraint, to the functions it invests, but is

power and stratification

so subtly present in them as to increase their efficiency by itself increasing its own points of contact.

(Foucault 1977: 206)

Bentham's original plan already involved a sort of budding where the guard who oversees the prisoners is himself subject to random inspections from his superior, the superior again subject to occasional inspections from a national inspector, who may again be subject to political control. The disciplinary relations easily multiply in this way from initially having society's deviants as their targets to increasingly becoming generalised to target normal citizens also.

Foucault further argues that this multiplication of disciplinary power relations is a previously overlooked aspect of what Marx identified as accumulation in capitalist society (Foucault 1977: 220–221). Whereas Marx understood the state apparatus as being fundamentally repressive, Foucault argues to the contrary that it is the comprehensive spread of disciplinary power relations that makes it possible to develop and maintain social order in a capitalist mass society. He consequently talks about the "disciplinary society" where the individual is disciplined from cradle to grave (Foucault 1977: 218). This broad diagnosis of society never becomes more than a sketch, however, because of Foucault's unwillingness to formulate general social theory.

Biopolitics and sexuality

Besides punishment, sexuality is probably the most important empirical topic in Foucault's analytics of power. He published three volumes of a *History of Sexuality*, but mainly the first volume, *The Will to Knowledge* from 1976, is relevant for the question of power. It basically analyses how knowledge and power affect the way we as subjects relate to our sexuality (Foucault 1978).

Foucault again takes his point of departure in a contemporary problem, this time gender struggle and ideas about sexual liberation. He then goes back to an earlier period and casts doubt on the widespread belief that the sexuality of modern human beings has been repressed and tabooed since the Victorian age. At the time when this taboo allegedly began, there was a virtual explosion of verbose discourses about sex. It is through this discursive construction that talk about sex is related to power. Foucault claims that sex becomes discursively constructed as a social phenomenon when various scientific disciplines begin to conceptualise human sexuality – both the normal and the pathological. It is of course a powerful act to be able to define who is normal and who is pathological, but

Foucault's point is further that power can hardly be exercised without defining these types of people.

Scientific disciplines are not the only sources of the discursive construction of modern sexuality. As the title of Foucault's book indicates, there was a widespread "will" to knowledge about sexuality during the 19th century. The state, science, literature and not least individuals articulated a desire to know every detail about the individual's sex life, not least in order to be aware of its possible dangers and pathologies. At the dawn of industrial capitalism, making the working class administer its sex life in a responsible manner dedicated to marital reproduction was important for productivity. To facilitate these ends, a series of social practices were developed during this period that codified individual sexuality into specialised scientific categories. Foucault claims that this codification, rather than a general cultural taboo or repression, is what ties sex and power together.

If we take a step back and reflect on how sexuality is connected with Foucault's analytics of power, it is perhaps easier to understand what the will to knowledge about sexuality has to do with power. A cornerstone in Foucault's approach is that power is a positive and productive force and not simply a negative force that restricts human action. No area illustrates this point more clearly than the attempt to regulate the population's desires. For the same reason, technologies of power in completely different fields often take inspiration from the historical connection between sex and power.

One example is a project, "Desire for learning", initiated by the Danish Ministry of Education in 2000. The aim of the project was to increase schoolchildren's desire to learn and avoid forcing them to do homework. The background policy document is packed with what may sound like erotic metaphors about desire, excitement and pleasure. The point here is not to identify a hidden, sexual agenda in this project, because there is none. The point is rather that the underlying technology of power draws on the same repertoire that Foucault identified. This technology of power is also termed "biopolitics", which we will clarify as the last of Foucault's conceptual tools introduced here.

Biopolitics can be understood as yet another technology of power that targets human behaviour. In contrast to the juridical conception of power – sovereignty – which is associated with the possession of a physical territory – biopolitics is oriented towards optimisation of the population and its biological qualities. Life, death, health, sickness, fertility, productivity and, in contemporary settings, lifestyle constitute essential biopolitical fields of intervention. Unlike discipline, however, biopolitics does not focus on individual behaviour, but on exercising care for the population as a biological entity, typically through the use of statistics on the

power and stratification

biological qualities and composition of the population. We can thus distinguish technologies of power depending on whether they aim to normalise the individual (discipline) or to create an optimal normal distribution within the population (biopolitics). An example is different strategies to fight crime following each of these technologies. Fighting crime through discipline would typically involve an attempt to rehabilitate and improve the morality of the criminal, whereas a biopolitical strategy would try to prevent high crime rates. Disciplinary and biopolitical technologies of power often overlap in practice, but their origin and inner logic are quite different in Foucault's view.

Bourdieu on symbolic violence

The first half of this chapter has introduced Foucault's analytics of power. Unlike Bourdieu's approach as detailed in this following, Foucault does not explicitly associate power with stratification. But although stratification is not addressed directly, it is a core ambition for Foucault to observe how social processes install divisions among masses of people, for instance via individualising architecture. Foucault further underlines that technologies of power influence the divisions we use to separate normal from deviant as well as for the continuous budding of new categories of deviant subjects.

Bourdieu studies how acts and positions taken by various classes contribute to the reproduction of a given cultural order and its structures of dominance. Unlike the classic "power over" perspective, it is central to understand power as wielded primarily in a nonconscious manner. Our ingrained habits and aesthetic preferences constitute our access to the social sphere. We seldom consider how the translation of these aspects into action intimately relates to the exercise of power.

In light of this relationship, Bourdieu's point of departure is that actions are subject to "interest" in two very different senses. First of all, we have a tendency to gain a taste for certain things at the expense of others, and such preferences are the product of the ways of life of particular social groups. We care about what we do and what we consume and these concerns and practices must be interpreted and understood with reference to our lifestyles. Our habits are relatively predictable when our social position and lifestyles are taken into consideration. The second sense in which actions are interested concerns the way we position ourselves vis-à-vis others. Again, this positioning must be understood on the basis of our membership of groups, classes or lifestyle communities. Constantly, we seek to position ourselves in relation to those whose tastes are different. We tend to think that "the others" have bad taste or no taste at all. Power is thus wielded through the attempt to establish a hierarchy between superior and inferior taste. Bourdieu always thinks relationally and hierarchically. A vision (a way of looking at the world) is always simultaneously a division (it is based on the establishment of a difference) (Bourdieu 1990: 210).

Bourdieu's emphasis on relationality is inspired by structuralism. French structuralist linguist Ferdinand de Saussure claimed that language is a system of differences (1998). Individual words do not primarily refer to particular objects, but rather to a system of differences that conditions the way we can make reference to objects. Hence, for Saussure it became vital to understand language as structure that conditions language use. The notion of a man, for instance, requires the notion of a woman, the notion of a father requires that of a mother, and the idea of parents that of children. A system of differences precedes our references to objects out in the world. On this basis, Saussure crafted two strategies of analysis. He dealt first of all in synchronic linguistics, analysing language as if it were frozen in time. In such a situation, the differences remain fixed and form a grammar and a system of meanings upon which any act of enunciation must draw.

The second strategy consists in diachronic linguistics, in which the evolution of language over time, and thus also changes in the system of differences, is analysed. The meaning, the connotations and the valorisation of a word may change over time, as we see for example in the usage of the term "homosexual". What was, at first, a social stigma becomes something in which to take pride. The word also changes from having primarily sexual connotations to become more of a designator of a certain lifestyle.

Bourdieu has carried out numerous diachronic studies, but most of them focus on the reproduction of given social systems, which means that the synchronic perspective takes precedence. Structuralists such as Bourdieu are typically interested in stability rather than change. Saussure emphasised how various words received their meaning by relating to other words in a grammatically given structure, and Bourdieu expands this perspective in order to analyse how various social groups mutually position themselves via cultural markers (1984: 467–470). The context might be one of gender (man vs. woman), religion (orthodoxy vs. heresy), or a social one (upper vs. lower class). In a way, one could say that for Bourdieu social differences are structured like a language.

In our daily lives, we act as if these differences were natural and not constructed, i.e. in a manner that parallels the notion of correspondence between words and objects, criticised by Saussure. When we claim, for instance, that a piece of music or a painting is beautiful, we believe that it is so in an objective sense (Bourdieu 1977: 214). We thus fail to consider how our notion of good taste simultaneously contains the ambition

power and stratification

of posing a difference in relation to others (just like we fail to consider how words do not refer directly to objects, but rather to a web of more primary semantic differences). Bourdieu's sociological project of enlightenment, by extension, is to demonstrate that judgments of taste is neither neutral nor objective. The cultural matrixes upon which we draw are intimately connected to the exercise of power.

Bourdieu uses the concept of symbolic violence to grasp this relationship (1991a: 164). The symbolic refers to all the systems or structures of meaning we use. An array of values are embedded in language, things it is possible to say and think, but even the very command of language can be an instrument of power. Command of language furthermore entails admittance to a number of institutions, not least institutions of education. Besides the significance of language, one may point to any system of meaning or notion of what is valuable, as aspects of the symbolic.

> Every power to exert symbolic violence, i.e. every power which manages to impose meanings and to impose them as legitimate by concealing the power relations which are the basis of its force, adds its own specifically symbolic force to those power relations.
>
> (Bourdieu and Passeron 1977: 4)

Symbolic violence is the type of violence that causes interest-borne actions to appear disinterested. For instance, those who are subject to such violence often recognise the dominant culture as superior, and thus no longer recognise the violence as such. The possessions and manners of the upper class evoke respect, admiration and humility.

Bourdieu usually discusses symbolic violence in the context of society or, with his preferred term, the social space. However, he also looks at narrower contexts, so-called fields, from this perspective. Here, too, a battle of positioning takes place, and the dominant agents tend to make their preferences appear as objective and neutral – as good taste within the given field. A field may be defined as a space structured around a particular, field-specific form of capital (Bourdieu and Wacquant 1996: 94–114). If we accept a provisory definition of capital as that which particular actors find valuable and wish to invest in, then we may conceive of the field as consisting of a number of actors, all of them interested in appropriating the capital of the field in question. The players of the field are all given by the same "illusio", i.e. by the same understanding that what occurs in the field is important and valuable. In somewhat simplified terms, school teachers, politicians and parents are interested in the school field; functioning clergy, academic theologians and church congregations are interested in the religious field, and so on. A field, then, is not the same as an institution. A field may be, but is not necessarily, institutionally embedded. For instance, the religious field in Christian societies is organised around institutional churches, but not all activity relevant to the field necessarily occurs here.

The number and nature of fields that exist in any given society is an empirical question. For instance, are mosques part of an overall religious field, or do they and the public churches each constitute their own separate field? This depends on which aspect of religious practice we focus on and the degree to which a struggle for a field-specific form of capital takes place within a given context. However, this response does not imply that the delineation of fields depends completely on the perspective selected by researchers as point of departure. Fields are institutionalised to a certain degree. The boundaries of a field seem somewhat rigid, which is not to say that they are impossible to challenge.

We find in Bourdieu, as in Luhmann, whose sociology will be introduced in the next chapter, the notion that the number of fields has increased and that in a historical perspective, the fields have become increasingly autonomous. Unlike Luhmann, however, Bourdieu maintains that some fields are more important than others. The field of power consists to a large extent of players from the upper class – in the economic as well as the cultural sense – and this is where the symbolic systems, upon which everybody draws to some extent, are established. The field of power is thus a kind of meta-field from which symbolic violence proceeds, and in which the exchange rate among the various forms of capital, for example between economic and cultural capital, is established. The field of power, in other words, is a very special field from which it is possible to intervene in the functioning of other fields.

Bourdieu has often been criticised for taking too little interest in counterstrategies. Symbolic violence does not always go unchallenged. If we look at language, the vulgar language and slang of the working class and of hip hop culture may be regarded as a break with proper, well-mannered language (Bourdieu 1984: 395). The focus on counterstrategies becomes more distinct whenever Bourdieu analyses so-called fields of production. The corresponding concept to symbolic violence is doxa. Doxa is anything that appears as established and unquestionable truth within a field, just as symbolic violence is the process through which something is established as beyond doubt and therefore natural and a matter of course.

If, for instance, a priest declares that he or she does not believe in God, it breaks with the established "truths" of the public church field. Reactions may involve a suspension from the post as priest or a so-called clerical case of doctrine. This example illustrates how doxa does not always remain unchallenged. Bourdieu therefore distinguished orthodoxy and heterodoxy, where the latter is what challenges the doxa of a given field (1991b). The hypothetical priest here is such a heterodox thinker, a

power and stratification

heretic, and (as usually happens) the heretic is punished. It is a demanding task to oppose the established hierarchies of power, preferences of taste, and doxical truths, not least because the prospect of losing is always imminent. The odds of success are somewhat increased, however, if one holds, in addition to one's involvement in a particular field of production, a position in the field of power or an alliance with one of its important players, e.g. a politician, an opinion maker or a representative of commercial interests.

Classes

Social space is differentiated. The symbolic violence exercised within it does not entail that everybody necessarily shares the same culture, but merely that those who are dominated recognise the dominant culture as superior. In order to conceptualise this condition, Bourdieu conceives of social space as given by the struggle over capital. Whereas fields of production are constituted by the struggle over a field-specific form of capital, e.g. religious authority in the religious field, the struggle of social space is about capital as such, regardless of form.

Let us briefly explain the relationship between social space and the fields. We may return here to the notion that action is characterised by interest. Naturally, this is the case with regard to fields as well as social space. We can easily be involved in struggles within the school field, over teaching material and methods, while simultaneously positioning ourselves in relation to other social groups. The struggles of, say, the school field are naturally influenced by struggles and positioning in social space (for instance, members of the middle and upper classes may articulate their points more concisely at parent-teacher meetings, thus effectively gaining more influence). The central point is, however, that fields are given by their autonomous dynamics, which may be affected by but are not reducible to what occurs in social space. As we have already described the struggles within fields, let us devote the remaining part of the chapter to social space and the forms of capital that according to Bourdieu are the most relevant in this setting.

Bourdieu adds three forms of capital to the economic form, i.e. possession of the means of production in Marxism and wealth. Before we look at these, let us recapitulate the definition of capital. Capital is something the players of a field are interested in appropriating and, according to Bourdieu, a resource that may be accumulated and transmitted. This raises three issues: systematic disparity in capital possessions; the composition of capital (for instance, Bourdieu claims that the difference between economic and cultural wealth is crucial); and the mechanisms that either reproduce or challenge the social distribution of capital.

Economic capital is the first and most important form of capital, for two primary reasons: It is often a precondition for appropriating other forms of capital (Bourdieu 1986: 252) and it is the form of capital that is most easily calculated, accumulated and passed on. Still, its significance tends to dwindle in a historical perspective. As a result of the general rise of welfare and the increased tax burden, the upper class increasingly chooses to invest in other forms of capital, e.g. education and culture. It is always a matter of establishing a difference, thus positioning oneself in relation to other classes, and should this become difficult with respect to one form of capital, one will often switch to another.

Economic capital is relatively easily defined as money and property, whereas cultural capital is a more complex matter. First of all, it concerns a degree of sophistication, i.e. the capacity to appreciate and understand "advanced" music, visual art, cinema, and other expressions of high culture. Access to these spheres is a resource in its own right. Finally, cultural capital exists in institutional form, e.g. it is embedded in schools, museums, universities, and so on.

Bourdieu also speaks of social capital, i.e. familial relations, connections and social networks in general, as well as symbolic capital, i.e. whether one's capital is recognised and valued by others. This means that all other forms of capital can become symbolic capital.

Bourdieu also conceives of capital in relational terms. The crucial aspect is not the quantity of wealth, but the difference between those who have a lot and those who do not have much. Bourdieu illustrates the social space in France with a diagram with one axis measuring degree of capital and the other its composition (for the sake of simplicity, Bourdieu here distinguishes merely between economic and cultural capital). Four classes are discerned on the basis of this diagram: the lower class, poor in terms of cultural as well as economic capital; the upper class, divided by Bourdieu into a cultural and an economic upper class, depending on the composition of their capital portfolio; and the somewhat blurred middle class, situated approximately in the middle of the diagram (Bourdieu 1984).

Now, Bourdieu's point is that these structurally given positions correspond to particular forms of life. Our positions in this social hierarchy are expressed through what Bourdieu calls "habitus", which is to say the manner in which we act and the things we have a taste for (Bourdieu 1990: 53). Habitus is thus to a great extent a habitus of class. The lower class, for instance, often have a taste for solid cuisine, for the concrete, for the quotidian and intimate, and one might thus continue to the point of having constructed a complete set of aesthetic preferences. Such preferences relate to a corresponding distaste for a different set of cultural values. The lower class perhaps have no taste for the restaurants of the

power and stratification

upper class, as one cannot "get a decent meal" there (in terms of satisfying one's hunger). The novels and films of the upper class are regarded as overly academic because one cannot really relax to them.

The lower class's disregard for upper-class cuisine is not necessarily acquired by experience. It is rather a matter of developing a preference for what is simply a necessity, yet simultaneously giving this preference the appearance of a free choice (Bourdieu 1984: 178). A person from the lower class claims not to like the fancy restaurants, which is a convenient notion, because he or she cannot afford to frequent them. By contrast, the upper class typically develops a taste for freedom – i.e. for anything that displays one's independence with regard to various limitations, economic or otherwise. For instance, one takes an interest in art, theatre, or other "unproductive" activities, typically regarded by the lower class as a waste of time. The upper class may thus precisely distance themselves from the lower classes. Concerning the habitus, Bourdieu writes that "It is a virtue made of necessity which continuously transforms necessity into virtue by inducing 'choices' which correspond to the condition of which it is the product" (Bourdieu 1984: 175).

As with the example of fancy restaurants, the way the lower class speaks of upper-class culture implies a certain recognition of it. Their lack of capital is thus deproblematised. It is not a case of not being able to afford fancy restaurants, but rather one of not wanting to. The class structure is extremely stable because it is tied to differences of capital and reproduced through a corresponding, or in Bourdieu's words, homologous, set of class habitus.

The concept of habitus describes a form of cultural unconscious. It consists of a number of dispositions, or a matrix, from which one may infer an array of preferences, attitudes and standards of appropriate behaviour. As with the advertising industry's distinction between various customer segments, it is common knowledge that if one reads the *Guardian*, one is likely to vote for centre-left parties, read "serious" novels (not only crime fiction), buy classic design items, and so on.

This is exemplified in the recurring Danish TV show "Do You Know the Type?" where a panel of advertising experts are competing to guess the identity of a particular famous person. After a brief tour of the person's home, the experts are often able to guess the person's identity with remarkable accuracy. The popularity of the program shows that we as viewers like to guess along with the advertising experts. We also possess the capacity demonstrated by the experts. We may be amateurs compared to them, but what they do in the TV show, we do constantly in our everyday lives.

The point is that habitus first of all makes it easier for us to maintain a consistent notion of ourselves. In situations requiring choice, we need not reflect extensively. Thanks to our class-specific habitus, we have virtually chosen in advance. Second, we view habitus – our own as well as that of others – as ordered and consistent, and this enables us to navigate among others. If we know of someone that they read *The Guardian* and attend the theatre regularly, we stand a fair chance of guessing the rest as well. The ability to draw on a habitus and to ascribe one to others is an enormous relief for the individual. Habitus helps us navigate, prioritise, and it provides a basis for making easy choices.

It is crucial to emphasise that Bourdieu sees classes as "classes on paper" (1987: 7). A group may exhibit class behaviour, i.e. behaviour that corresponds to a particular location in social space, without being conscious of belonging to any class. A class is simply a group with a roughly similar habitus – nothing more. The notion is closer to Weber's idea of status groups than to Marx's classes (Bourdieu 1984: xiii).

A position within the class structure tends to structure the actions of individuals in a particular way. However, one should bear in mind that Bourdieu regards action as informed by interest, even strategy, and that in this light it is possible to act in various ways. He distinguishes between three fundamental strategies. A group may follow its habitus and thereby contribute to its reproduction. However, because this also presupposes a reproduction of the difference and distance from the habitus of others, it contributes to the reproduction of the class structure of the society in question. Second, one may aspire towards the way of life of other, higher-ranking classes. This strategy likewise follows from one's habitus, as it carries the implicit notion that other habituses are superior. This strategy also contributes to the reproduction of the class structure. Social mobility does not mean that the classes disappear, but merely that some individuals move from one class to another.

The middle class may, for instance, attempt to mimic the upper class. They may buy imitation antiques, poster versions of expensive paintings, and sit in the cheaper rows at the theatre. Many immigrant communities use the same strategy. As their capital is often not recognised (knowledge of Turkish avant-garde literature is not likely to be rewarded with high social status in the United Kingdom), immigrants may attempt to become as British as possible. People who live in ghettos would perhaps rather move into suburban single-family housing, but this merely aggravates the contrast between the capital-poor ghettos and such suburban areas. Once again: The upward mobility of individuals does not necessarily mean that the class structure changes – often quite the contrary.

Attempts to climb the social ladder are not guaranteed to succeed. Bourdieu sees mobility as the exception rather than the rule. Quite often, the upper classes react to middle-class imitation by establishing new distinctions. Class struggle is also a struggle of classification. When

power and stratification

everybody buys Monet posters, this no longer expresses good taste. Once everyone can afford to travel to the Canary Islands, the upper class moves on to more exotic destinations. Furthermore, the middle class tends to exaggerate upper-class lifestyle in their appropriation of it. At least the upper class tends to think so. They lack the ease that comes from not having fought for one's privileges.

The same goes for immigrants, who are often seen as too rigid in their appropriation of "nativeness". No matter what efforts they make, a difference will always be established which can reassure us that we are the true natives. Being social, for Bourdieu, is synonymous with establishing differences.

The third strategy consists in challenging the valuation of the various forms of capital: sticking to one's own habitus, but with no implicit acceptance of its inferiority. Bourdieu has several examples of this strategy in his analyses of specific fields of production, but few in relation to social space. He provides the example that the working class may stick to their physical capability (their bodily capital, one might say) as an area of superiority over the upper class (Bourdieu 1984: 179). Another area might be the capacity for heavy drinking, although that may not constitute an obvious route to social change. The possibility of strikes and political protest is a third and more sober strategy, in which Bourdieu begins to take interest in the final period of his authorship. Bourdieu took active part in the development of counterstrategies, not least via his membership of the Association for the Taxation of financial Transaction and Aid to Citizens (ATTAC) movement.

The fact that Bourdieu offers relatively few examples of resistance to the class structure is naturally due to the rarity of individual working-class players in the field of power. Not everybody has equal opportunities in the struggle to set the value of the various forms of capital. Even successful counterstrategies therefore often have elites as their champions. With his position as professor of sociology and his role as an intellectual, Bourdieu belonged to this elite, and he employed his position within the field of power in the struggle for the cause of the inferior classes.

Centre and margin

In this chapter, we have attempted to show how two of the foremost representatives of modern French sociology coin new concepts in order to understand power and stratification in a more nuanced way than classic sociology. Bourdieu and Foucault develop sociological concepts that draw on insights from the disciplines of philosophy and history, but still offer unique sociological insight into stratification and the exercise of power.

Both thinkers seek to analyse the exercise of power in society in a manner that is sensitive to the symbolic and linguistic aspects of the latter. The symbolic aspects of power are of utmost importance when it comes to the subdivisions of society. Bourdieu focuses on the vertical stratification of habitus among the social classes, whereas Foucault is more interested in the conceptual segregation of the normal from the abnormal, the healthy from the sick, and so on.

Despite their conceptual differences, Foucault and Bourdieu both operate with an implicit dynamic between the centre and margin of society. Their clear interest in the outsiders of society goes beyond political sympathy for initiatives to improve conditions for the disadvantaged. It is an analytical interest in the social relations surrounding the margins of society, because they demonstrate what carries social value and is regarded as normal. This is why Bourdieu put so much effort into thorough sociological analysis of social misery. However, the margin is not merely the contrast based on which the social middle forms its identity. It may also be regarded as a social laboratory. Foucault, for instance, analyses how technologies of power have been applied first to deviant segments, e.g. criminals, the insane or sexual deviants, before being applied more generally in the sphere of normality. Thus, there is an interplay between centre and margin. But this does not imply that individuals on the rim of society have free passage into the sphere of their betters.

This type of recent French sociology is often criticised for holding an overly socialised view of the individual and portraying humans as mere objects of power. Foucault's power analytic certainly gives the impression that discipline forms the individual, and not vice versa. Discipline seems to imply a political logic that spreads throughout society's institutions, thus following the individual from cradle to grave. With Bourdieu, one may likewise get the impression that the individual's social background, not least its habitus, and not the individual's own will or strategies, is what structures its actions. Almost all his theoretical concepts are about the reproduction of social differences, which does not seem to open the door to social mobility or leave room for the individual's own strategies.

Hence, Foucault's and Bourdieu's theories are primarily about the ways in which relations of power and dominance affect the subject. It is worth mentioning, however, that both have clear ambitions to avoid the determinism for which they are often criticised. They both heavily emphasise the analysis of the social from a relational perspective in which individuals, although they are subject to power and dominance, act strategically or generate resistance to the structures to which they are subject. Foucault's concept of the tactical polyvalence of discourses implies precisely this

power and stratification

possibility of turning power on its head. With Bourdieu, it is likewise worth emphasising the generative capacity of habitus, which affords individuals a strategic space of action. Both attempt to analyse power as something more flexible and prone to change than what we find in traditional conceptions of power. It is thus not completely off the mark to characterise these theorists as structuralists – but both have an eye for what breaks the structure to generate social change.

chapter 6

System and differentiation

Luhmann and Habermas

We saw earlier how the classic sociological thinkers tried to conceptualise the process whereby traditional society was transformed into a modern one. Almost all accounts of modernisation involve some sort of disintegration or at least increased specialisation. Modern society simply contains more differences or distinctions than the traditional, which is typically labelled under the headline of differentiation. All classic sociological theories point to a sort of separation between spheres or rationalities in modern society, but it is perhaps clearest in Durkheim's theory of the division of labour.

The counterweight to differentiation is integration. Although modernisation produces more differences and separate subsystems, it is still possible to reintegrate society as a social order. Integration is how sociology solves the classic problem of order, which we previously discussed in terms of the "social question" (see Chapter 1). Contemporary sociologists may not always use the terms differentiation and integration, but in many cases the theories still concern the interplay between a differentiation of societal subsystems and the question of how societal functions are now integrated in a new and more complex way.

In this chapter, we introduce the dominant discussions in postwar German sociology about these topics. This generation and its French contemporaries (see Chapter 5) have had tremendous influence on European sociology. The chapter introduces two leading German theorists, Niklas Luhmann (1927–1998) and Jürgen Habermas (1929–), and the tradition of systems theory in sociology. Before going into each theory, let us look at a few common identifiers in their respective approaches to sociology.

First, the two German theorists are more directly preoccupied with communication and its societal impact than Foucault and Bourdieu, who thematised the symbolic and discursive aspects of power. In broader terms, however, it is common to refer to the "communicative turn" in the whole postwar generation of sociological theorists, because they all start from a critique of how the material conceptions of power and structure dominates classical sociology. Second, Luhmann and Habermas distinguish themselves clearly from their French counterparts by not attempting to develop their theories through specific empirical studies. They go, so to say, the opposite way and build comprehensive, general theories of society that may initially seem difficult for readers to grasp. Their claim is that a systematic use of their massive conceptual frameworks will enable a better understanding of the complexity in modern society. Third and finally, both Luhmann and Habermas are more preoccupied with society's general structure and mode of functioning than with individuals and the microlevel.

Luhmann's systems theory

Before we turn to Luhmann's own conceptual framework, it is useful to focus on what he distances himself from. In his article "The Concept of Society" (1992), Luhmann argues that the social sciences are trapped in three traditional ways of thinking about society that constitute a hurdle to new insights. First, it is common to think of a society as a group of people united in a community. According to Luhmann, however, society is not composed of people, but of communication. Individuals are simply the external environment of society's communicative systems. No individuals can independently control society's communication, because communication operates according to its own logic. It may sound strange at first that human beings are not part of society, but Luhmann claims that our seemingly intuitive understanding of society as a community of people is built on an outdated and fallacious theory of society.

Equating a society with a specific country is the second hurdle in social sciences. We often talk about Sweden as a society distinct from Danish society, French society, and so on. Again, this may sound intuitive and simple, but it is in fact another outdated theory of society from the nation state that we have come to perceive as intuitive. It is problematic because societal systems today form a world society and do not adhere to national borders and because it is a mistake to even think of society in spatial terms as if you could walk in and out of society. We will return to this point below.

92   system and differentiation

Third, Luhmann seeks to overcome the classic distinction between subject and object in the social sciences. One example is in positivist sociology where society is studied as an objective set of facts given independently of our observation. This is particularly problematic for the social sciences, because our study object – society – also includes the subsystem of science from which our observations are made. Sociologists are, in Luhmann's words, a "rat in the labyrinth" (Luhmann 1988: 24), so they should always consider from where they make their observations and with which distinctions they observe the world. Here, Luhmann is not far from Habermas, who is similarly critical of positivism and the strict distinction between scientist and study object.

Luhmann presents his general systems theory in the book *Social Systems* (1996). His point of departure here is the distinction between system and environment, which can be understood simply as a distinction between something that belongs in a given communicative context (system) and something that does not (environment). Whether we distinguish between legal and illegal, female and male, or true and false, we can only observe social phenomena if we distinguish them from something else. It is therefore essential to know precisely which distinctions are used to observe society in sociological studies.

Another fundamental characteristic of systems is self-reference. When a system observes something as belonging to the system, it refers to itself and thereby reproduces the system's boundary towards the environment. The opposite operation where the system relegates something to its environment is called other-reference. Luhmann understands self-reference and other-reference as mirror images. For example, science usually claims that the basis of astrology is unscientific because it builds on false assumptions. On one hand, this type of communication clearly constitutes other-reference, because science excludes astrology and thereby relegates it to the scientific system's external environment. On the other hand, it also serves to enforce and reproduce the scientific system's own criteria. Even when the scientific system excludes something, it indirectly refers to itself. On a general level, systems create order by drawing a distinction, but the act of drawing this distinction reproduces the system in a continuous process. This recursive process is also called autopoiesis, which means self-creation or self-reproduction. Luhmann argues that all social systems first and foremost seek to reproduce themselves, which is what makes them impenetrable to external control.

Traditional systems theory before Luhmann largely understood systems as either open or closed. Open systems theory focuses on how a system depends on and adapts to its environment, whereas closed systems theory sees all systems as operating entirely by their own logic. According to Luhmann, autopoietic systems theory combines the two and sees the

system and differentiation

system as operationally closed, but cognitively open. Operational closure means that a system is closed around its own operations and no other systems can perform the system's constitutive operations for it. The constitutive boundary setting of a system can only be established by the system's own communication, which makes it relatively immune to control from the outside. Systems are cognitively open because their communication can address anything and not merely internal elements of the system itself. The system can communicate about anything, but only by using its own particular mode of drawing distinctions, as we saw in the example about science and astrology. In conclusion, systems are both open and closed because they can address anything as a topic of communication, but only through distinctions and communication codes controlled by the system itself.

We can illustrate the difference between system closure and openness by thinking of a trial in court. A legal system is closed around its own particular operation, which is to make legal decisions, typically in the form of a verdict on the lawfulness of a given matter. Decisions are made on the basis of existing, valid law, which is the communication medium of law. Legal decisions cannot base themselves on anything, but must refer to existing law in the decisions, which in turn becomes part of future existing law. In spite of this operational closure, a court case also includes matters of a factual nature, which are used to determine how a specific case should be evaluated in light of the existing rules. Law is thus not completely independent of its environment, but is precisely cognitively open towards all factual matters of significance for the legal decision. Facts in themselves can never constitute law; a judge would not declare murder to be legal just because someone had proven that it was factually possible.

The concepts from Luhmann's systems theory presented until now can be understood as building blocks or as logical assumptions behind a systems theoretical analysis of society. They may be used to analyse a specific system such as law or the mass media. The core distinction between system and environment can also be used to explain Luhmann's theory of the functionally differentiated society as detailed in the following section. In a broader sense, systems theory can be boiled down to the basic idea that all communication is selective and operates by distinguishing something from something else. It is therefore essential in communication processes which distinctions are used to distinguish system from environment and how these distinctions also refer to themselves.

Functional differentiation

Similar to Durkheim, Luhmann's basic idea is that society gradually develops into an increasingly complex entity. To handle this complexity, society must differentiate itself into specialised subsystems with different functions. For example, if an organisation went from 10 to 100 members within a short time span, this would create the need for more specialisation and internal differentiation. Growth in size might create a need for formalised rules, members with specially appointed positions, and a formal budget. A similar process happens when societies become more complex, but on a larger scale. In Luhmann's view, the development from low to high complexity in society is not a simple linear increase, but also a qualitative change in the principles by which society is differentiated. In sum, "differentiation" is a process in which society grows more complex and develops subdivisions, and the "differentiation form" is the principle by which the process is structured.

In "Inclusion and Exclusion" (2002), Luhmann describes a historical succession of three forms of differentiation, which have dominated in various historical periods to regulate how individuals are included and excluded by systems in society. Early societies were characterised by a "segmentary" differentiation form that divided society into homogeneous and mutually exclusive units, for example tribes or villages. Each segmented tribe had to contain and perform all functions from within, because there was no overarching society to regulate, for instance, legal codes or a monetary system. All communication in a segmentary society begins and ends at the tribe's border, and because the tribe has to perform all functions by itself, the threshold for how much complexity a segmentary society can handle is very low. Luhmann adds that the key distinction in a segmentary society is between being inside or outside the tribe.

Complexity increases with the gradual development of stratificatory differentiation (i.e. feudal society). Stratification means that society is ordered hierarchically. Everything is oriented towards a vertical distinction between those who are above or below. At the top of the hierarchy is typically a king or emperor, who in some contexts even claims to have legitimate authority directly from a god. A stratified society can handle much larger degrees of complexity than a segmentary society, because hierarchy enables a coordination of societal communication between different layers in society and between the corresponding institutions such as army, church, kingdom or nobility. The hierarchical differentiation of social strata further enables complexity, because problems and solutions can be worked out on a much larger scale, for instance in the organisation of mass warfare or the development of major public institutions.

As we saw in Bourdieu's work (see Chapter 5), some sociologists still understand contemporary society as being fundamentally stratified in a more or less fixed class structure. Luhmann does not share this view and argues that stratification is no longer the primary form of differentiation. The development of modern society – a protracted development that took

system and differentiation 95

off especially in the 18th century – involves "functional differentiation". Society is now primarily differentiated into functional subsystems, or function systems, each controlling communication around their respective functions. Luhmann describes a totality of nine function systems – politics, law, economy, education, mass media, religion, art, science and family – and dedicates a book to each one. Ultimately, it is an empirical question exactly how many and which systems develop sufficient autonomy to constitute a functional subsystem. Other system theorists discuss whether, for instance, sports or health has this status.

Function systems are not spatial entities and do not start and stop at national borders. The scope of all function systems is modern society as a whole, but each system communicates from a very selective functional perspective. They only "exist" in communication, so to speak, they basically work by codifying societal communication according to their respective functions. For example, the economic system is not limited to communicating about trades and exchanges in economic institutions such as businesses or the stock exchange. It can communicate about everything in all parts of society, but it only does so with the available communication media of the economic system, which is money.

In a similar fashion and as described earlier, the legal system can communicate about all factual questions with relevance for a given legal question, but only in legal terms and not, for instance, to decide to sell a legal decision to the highest bidder. What is truly special about function systems in Luhmann's account is their selective responsiveness. On the one hand, they are incredibly responsive to communication that is coded into one, particular communication medium distinctive to the system in question; on the other hand, they have developed over several centuries to become highly insensitive to and simply ignore all other concerns. Other function systems are unable to interfere in each system's mode of functioning. So, for instance, a political regulation of the economy can only hope to work if it is coded into the economic system's form of communication, which is monetary payments.

The function systems are also autopoietic as described earlier, which means operationally closed around their own particular type of communicative operation. As a consequence, function systems are not geared to accommodate moral concerns just as there is no function system of morality in Luhmann's view. Any society obviously communicates about moral questions and some individuals undoubtedly act on their moral views. In Luhmann's understanding, however, it does not mean that modern society is integrated through a common set of moral values. This may sound counter-intuitive and like a great loss, but it also constitutes a major step forward. The functionally differentiated society is able to handle immense levels of complexity, precisely because it has developed highly specialised functional subsystems that do not need consensus on moral norms in order to work. A dramatic consequence is that a functionally differentiated society does not consist of integrated parts of a whole as we typically think about it intuitively. Or as Luhmann ironically writes:

> [I]n a sense, the whole is less than the sum of its parts. In other words, functionally differentiated societies cannot be ruled by leading parts or elites as stratified societies (to some extent) could be. They also cannot be rationalized by means/ends chains as a technocratic conception would suggest. Their structural complexity can be adequately formulated only by models that take into account several system/environment references at once.
>
> (Luhmann 1982: 238–239)

The lack of integration of shared norms in Luhmann's theory of the functionally differentiated society makes a central, political regulation of basic social norms equally inconceivable. We will return to this later as a prime target of Jürgen Habermas's critique. Luhmann only describes and analyses how society actually functions and not how it should be, nor how these ideals could be realised through democratic procedures. The theory of functional differentiation is not undemocratic per se, but the impossibility of integrated shared norms of course makes democratic control less likely or at least limits the scope of what can be subjected to democratic, political control.

We are intuitively used to thinking of the state as a central governing unit that coordinates and arbitrates between all its constituent parts such as economy, civil society and the private sphere. In Luhmann's view, these intuitive ideas say more about the self-description of the political system than it says about how societal communication actually functions. The communication of functionally differentiated systems must be analysed within the framework of the so-called world society where national borders are at best a subdivision within each function system. Inspired by this point, German sociologist Ulrich Beck (1944–2015, see Chapter 8), criticises the social sciences of "methodological nationalism", i.e. of being trapped within the context of the nation state (Beck 2006). Luhmann is also on par with Foucault, who criticises the outdated juridical power conception for being nothing more than the self-description of absolutist monarchy. Luhmann and Foucault agree that many of our normal concepts of power and politics are in reality obsolete theory or old self-descriptions of state institutions. Over time, these self-descriptions have slipped into everyday language to the extent that we now intuitively accept them as truthful descriptions of reality.

system and differentiation

The last aspect of Luhmann's systems theory to be introduced here is the great significance that he ascribes to communication codes and media. This point is important because many empirical applications of Luhmann's theory concern how difficult it is to coordinate communication that operates in different codes. Luhmann distinguishes between code and medium as two separate but interrelated ways to characterise the communication form of a system. Communication media have a looser structure than codes and may appear in various forms. Communication codes, on the other hand, have established a more fixed, binary form, i.e. they always have two sides. For example, the legal system draws on existing law as its medium, but in its operations, law codifies everything into a binary form that distinguishes legal from illegal. There can be nothing in-between the two sides of a code, but in principle a code can be related to more than one medium and thereby identify more complex situations. In the economic system, communication codes only identify whether or not payment is made. Money is the typical communication medium, but in principle a cow or a car could constitute economic communication.

Some, but not all function systems have developed what is termed symbolically generalised communication media. The concept, which Luhmann borrows from American sociologist Talcott Parsons (1902–1979), designates a special set of standardised, symbolic codes that are used to communicate within a subsystem with the aim to perform very general functions in society. Symbolically generalised media ease communication tremendously because participants do not have to clarify every single aspect of the themes they communicate about, but may instead take a lot of standards for given.

The best example is money, which is defined as a symbolically generalised communication medium by Parsons, Habermas and Luhmann. Most people know that the value of money is only symbolic or at least dependent on being a recognised mode of payment by the receiver. Nonetheless, money works as a common standard under normal conditions, and it makes economic transactions significantly easier, because it filters out a lot of irrelevant information about the other participants in the communication. You do not need to know anything about the other person in an economic transaction to be able to exchange payments through money.

Money is by far the most concrete symbolically generalised medium, but there are others. Both Parsons and Luhmann understand power as the symbolically generalised medium of the political system, even though there is of course no explicit currency of power. If a decision is made by a person or an institution in a decision-making power position, the decision is normally recognised without everyone testing whether the power holder is willing to go to extremes to enforce the decision.

system and differentiation

Not all function systems necessarily develop their own symbolically generalised communication media, but it is a characteristic step in the development of high system complexity and autopoiesis. Besides money and power, we can mention love, defined as the generalised medium of the family system, and truth, defined as the generalised medium of the scientific system. In each case, the generalised media can never achieve absolute and final control of communication, because all symbols or currencies may lose their value over time. A sort of inflation might occur where the general trust in a communication medium decreases. Nevertheless, the generalised media work under normal conditions and thereby reduce the necessary amount of information to a fraction of what would have been necessary without them.

A key topic for systems theoretical analyses is how different function systems coexist and interact. Connections between systems are initially very challenging, because all systems communicate with their own codes and communication media. Systems can thus not interfere in each other's operations, but Luhmann does describe the possibility of a so-called structural coupling between two function systems (Luhmann 1996). As an example, a constitution works as a structural coupling between the legal and the political systems, but still on the condition of each system's autopoiesis, so the constitution will be understood politically by the political system and legally by the legal system.

As an example of empirical application, the Danish systems theorist Niels Åkerstrøm Andersen has used Luhmann's concepts to analyse the relations and tensions between private and public forms of management. In empirical studies of outsourcing, partnerships and contract management, Andersen has demonstrated the resultant couplings between the subsystems of law, politics, and economy. Most of these Luhmann-inspired analyses conclude that it is at best very difficult if not impossible to achieve the required coordination between different function systems to make a program such as outsourcing function as planned (Andersen 2003; 2006).

Luhmann's theory of functional differentiation is also useful to analyse the difficulties of managing or governing other complex, social problems. No function systems can control each other, and there is thus no overarching or central engine for governing a functionally differentiated society. In *Ecological Communication* (1989), Luhmann analyses the failure and inability of the economic system to handle large environmental problems. The consequences of these steering problems are not always as bleak as this, of course. The basic theoretical point is that because Luhmann does not automatically expect societal systems to integrate seamlessly, his theory is well equipped to analyse the conflicts that occur when society's subsystems have problems coordinating their efforts.

system and differentiation

Habermas's theory of the public sphere

Whereas it is difficult to identify a normative horizon in Luhmann's work, it is for Habermas vital to work out the principles of a normatively founded social theory. The basis for this endeavour is a critical interrogation of our modern predicament. He conceives of modernity as an incomplete project. Its goal is human freedom and self-realisation, but these values have not yet been fully realised. The task of sociology is to point us in the direction of achieving these goals. In Chapter 1, we argued that sociology as a science is empirically directed, and in this light one might view Habermas's normative emphasis as an indication that his project is more philosophical than sociological. Things are not this simple, however, and for two reasons.

First, in the so-called positivism debate, Habermas convincingly shows that allegedly value-neutral science is actually tied to a technical-instrumental interest in gaining control over nature. Habermas also operates with a practical and emancipatory interest. Research based on a technical-instrumental interest tends, through its alleged neutrality and its naïve technological optimism, to mediate a false consensus whereby a given social order appears in an unproblematic light. Positivism, in other words, also implies a certain normativity. No matter what position one chooses, or perhaps precisely because one must choose one's position at the expense of another, one's position always comes with a normative perspective. Consequently, a theory of society must be a critical theory. A critical theory is characterised by, among other things, being reflexive with regard to its own normative foundation, or better, its interestedness – in Habermas' case an emancipatory one.

Second, it is central to understand that Habermas is no classical philosopher, if by this term one understands a person attempting to arrive through thinking at the nature of a good or just society. Habermas belongs to the second generation of the so-called Frankfurt School (central first-generation figures were Theodor W. Adorno, Max Horkheimer and Herbert Marcuse, whose particular brand of theory is often named critical theory), who, inspired by Marx, conducts so-called immanent critique. In Habermas's version, this consists in proceeding from the ideals that are immanent in the project of modernity. One might, for instance, follow the tireless first-generation critical practice of showing how the alleged free will – which is one of the central pillars of modernity – is not so free after all, given that it is constantly manipulated by advertisements and ideology.

Such critique is sociological because it proceeds from ideals that actually occur empirically in society (in our example the notion of the free formation of will) and because it points to the defective breakthrough of

100   system and differentiation

these ideals in institutions and in life (e.g. through deformation of free will through advertising). Critique becomes a critique of what is given (degenerative tendencies) on the basis of what is given (the immanent but unredeemed ideals of modernity).

Habermas delivers this form of immanent critique in his work about the emergence and decay of the bourgeois public sphere. The bourgeois society referred to by Habermas is the one that emerged over the course of the 19th century. People began to gather in private salons and coffee houses to discuss matters of public interest, e.g. art, moral questions, literature, and to some extent politics. The idea of the public at this time was founded on equal access to and participation in discussion and on a notion of the precedence of the good argument. The precondition for realising these ideals was that the public sphere remain relatively independent of the economic and political system. Whereas the bourgeois public sphere used to be acclamatory, i.e. served the function of applauding political power (Habermas 1991: 5–14), the separation from the political field makes a critical attitude towards political decisions possible.

In the Italian renaissance, not least evident in the work of Niccolò Machiavelli, an initial detachment of the political from the theological took place – God's will and the political ruler's will no longer coincided. During the 19th century, the notion emerged that the political leadership's will and the people's will did not automatically coincide. This was, in a sense, a democratic revolution. Classic Marxism also focuses on this period, but whereas many of Marx's disciples view the working class as the politicising force, Habermas focuses on the bourgeoisie, and he focuses on the individual's capacity for and access to the exercise of reason rather than on social movements.

Habermas's work on the emergence and fall of the public sphere has quite a disheartening story to tell. The conditions that make the public sphere possible, e.g. the development of autonomous media, the abolition of individual ties to agrarian production units, urbanisation, and the emergence of private contract law, are the same conditions that subsequently contribute to the subversion of the public. If we begin with the media, Habermas notes that the political pamphlets of the time express popular moods independently of politicians and the state apparatus. This, however, changes with the advent of mass media, which is primarily interested in entertaining for profit. The new media often fail to persistently draw attention to relevant issues and thus cease to be a corrective to the political level. Rather than carrying the perspectives and attitudes of the populace into public space, the media become a top-down information channel, i.e. from politicians downwards. This development transforms the public sphere and reduces the individual from being a producer

system and differentiation 101

of culture into a consumer of culture (Habermas 1991: 159–175). Habermas describes this change as a re-feudalisation of the public (Habermas 1991: 142–151).

> The communicative network of a public made up of rationally debating private citizens has collapsed; the public opinion once emergent from it has partly decomposed into the informal opinions of private citizens without a public and partly become concentrated into formal opinions of publicistically effective institutions. Caught in the vortex of publicity that is staged for show or manipulation the public of nonorganized private people is laid claim to not by public communication but by the communication of publicly manifested opinions.
>
> (Habermas 1991: 247–248)

In addition to the transformed function of the media, Habermas mentions a broad range of affairs that place the public sphere under pressure. The state and private firms take over functions that were previously handled in civil society or at least derived their legitimacy from it. Free trade is subverted, yielding to a number of oligopolies. Organised interests dominate political discussion. The safeguarding of interests takes precedence over a rationality of listening and discussion.

We will mention two criticisms of Habermas's analysis of the bourgeois public sphere, which further specify his contribution. An oft-repeated criticism holds that the notion of the public sphere as a fundamentally open, equal, and free sphere is naïve. The strongest argument does not necessarily win, but rather the one proposing it, i.e. the one with most symbolic capital and the strongest rhetoric. Whereas Bourdieu views language as a means to exercise symbolic violence, Habermas regards understanding and consensus as its telos. Why else have a conversation at all? Another, equally frequent criticism is that access to the political was precisely not equal. Only a few had access, and as the debate societies belonged to the bourgeoisie, no other classes contributed to political discourse.

These two criticisms cause Habermas to specify the nature of what he calls the ideal speech situation. It is not an empirical phenomenon, but rather a set of values that must be presupposed in order for conversation to make sense. Simultaneously, it is the ideal against which to measure a perverted conversation. In the book on the public sphere, Habermas focuses on the institutional embedment of the ideals of equality, freedom and rationality in the guise of a public sphere, but he later shifts his attention to language itself. Just as Kant claimed that the lie cannot be primary – it is only possible to lie if the other presumes that one speaks the truth – Habermas holds that persuasion and other kinds of manipulation cannot be fundamental to language.

In order to get a conversation started at all, we must assume that our interlocutor speaks the truth, is sincere, and that his or her propositions are morally defensible. Once more we find that Habermas practices immanent critique. Language holds certain immanent ideals upon which we draw in our conversation. This ideal was realised to some extent in the bourgeois public sphere that emerged in the salons and coffee houses, and the task today is to establish institutions in which this potential may once more unfold.

If we read Habermas's story of the glory and decay of the public sphere as merely a historical description of changes in society, then it is, as already noted, a sad tale. If, however, we read the work on the bourgeois public sphere in light of subsequent work, it becomes essential that the coffee houses and salons institutionalised something immanent in language. A potential was involved which may be redeemed at any time. This theoretical upending, i.e. the shift from an institutional understanding of the public sphere's critical potential to a more linguistically and communicatively founded understanding, will be introduced in the following. We thus move from an analysis of the public sphere to a full-blown theory of society. This only means that the thesis of decay is delivered in an alternative form, now supplemented by an explicit critique of Luhmann's systemic perspective.

System and life world

Habermas largely accepts Luhmann's analysis of state and market as functioning systemically through the media of power and money. However, according to Habermas, a broad range of other types of behaviour cannot (and should not) be explained in systemic terms, for instance what occurs in families and in the public sphere. These spheres continually draw on a so-called life world, i.e. a reservoir of common meaning and significance.

The point is not merely that something exists alongside systemic integration that Habermas names social integration, but also that social integration is the primary type (1987: 154). Systemic integration builds on social integration and relieves it. However, this is possible only in some spheres of society. If symbolically generalised media are introduced in, say, family or the public sphere, the result will be a number of pathologies. Habermas speaks here of the colonisation of the life world by systems. The crucial difference between the two forms of integration is that in systems, action is coordinated through strategic and instrumental rationality, whereas in the life world, a communicative rationality unfolds, or ought to unfold.

Communicative action, according to Habermas, aims at understanding. As opposed to strategic action, the referent of action in communicative actions is no mere means to an end. In communicative action, on the one hand, one listens to the objections of the other with the intention of reaching a common understanding of the situation and of what to do about a problem. In strategic or instrumental action, on the other hand, the goal stands outside of interaction (e.g. in the guise of profit or power) and therefore cannot be changed through it.

Communicative action is furthermore characterised by the establishment of consensus without force or economic coercion. This is possible because the interlocutors may refer to the aforementioned common life world, that is, the linguistically given and culturally founded resources which one draws upon in a conversation. It is a form of cultural grammar actively drawn upon by actors, whether or not they are fully aware of it. The life world is, one might say, our entrance to the world. It is thus not a region of the social on the same level as, say, the market or the state, but rather a precondition of cultural knowledge, social solidarity, and personal identity. The life world thus consists of three components: an objective one (culture), a social one (solidarity and communal feeling) and a subjective one (identity) (1987: 120, 126, 131).

The consequence of the impeachment of systems upon regions in which the rationality of the life world ought to be primary, e.g. family or the public sphere, is that a large number of pathologies arise. As far as cultural reproduction, one will experience a loss of meaning; as far as social integration, one will experience anomie (a concept Habermas borrows from Durkheim, see Chapter 3); and as far as socialisation (the subjective component), psychopathologies will emerge in individuals (1987: 145). One sees, in other words, a tendency towards decay in all three components of the life world.

Habermas's notion of systems as alien to the life world is primarily philosophical in its foundation, and yet this is the Habermasian idea that has inspired the greatest number of sociological analyses. Let us here mention the widespread critique of clientilisation. With the introduction of so-called new public management and other forms of result-oriented management, the citizen who approaches a state institution (e.g. a job centre or social office) is often put in a situation where his or her case will only run its smooth course to the extent that the citizen adjusts, acts like a specific type of client. Initiatives meant to prevent individuals from adjusting to life as a social client and instead take a job are bound to distort the citizen's will, norms and behaviour.

Habermas thus agrees with Luhmann that systemic media exist in the family and the public sphere, but unlike Luhmann he views this as a problem. This emphasis on the limitations of steering media is perhaps

104 system and differentiation

in itself a fair critique of Luhmann. As a diagnosis of contemporary society, however, the notion of systems colonising life worlds is reductive. We shall here address three problems.

First, systemic elements are present in life worlds and life world-founded elements in systems. Whereas Luhmann explicitly warns against associating systems with physical organisations, Habermas does so deliberately and thereby misses the fact that power is exercised in the family and in a nonpathological manner. It would be impossible, for instance, to raise children without exercising power. Another example is that the democratic public sphere in many countries is centred around state television and radio stations that are subject to strong political control as well as market competition. The point is not that Habermas's thesis of decay is once again proven right, but rather that it is problematic to place concrete institutions and various social rationalities on the same level.

Habermas views the life world as a foundation for consensus. It is clear that a common life world is a precondition for understanding one another. In a more normative perspective, it is also crucial that we are able to constantly correct one another and attain an understanding of each other's positions: "When you said that, did you then mean to say ...?" But can one infer from this the possibility of consensus? Another critique, then, is to say that enlightenment and debate do not necessarily lead to agreement, or better that not all communication has this as its aim. Politics is also about interests and struggles. One could therefore ask, could a notion of the goals embedded in language take the place of class theory and the way interests are derived from them? Generally speaking, the problem is that it is not clear whether Habermas's theory is normative or descriptive. Is it a moral philosophy undergirded by sociological analysis, or is it a contemporary social diagnosis with normative implications? If the latter is the case, then Habermas's conception of politics clearly gives us only half the story. Habermas's focus on language causes him to overestimate the possibility of social integration and to underestimate the potential for conflict.

Third, in continuation of the preceding criticism, one might ask whether a common life world in the singular exists at all. Are modern, pluralist societies not characterised by a multiplicity of life worlds that do not always come together? Habermas seems to have addressed this objection in his latest works (Habermas 2008: 99–148), where he raises two important questions. One deals with religion and other fundamental articles of belief. Are religiously founded propositions alien to the bourgeois public sphere? No, contends Habermas, not if they can be relativised within the political conversation. He seems here to establish a distinction between a religious life world and some derivative concrete propositions for political action that may be relativised. The question is whether such a

system and differentiation

105

distinction can be practically maintained. Wouldn't a religious fundamentalist be a political fundamentalist as well?

Of more interest is Habermas's proposed new way of thinking integration – a way that does not proceed from a notion of cultural homogeneity. Habermas has advocated so-called constitutional patriotism in various contexts. The common principles to which everybody in a society can agree are no longer substantial, cultural values, but rather a common emotional investment in the principles of the constitution and in democracy. Habermas here returns to the public sphere, because this emotional attachment to the constitution, which is the foundation of political discourse, is established precisely through participation in such discourse.

Horizontal and vertical differentiation

In this chapter we have discussed two recent theories of social differentiation. We shall attempt here to make a concluding review. Whereas classic sociologists such as Durkheim described differentiation as virtually a linear process, Luhmann and Habermas add substantial insight into the subsystems and sub-rationalities into which society is differentiated. Furthermore, they both develop far more advanced conceptual apparatuses for the analysis of current problematics concerning differentiation and integration.

A common trait in Luhmann's and Habermas's theories is that they primarily describe horizontal differentiation, i.e. the division of society into subsystems that are in principle parallel in distribution. This means that vertical distribution, i.e. the class structure of society, does not receive much attention. Luhmann believes that stratification is no longer the primary form of distribution in society, and sees functional differentiation as being a far more fundamental process. Habermas's theory likewise has little to offer as regards the analysis of class structure.

If, instead of differentiation, we emphasise the aspect of integration, the difference between Luhmann and Habermas is more pronounced. Luhmann rejects the idea that a functionally differentiated society needs close normative integration. Possibilities for sociological analyses far wider in scope arise if one rejects the notion of general integration of steering as well as social norms in society. Problems of steering and the collapse of social norms may well be real problems, but they cannot be solved by forcing a simplified concept of unity, such as integration, on a complex and highly differentiated society. Conversely, Habermas's view is that modern society is in a sense integrated too easily, given that systemic integration and generalised control media are so effective that they trump everything else. His diagnosis of modern societies is that they often tend towards a deficit in terms of social integration. Communicative rationality makes itself heard with great difficulty over the dominant systemic rationalities. Against this backdrop, Habermas recommends a strengthening of the democratic public sphere or a new constitutional patriotism.

Finally, it is worth mentioning a crucial difference between Luhmann and Habermas, namely the relationship between the descriptive and normative aspects of their theories, i.e. between describing states of affairs and addressing the norms for how things ought to be. Luhmann rejects the normative perspective because he believes that virtually all normative theory attempts to appraise society on a grossly simplified scale. Habermas, via immanent critique, attempts to integrate the descriptive and the normative into one perspective. Many find that this approach provides a more complete theory of contemporary society and a critical potential, whereas others find that the heavy moral standard hampers the theory's analytical impact.

system and differentiation

chapter 7

State and market

Althusser and Boltanski & Chiapello

Sociology asks questions about the character and basis of our social being. What we believe, what we are, our identity, our feelings and intuitions, how we perceive one another, and finally our conception of the common and of society; all these things must be conceptualised with reference to a prior social formation. In this chapter we focus on how two central institutions, the state and the market, contribute to our social identities. We have chosen to do this by discussing three sociologists, namely Louis Althusser (1918–1990), whose theory of state and ideology is discussed in the first half of the chapter, and Luc Boltanski (1940–) and Ève Chiapello (1965–), who have contributed significantly to describing and theorising contemporary capitalism's novel ways of producing subjectivity. We will become acquainted with Boltanski and Chiapello's work on the spirit of capitalism in the second part of the chapter.

We have several reasons for focusing on these elements. It is obvious, first of all, that precisely the state and the market are the most important social institutions today. The state intervenes in and regulates practically all aspects of common life. Our life paths run through a number of state institutions, from nurseries and day-care centres, over educational and cultural institutions, to hospitals and nursing homes. We live in a society ruled by law and are thus subject to rules which, if broken, are sanctioned by police or other executive authorities. Correspondingly, the market regulates and shapes a wide range of services and not least our consumption. Practically anything can be commercialised and capitalised on. Even love, or in any case sex, can be bought with money. Many social fields, e.g. art, are subject to the logic of the market, although they cannot be reduced to this aspect.

State and market should not necessarily be understood as two isolated fields. As soon as we widen our scope beyond public institutions, e.g. libraries and hospitals, to include public regulation and management as well as legal sanctioning of our behaviour, it becomes more difficult to discern the limits of the state. The same goes for the market. There are stock markets where money, raw materials and financial assets are traded, and there are shops where buyers and sellers meet to exchange commodities, but a capitalist society is not limited to such institutions. We are not interested in the market as an autonomous field, isolated from other social systems. We do not wish to conduct economic sociology, nor are we about to introduce a sociology of the state. What we are concerned with is how modern societies are shaped by the state and in what sense they may be described as capitalist.

Althusser and Boltanski/Chiapello regard state and market as absurd systems in need of continuous legitimisation. Althusser sees the state as an instrument of the ruling class, serving, like a kind of machine, to transform a surplus of violence into legitimacy. According to Althusser, the fundamental inequality, antagonisms of class, must be covered up by means of ideology. Boltanski and Chiapello also see capitalism as an absurd system, given that its raison d'être is to generate profit. The fact that some receive more than others and that most people do not own what they produce calls for legitimisation, and this is precisely what is offered by various justification regimes.

However, the three sociologists diverge significantly in their critical stance. Whereas Althusser's project is classically normative in its attempt to overcome the capitalist system he criticises, Boltanski and Chiapello are interested in the ways in which the system itself produces criticism. In other words, it is a difference between critical sociology and sociology of criticism, i.e. between a sociology that conceives of its own work as critical and a sociology that examines criticism and critical capacities.

Althusser's Marxist sociology of the state

Althusser was active in the French communist party, and he viewed the party's and the movement's crisis as related to theoretical problems. Most importantly, Althusser felt that the Marx reception of the time lacked a theory of politics and political practice, and of the crucial nature of "super-structural phenomena", e.g. of how ideology produces subjectivity. The idea, which was common in much Marxist theory of the day, that everything can be explained by reference to economics, was excessively reductive, according to Althusser.

As is commonly known, the revolution was realised in Russia rather than in a country where capitalism had developed the furthest. And in the West, workers went to war against each other during the First and Second World Wars. The former fact indicates the need to develop a nonreductive conception of the political as a semiautonomous field; the latter indicates the need for a theory of the role of ideology in shaping the consciousness of individuals. In the following, we will outline Althusser's attempt to solve both tasks: first Althusser's contribution to the development of a theory of the state and then his contribution to the understanding of how ideology functions.

Whereas many reacted to the crisis of Marxism by abandoning all Marxist insights, Althusser made the opposite move. The crisis was to be overcome through a rereading of Marx's texts in order to bring out their unrealised potential (Althusser 2006: 12). Althusser thus became known for the so-called symptomal reading, which consists, briefly put, of three analytico-theoretical devices.

First, the reading worked backwards, starting from the mature elements of the work, which would then influence the reading of less mature elements. Althusser claims, for instance, that the young Marx remains mired in a humanist and idealist tradition (represented by the influence from Hegel and Feuerbach and the prominent notion of (false) consciousness, among other things, and that Marx's works should therefore be read with the later, more scientifically founded works as point of departure.

Second, one source of difficulty is that Marx was often tied up in the concepts of his time and that readers therefore often overlook the radical nature of his work. A reinterpretation or a fresh reading of a number of central concepts therefore requires that the reader retrace the problems Marx grappled with.

The third form of symptomal reading pertains to external reality, i.e. not to Marx's writings. In the analysis of social reality and the reading of ideological texts, the ruling notion is that on the one hand there is a drive to cover up fundamental antagonisms (e.g. between workers and employers, via the notion that the worker's wages correspond to the value they add to the products of their trade). On the other hand, such antagonisms can never be fully eliminated and therefore surface in the guise of "symptoms". With this method Althusser develops the traditions of immanent critique, also drawn upon, as we have seen, by Habermas, albeit in a less conflict-oriented manner. Concerning Marx's notion of critique, Althusser writes:

> Marx tied critique to that which, in the real movement, grounded critique: for him, in the last instance, the class struggle of the exploited,

110   state and market

which could objectively overcome the domination of the bourgeois class because and only because of the specific nature of the existing forms of their exploitation: the forms of capitalist exploitation.

(Althusser 2006: 17)

The fundamental tension to which the symptoms can be retraced in this third form of symptomal reading is the class struggle.

By extension, Althusser's theory about the function of the state carries a double agenda. It serves, first, to understand the activity of the state against the backdrop of a fundamental and structural tension, or better, conflict or antagonism (the class struggle). The state is a tool with which the ruling class may better maintain its position of power. Second, the state seeks to eliminate awareness of its conflictual basis and to cover up fundamental conflicts. It conceives of its own task as delivering public services and facilitating a neutral legal process (Althusser 2006: 78).

The state is commonly perceived as a neutral instrument, a bystander to the class struggle, and for this very reason it is crucial to gain control of it in order to win in the class struggle. This is the grounds on which to understand Marx's often misconceived theory of the dictatorship of the proletariat. Dictatorship is often understood to be a specific nondemocratic form of rule in which the few rule over the many. Althusser's point is that Marx is constrained by the language of his day. What Marx is getting at is that the class struggle is precisely a struggle, and that the opponents of the working class will not surrender voluntarily. In order for the revolution not to be rolled back, the state apparatus must therefore be appropriated and the former ruling class forced to play by the new rules. This is not a case of an elite ruling the many. Marx rather conceived of a form of radical or basis democracy in which the distinction between rulers and subjects would be dissolved. From this also follows the notion of the withering away of the state, which does not imply the disappearance of state regulation, but merely the substitution of the class state with a state that does not reproduce a repressive system (Althusser 2006: 69–91).

Until then, however, the state is to be viewed as an instrument of the ruling class. But the term "instrument" says nothing of the state's manner of functioning; it only addresses the particular interests it serves. In order to deal with the question of functionality, Althusser turns to Lenin's notion of the state as a machine. Through this metaphor, Althusser seeks to direct our attention to two aspects of state activity.

First, the state is a complex entity. Like any machine, it consists of several elements with their respective forms and functions. These parts are the so-called apparatuses. One may speak of an administrative, a political, a repressive, and an ideological state apparatus – and this list is not necessarily exhaustive (Althusser 2006: 101). Whereas the administrative state apparatus undergirds the status quo via "neutral" facilitation and public service, and the political state apparatus does so via legal power, laws, and so on, the repressive state apparatus deals in corporal violence, and the ideological apparatus produces submission through ideology.

Second, a machine, in the lexical definition of the word, is a contraption that transforms one form of energy into another. The foundation of the state is class society and the violence upon which it rests, and its purpose is to transform the surplus of violence into legitimate force, thereby consolidating the regime's continuance.

At this point we may turn to the much criticised model of basis and superstructure, of which Althusser was not entirely uncritical. The fundamental intuition behind the model is, however, correct: The precondition for the activity of state apparatuses is a capitalist class society. The metaphor becomes reductive, however, if it produces the notion that the economy manifests itself directly in all aspects of social life. Althusser chooses instead to speak of "overdetermination" and "determination in the last instance" (Althusser 2006: 59). Yes, the apparatuses contribute to the reproduction of class society, but they do so with a view to the general interest of the bourgeoisie, which is in no way reducible to the interest of an individual capitalist. One precondition for capitalism, for instance, is the occasional bankruptcy of individual capitalists. Such cases demonstrate a clear divergence between the individual capitalist's interest in survival and the capitalist imperative that unprofitable production be shut down. The last instance, in which determination must necessarily assert itself in its pure form, is a situation that threatens the very existence of the system. Althusser writes:

> That is what the state is: an apparatus capable of taking measures against the will of a part of even a majority of the bourgeoisie in order to defend the bourgeoisie's "general interests" as the dominant class.
>
> (2006: 77)

The dominant ideology, in other words, is not necessarily that of the ruling class. It can be any horizon that serves to maintain the status quo: religious notions, nationalism, liberalism or something else entirely.

Another unfortunate consequence of the metaphor of basis and superstructure is that it often discourages enquiry into the modes of operation and the complex interplay of the individual apparatuses. The state is a complex entity. The ideological state apparatus has its peculiar specificity, which should be investigated in its own right, but it is simultaneously clear that this apparatus produces services that are central to other apparatuses. The repressive state apparatus requires ideology as its supplement, e.g. in the guise of troop morale, and the administrative apparatus rests upon an administrative ethic: the notion of the neutral civil servant's vocation. The apparatuses are relatively autonomous in the sense (just outlined) that they depend on one another, but also in the sense that the individual apparatuses may stand in mutual opposition. In the following we will primarily focus on the function of the ideological apparatus.

Ideology as interpellation

Althusser finds in Marx's work two notions of ideology and the rudiments of a third, which he sets out to develop. The young Marx, in continuity with Feuerbach, focused on the alienation of humans with regard to religion and later the production process. According to Althusser, this is an idealist, humanist and essentialist conception of ideology, as it proceeds from a notion of the true nature or essence of the human being. Althusser finds the second conception of ideology in Marx's analysis of commodity fetishism (Marx 1990: 163–177). The central point here is that humans treat commodities as if they possess a life or magical substance of their own, whereas human relations are simultaneously instrumentalised. Althusser regards this theory too as idealist, because it still implies that some social substance is incorrectly reflected (Althusser 2006: 127).

Althusser's third and original approach is to conceive of ideology not as an erroneous human notion of social reality, but rather as a form of practice. The task thus becomes to theorise the ideological production of consciousness and subjectivity. Althusser is a materialist, which should not be understood in terms of a reverse relation between ideas and matter, as the model of basis and superstructure sometimes seems to suggest, but rather as the ambition to analyse how our modes of thought and being are formed. Althusser thus moves away from a philosophical approach to ideologies (testing their internal consistency or their correspondence with external reality) towards a sociological one, deploying the notion of ideology as a theory of socialisation.

It is often claimed that Althusser's theoretical innovation consists in shifting the focus of Marxism from production to reproduction. Indeed, Althusser takes interest in the function of ideology, that is the working of the superstructure, but this is to be understood as a completion of Marx's theory. It is not a case of economics and capitalism declining in importance, but rather one of the economy requiring the respective state apparatuses to produce autonomously services vital to its functioning. If we view the ideological state apparatus in isolation, it reproduces first of all the skills of workers (Althusser 2006: 43–44). The more technologically

state and market 113

advanced the economy, the greater the importance of knowledge and technical skill. To maintain labour power, the labour force must regenerate, which causes Althusser to speak of the family as part of the ideological state apparatus. Third, the notion of wages as fair compensation for one's labour, as well as other notions central to the economy, must be communicated and sustained, and finally, the notion that the overall system is legitimate must be upheld.

The shift from production towards reproduction should be interpreted as a shift from something regarded as stable and autonomous to something in constant need of recreation. In lieu of a vulgar philosophy of history in which capitalism unfolds according to its innate laws and in which there is no space for political action, Althusser emphasises how capitalism requires agency in order to be reproduced. Althusser has elsewhere referred to his materialism as "aleatory". His point is to emphasise contingency as well as the space for action present in any historical context. He even claims that a social formation that fails to reproduce the conditions of production cannot be sustained even for one year (Althusser 1971: 1).

Ideology manifests itself for instance in school, where the acquisition of linguistic competence and of the ability to sit still and comply is essential for the subsequent capacity to receive instruction in the workplace and accept the division of labour. We have previously mentioned aspects of the family as part of the ideological state apparatus, and one might add the media, political parties, culture and religion (Althusser 1971: 17). Unlike the repressive state apparatus, all these institutions stem from the private sphere. But their importance for the reproduction of the state and submission to the given order is great enough for Althusser to justify naming them state apparatuses.

So far we have mainly focused on the relationship between the state and the ideological state apparatus. As promised, we will now look at how ideology creates particular forms of subjectivity. In this context it is important to look at Althusser's conception of the process of socialisation.

Not all ideologies are alike, of course, but according to Althusser, ideologies as such have an "eternal" status. In other words, there is no such thing as a society free from ideology. Ideologies are an essential element of any social formation, as the subject represents its relation to society through an ideological horizon, e.g. through the notion of being a citizen of a state or a recipient of wages in a capitalist economy (Althusser 1969: 209–210, 213–214). Ideology therefore does not distort a social reality – ideological notions are not necessarily false. Instead, the main issue for Althusser is that ideologies mediate a particular way of relating to society. The individual – or better, the subject – relates to society in an imaginary manner (Althusser 1971: 35, 38–39). Because this notion may come off as somewhat opaque, let us briefly cover its meaning in Althusser's thought.

Althusser does not elaborate much on imaginary identification, but he was inspired by French psychoanalyst Jacques Lacan's article "The Mirror Stage as Formative of the I" (1977). It is Lacan's thesis that between the ages of six and eighteen months, the child views itself as an autonomous whole rather than as motorically undeveloped and dependent on adults. This notion is a precondition for the child's development. Via reflection in its "mirror image" (its body imago) the child is formed as an "I". This typically occurs when the child regards itself in a mirror or perceives itself as reflected by the mother's care, or the care of other persons. Any kind of representation of the child's environment is therefore a misrepresentation, as it starts from the notion of being a fully developed and independent I. The child believes that he or she is fully formed and in control of his or her surroundings, which is not the case.

According to Althusser, the subject's perception of itself as an autonomous individual (the imaginary identification) entails that the subject systematically plays down the importance of the social environment for the formation of it. The subject's notion of being an autonomous individual is only possible on the condition of accepting a social role, e.g. that of a citizen. Althusser thus claims that Lacan's theory is useful in terms of explaining how the adult person relates to society. The imaginary, then, refers to our notion of being the point of reference of our perceptions and experiences. We do not view our subjectivity as derived from something else.

However, more than imaginary identification is involved here. The notion of a self presupposes some roles, or in Althusser's term, positions, to step into. Althusser here speaks of the symbolic, i.e. the "moulds" that structure our identity. Althusser formulates the relationship between imaginary and symbolic identification as follows:

> The category of the subject is constitutive of all ideology, but at the same time and immediately I add that the category of the subject is only constitutive of all ideology insofar as all ideology has the function (which defines it) of "constituting" concrete individuals as subjects.
>
> (1971: 160)

Put differently, the precondition for us to accept the messages and norms of ideology is that we perceive ourselves as the active part. We are the ones who build our identities. We are not mere products of social formation.

Imaginary and symbolic identification thus refers to two different senses in which we are subjects. We know the word subject first of all from the

state and market   115

distinction between subject and object, with the subject as the active pole and the object as passive pole. The concept of imaginary identification refers to this experience of being one's own master. In its other use, the concept of subject carries the exact opposite meaning. To be someone's subject is to be ruled by them. For instance, the king's subjects are those who owe him unconditional obedience. They are subjected to his will. In other words, this symbolic identification is about stepping into certain positions in society, which is why Althusser speaks in this context of subject positions.

Althusser develops the concept of interpellation to describe this double inscription of the imaginary and the symbolic. The term interpellation conceptualises an act in which the subject is constituted, via an "addressal", as subject to a social role. This may take place, for instance, when somebody hails you in the street and you turn around, thereby acknowledging that the hail is addressed to you in particular. A classic example is the Führer addressing his subjects in the name of the homeland, or the police officer shouting "Hey, you there!" (Althusser 1971: 163).

Interpellation thus conceptualises the illusion of always already being a subject – or to put it differently, the notion that the imaginary identification is primary and therefore takes place independently (Althusser 1971: 158). The subject does not perceive that it is constituted via the addressal. The subject's blindness to the constitutive nature of interpellation causes the ideological call to appear as trivialities, truths, personal preferences, or choices. Ideology thus has a naturalising function. It diverts attention from the temporal, from the fact that all ideas and notions are social in origin, i.e. acquired, and that they might therefore have turned out differently.

Strongly put, we might say that the concept of interpellation seeks to capture how we as laymen tend *not* to think sociologically. We are accustomed to ascribing all events to an active subject: "I want ...", "I became angry ...", "I didn't like ...", and so on. And we thus fail to perceive how society acts through us, how it shapes our thoughts, and how it blocks our paths or alternatively guides us towards social ends. In this way Althusser's concept of interpellation reminds us of what Bourdieu coined symbolic violence.

The idea of a social contract, e.g. the Hobbesian notion discussed briefly in Chapter 1, draws precisely on the notion of the individual as the foundation of society rather than its product. Individual citizens are supposed to have freely elected the exact form of society and state to which they are subject. It is up to us to evaluate the legitimacy of the state. Althusser would reject this as a misconception. The state interpellates us as good citizens, and our support for the state thus derives from the socialisation to which we are subjected by the ideological state apparatuses. The state addresses us, and we respond as if we had elected the state, i.e. independently of the symbolic violence it perpetrates.

If ideology is formative of subjects, and consequently also of scholars – perhaps even of Marxists – then the question is how to criticise ideology at all. Does such critique not presuppose a position beyond ideology? Althusser's answer is twofold. First of all, the working class must necessarily have its own ideology. If nothing is external to ideology, it becomes a matter of substituting one ideology for another. Although Althusser does not explicitly deal with French syndicalist Georges Sorel, one might refer to his theory of the myth of the general strike as the mobilising horizon of the working class. As for the second response, let us first read Althusser's own formulation:

> Ideology never says, "I am ideological". It is necessary to be outside ideology, i.e. in scientific knowledge, to be able to say: I am in ideology (a quite exceptional case) or (the general case): I was in ideology. As is well known, the accusation of being in ideology only applies to others, never to oneself (unless one is really a Spinozist or a Marxist, which, in this manner, is to be exactly the same thing). Which amounts to saying that ideology "has no outside" (for itself), but at the same time "that it is nothing but outside" (for science and reality).
>
> (Althusser 1971: 164)

The science to which Althusser refers is Marxism. Marxism is scientific because it enquires about the institutional source and function of ideologies. This takes us to the somewhat paradoxical conclusion that one can only escape ideology by recognising that one is trapped within it. Claiming to be beyond ideologies, which is in vogue after the fall of the Berlin Wall, is itself an ideological operation – perhaps even the ultimate one. The scientific character of Marxism consists in its recognition of holding a position within a political struggle. One cannot escape ideology, and the scientific approach thus consists exclusively in constant critical reflection on the ideological – even in one's own thought. If the critique of ideology is conceived of as merely a question of criticising ideologies, then one has only halfway understood the matter. Critique should imply self-critique. Just as the state must constantly reproduce itself, so must the critique of ideology perpetually regard itself critically to avoid stagnation and capture by the status quo.

The latter reflection happens to be the point of departure for the work of Boltanski and Chiapello. Whereas Althusser primarily focused on 1970s capitalism and state power, Boltanski and Chiapello are concerned with the self-legitimation of contemporary capitalism. Capitalism has absorbed the criticism of the 1970s, aimed at standardising, routine forms of labour,

state and market   117

making it paradoxically a form of "leftist" capitalism based on creativity, flexibility, and project-based endeavours. 1970s critique of ideology has, in other words, become ideological, if by ideology one understands ideas that serve to reproduce the status quo (in this case capitalism).

The project spirit according to Boltanski and Chiapello

Boltanski and Chiapello, like Althusser, emphasise structural as well as historical aspects in their conception of capitalism. Capitalism is defined by a movement towards the capitalisation of ever more aspects of social being and by the ambition of producing and selling at maximum profit. It is an "absurd" system where workers have no rights over what they produce, and it therefore demands perpetual legitimisation (Boltanski and Chiapello 2005: 4–7).

Whereas Althusser thematised a tension between basis and superstructure – ideology never quite succeeds in erasing the traces of capitalism's fundamental contradiction and exploitation – Boltanski and Chiapello are mainly interested in tensions found within the superstructure. They investigate the interplay between three phenomena: capitalism, the spirit of capitalism and the critique of capitalism. The basis is still to some extent an impetus (new modes of production demand new forms of justification) but this is not the locus of the primary conflicts and tensions – they are found in the responses to new challenges. Like Althusser, Boltanski and Chiapello are heavily critical of the basis and superstructure model. As opposed to Althusser's reconstruction of the model, they reject it entirely, and with it the entire body of Marxist analytics:

> Effecting a marked separation between ideas and the real world, and ignoring the interconnection, their interwoven, conjoint production, their reciprocal influence, such a conception always prompts a lapse into narrow definitions of ideology as a mask or mirror, constantly posing the question of the chicken and the egg. It prevents researchers from engaging with the complexity and indeterminacy of the production of historical realities in order patiently to untangle its threads.
>
> (Boltanski and Chiapello 2005: xix–xx)

In lieu of ideology, Boltanski and Chiapello now speak of the spirit of capitalism. Capitalism needs legitimisation, but legitimisation is not necessarily a manifestation of distortion, symbolic violence, depoliticisation, or the like. Any given spirit may be criticised. Not by virtue of obscuring something that people, from a scientific (i.e. Marxist) point of view, would agree is repressive or unjust, but because the world is always up for various forms of justification and criticism.

For Boltanski and Chiapello, Althusser's critical theory is but one of several possible ways of thematising capitalism. Their analysis of the spirit of capitalism is inspired by two bodies of thought. One is so-called actor-network theory. A key principle in this tradition is to follow the actors (or actants). For Boltanski and Chiapello this implies sober characterisation of agents' justifications of their actions and their criticism of others agents' actions. As we have shown, Althusser practiced a hermeneutics of suspicion in which Marxist theory/science made possible an epistemological break with ideology. Boltanski and Chiapello are not interested in moving beyond ideologies (2005: x). Instead, they investigate how conflict arises between actors over the fairness of various issues, i.e. potentially anything of common interest.

The key idea is that actors have a sense of justice which they may exercise with relative independence. They may argue their case, provide relevant information, criticise states of affairs that appear unjust in relation to a particular regime of justice, and they may have the capacity for abstract thought, i.e. to extrapolate beyond the particular situation. We are thus far from Althusser's relatively pessimistic view of subjects as lacking opportunities to form autonomous attitudes and opinions.

Second, the thesis of the spirit of capitalism is of course inspired by Weber's work on the protestant ethic and the spirit of capitalism. As we saw in Chapter 2, Weber found that Protestantism undergirded capitalism, which for him served to explain the breakthrough and success of capitalism in protestant countries. Unlike Weber, however, Boltanski and Chiapello claim that capitalism is in need of legitimisation not only in its initial phase.

They identify three spirits – each with a corresponding mode of production (Boltanski and Chiapello 2005: 16–19): During the 20th century, a bourgeois spirit dominated in which free entrepreneurship and breaking the constraints of agrarian society were central. The period 1940–1970 was epitomised by an industrial and bureaucratic spirit with career opportunities, in the guise of hierarchical ascent, meritocracy and impartiality, as the central value. Finally, the project spirit with focus on self-realisation and organisation broke through in earnest during the 1980s.

In order to break through and attain stability, these three spirits (and the list is not necessarily exhaustive), must convey an answer to three respective questions: The spirit must first of all attempt to explain what motivates individuals (e.g. emancipation from the bindings of agrarian society in the case of the bourgeois spirit). Second, it must make claims concerning what is just (e.g. meritocracy in the industrial and bureaucratic

state and market

spirit), and finally it must establish ways of attaining comfort and security (e.g. through the capacity to participate in networks, mobility, etc. in the project spirit).

The project spirit, or the new capitalism of which it is part, demands flexibility, dispersal of knowledge, teamwork, networking skills, and so on. (Boltanski and Chiapello 2005: 90–96, 108–128). With reference to philosopher Gilles Deleuze's (1995: 177–182) distinction between discipline and control, one might contend that the new capitalism marks a break with discipline as an administrative strategy. Management is no longer a question of fixating, standardising, limiting, normalising and securing uniformity. Rather it is about facilitating, dynamising, activating, innovating and generally setting things in motion. One must, in the words of Jan Carlson, former CEO of Scandinavian Airlines System, "tear down the pyramids". Creativity, knowledge sharing and the capacity to cooperate have become the most essential resources for modern corporations. This new spirit obviously didn't arise out of thin air. It has, according to Boltanski and Chiapello, a number of preconditions in what is often named the new economy or new capitalism.

First, the mode of production has changed. Since the 1950s, there has been a tremendous shift in business financing methods. With the increasing significance of finance capital, power has shifted internally in corporations from managers to shareholders. Financial markets have been deregulated, which has afforded increased mobility of capital. Finally, outsourcing of production to third-world countries with lower wage rates, more lenient tax regimes and modest to nonexistent environmental legislation has made capital less bound to national economies.

Second, corporations and their productions have undergone a change in character. Corporations have become bigger and more international. Mass production is now the norm. But it is not necessarily a question of producing many entities of one product. Commodities are produced with a constant set of basic components, whereas certain identity-bearing elements may vary almost infinitely: A mobile phone can be customised with various skins, ring tones, and so on, even though the phone is basically the same. The corporate structure has also changed. There used to be a strong link between managerial functions, departments of research and development, and marketing on the one hand and production on the other, but today this link is often broken. Typically, marketing departments are located in the corporation's country of origin, whereas production has been moved overseas. Corporations are organised in terms of networks whose respective elements, so-called nodes, may be coupled or decoupled at will.

Third, management and administration hierarchies have been replaced by more horizontal structures. Individual employees are no longer bound to one job function; they may relocate depending on the tasks available. Management in terms of framing work conditions and setting up goals has largely replaced micromanagement. Correspondingly, employees are more capable of planning their own work activities, and are no longer secured or constrained, depending on one's viewpoint, in their positions by union ties. Even the very idea of a job has changed. The distinction between education and work – and between work and leisure – is replaced by an ideal of lifelong learning and self-improvement (2005: xxxvii–xl).

Boltanski and Chiapello make the interesting point that these changes may indicate that the left's post-1968 critique of standardised labour has broken through (2005: 169–198). Historically, capitalism has been subjected to two forms of criticism: social criticism, e.g. of exploitation, inequality, immiserisation and selfishness, and an "artistic" criticism aimed at the lack of opportunities for self-realisation and -improvement (2005: 38–40). The artistic criticism is a criticism of verticality, control, technification, standardisation and alienation. The ambition is to transcend the prevailing formats and structures. This form of critique has, from the perspective of the critique of capitalism, dug its own grave by succeeding.

The work of Boltanski and Chiapello has an empirical basis. They have pinpointed the project regime and the project spirit by reading large bodies of management literature. Like Foucault, they are interested in concrete instruction concerning good and proper behaviour, and they claim to find such instruction in the management literature. This literature from the 1990s is characterised by distaste for hierarchies and administration; the manager is coach, tutor, catalyst, a source of inspiration or some other category with no direct connotations of superiority and subordination. Management becomes a tool for self-management, and control becomes self-control. There is a general distaste for quantification and rigid normativity, and a parallel promotion of situational discernment, emotional rationality and intuition. Rather than knowledge, the capacity for quickly acquiring knowledge is the central issue (Boltanski and Chiapello 2005: 70–86). After this look at the latest phase of capitalism, we will return to the nature of critique and the dynamics it affords.

The infrastructure of criticism

Boltanski and Chiapello conceive of capitalism as fundamentally devoid of norms and values. To motivate labourers and consumers it must therefore draw upon external resources. There is, however, no guarantee of a perfect interplay between capitalism and the normative/critical horizon upon which it draws. A criticism, or a legitimisation, depending on the outcome of the test in question, may have three different effects. It may delegitimise previous spirits, which is what happened in 1968 when artistic criticism pushed social criticism off the stage. Criticism forces capitalism and capitalists to justify themselves and therefore also pressures capitalism into taking a more "humane" course. Finally, somewhat more pessimistically, criticism may lead to greater opacity and more conflict, making it difficult to act and navigate (Boltanski and Chiapello 2005: 27–28).

In *On Justification: Economies of Worth* (2006), Boltanski and Laurent Thévenot distinguish six different regimes of justification, which makes for a more nuanced conceptual apparatus than the distinction between social and artistic criticism. These regimes all have a metaphysical and empirical pole. The justification regimes all contain a coherent conception of justice, which constitutes the metaphysical pole. They each have their own grammar, and in order to unpack this grammar, Boltanski and Thévenot look to a range of paradigmatic examples form the history of philosophy. Boltanski and Chiapello's method is here akin to Weber's, who articulated the capitalist spirit with reference to its grammarian, Benjamin Franklin (See Chapter 2). The empirical pole consists of the concrete application of the regimes. The project regime, described by Boltanski and Chiapello in *The New Spirit of Capitalism*, is for instance traced via management manuals written for mid-level managers.

The six justification regimes identified by Boltanski and Thévenot are inspiration, domesticity, opinion, citizenship, market and industry. The grammar of the inspiration regime is articulated by St. Augustine, whose book *On the City of God* founds a notion of justice based on grace and on a direct relation to an external authority, which in Augustine's case is God. The grammarian of the regime of domesticity is J. B. Bossuet, who ties greatness to hierarchical positions and to the familial importance of intimacy. The opinion regime is derived from Thomas Hobbes' *Leviathan*, with the central notion that a great man is someone who is regarded as such by others. The regime of citizenship is modelled on Jean-Jacques Rousseau's *On the Social Contract* and associates greatness with the renunciation of one's singularity and the exclusive regard for the common life. Adam Smith, unsurprisingly, is the grammarian of the market regime, in which wealth is the source of greatness. The fundamental idea of the market is that by striving for private goods, one may contribute to the whole. Finally, Henri de Saint-Simon is the grammarian of the industrial regime, where value is ascribed to production, planning, organisation and investment. We will not go into detail with these regimes, except to underline the notion of several justification regimes that may either oppose one another or underpin each other.

What is a justification regime? It is first of all an entity to which one subscribes whenever one criticises a perceived injustice. The point of departure for all these regimes is the equality in value and rights of any and all members of the "city", i.e. of the social group affected by the object of the critical test. Inequality, in other words, calls for justification. It is tolerated only if it contributes to the common good. This entails that "lesser men" (those who, according to the justification regime in question, do not immediately contribute to the common good) must have the opportunity to become "great men", if they have the capacity and motivation. Once again, the central notion is that inequality must be legitimised. Another precondition for a test concerning justice is the possibility of testing various elements of conflict against each other. Hierarchical ordering must be possible, e.g. with regard to investment of power, wages, status or prospects of development.

A justification regime is a double-edged sword. On the one hand it can be used to justify inequality. One may explain, with reference to a specific ideal, why some are greater than others, e.g. in terms of wealth. On the other hand, justifications may be used for purposes of critique, proceeding from the claim that perceived inequalities are not justifiable within the prevailing regime. Chiapello (2003) thus claims that the theory of the new spirit of capitalism reconciles two notions of ideology: Marxism's negative notion of exploitation, illusion, distortion, and so on and the more positive notion of anthropology, in which ideology is almost synonymous with culture. Whether this reconciliation is entirely successful, and whether there is anything irreconcilable between the two positions, will be discussed in the following section.

A critical test is motivated by indignation and by a perceived discrepancy between the prevailing state of affairs and the ideal one. The test proceeds from an inequality (as mentioned, equality is the ideal of all justification regimes). A justification regime may on the one hand defend inequality – all regimes distinguish between lesser and greater men, i.e. between those who contribute to the common good and those who do not. In the project regime, for instance, the mobile, innovative, flexible, adaptive, trusting and cooperative subject contributes to the common good, whereas the authoritarian, intolerant, rigid, stationary stickler for the rules is viewed as a problematic player. However, on the other hand, a justification regime may also lead to change, should it become evident that the lesser man actually contributes to the common good and that his inferior position therefore is unfair.

A test may have three different outcomes (Chiapello 2003: 28–30). The criticism may point out that a given justification regime has not been correctly applied, for instance that biased considerations are involved. The goal here is to improve the test. One might for instance anonymise an exam to minimise the risk of personal sympathies or aversions influencing judgment. Second, it may be contested which justification regime

state and market 123

is the right one. For instance, should loyalty or efficiency be the core value of a situation or institution? Finally, the assessment of a particular situation may be contested, and the solution consists in a compromise involving elements of various justification regimes.

Boltanski adds a fourth possibility, namely that of disabling criticism via microlevel dislocations. Boltanski has devoted an entire book to this issue alone. In *La souffrance à distance* (1999), he looks into the difficulties of transforming moral indignation into action. The way the media function makes it difficult to focus for very long on one topic, which causes perpetual shifts among issues.

Critical sociology or the sociology of criticism

We mentioned in the opening chapter that sociology exists both in the form of theories of society and of notions in society of the social – and that the two are necessarily connected. The same applies to criticism, and one might thus conclude that there is a need for Althusser's external perspective as well as Boltanski and Chiapello's internal one. Chiapello writes the following concerning her work with Boltanski:

> We then oscillate between a conception based on the concealment of the balance of power and one that focuses on a notion of justice. However, there is no need to choose between these two conceptions, inasmuch as it is precisely this double dimension of the idea of legitimacy that makes it possible to shift from ideology-as-distortion to ideology-as-integration.
>
> (Chiapello 2003: 165)

In this book we are more sceptical and argue that the tension between the two perspectives should be maintained. It is probably true that Althusser's view of the critical capacity of so-called ordinary people is much too limited. However, reducing criticism to actually proposed arguments is equally unsatisfactory. Boltanski and Chiapello's approach to criticism has an extremely descriptive and relativistic quality to it. The foundation of the demands for justice becomes quite feeble. The pragmatic criticism to which Boltanski and Chiapello subscribe has as its basis only the notion that things might be different. Criticism is thus reduced to the critique of fatalism. Its normative foundation is that things might be different and thus not how they ought to be. The foundation of Marxism is different. Here, criticism is connected to structural features, which may in turn be acknowledged or disavowed. Boltanski and Chiapello would most likely reduce Althusser's role to that of a grammarian, to one of many attempts at a justification regime, whereas Althusser in turn would maintain that the theory of the new capitalism is no scientific theory because it does not enable an epistemological break with the self-conception of actors.

In conclusion, let us suggest a way to critically assess the project regime and the project spirit or, in others words, a strong Althusserian critique of the social state indicated by Boltanski and Chiapello.

From an Althusserian point of view, it is problematic that it is almost impossible to criticise the spirit and regime of projects. Who would not want freedom and the opportunity to develop and innovate? An Althusserian point might be to say that this is not a matter of capitalism becoming more just. It might as well simply have become more efficient at utilising human resources. The ideology of management has now found ways to exploit our emotions, fantasies and desires. The ideological aspect of the new spirit consists in the way it covers up the dark sides of the new capitalism. And what might these dark sides be? We may here draw on the distinction between social and artistic critique.

As far as social critique is concerned, i.e. the classic critique of inequality and exploitation, one might argue – in tune with Boltanski and Chiapello (Boltanski and Chiapello 2003: 355–365) – that the mobility of mobile population segments is maintained at the expense of the immobile population segments. A consultant may travel far and wide only on the condition that a secretary takes care of messages, clients, bills, invoices, and so on. For this inequality to be just, it must contribute to the common good, which is perhaps not always the case. Whereas Marxism settles this question with reference to labour value theory and the corresponding notion of exploitation, Boltanski and Chiapello view the matter in purely pragmatic terms. The answer simply depends on who emerges victorious from a dispute concerning justice. However, one should not stop at this. There is a more fundamental type of inequality. It is not the inequality of mobile versus immobile segments, but of those who are plugged into a given network versus those who are excluded. The contemporary problem should perhaps be articulated in terms of exclusion rather than exploitation: a series of loose contracts carry the drawback of temporary or long-term unemployment; the focus on change makes employees who are incapable of adapting, e.g. senior staff, redundant; mobility makes it difficult to form and maintain intimate social relations, and so on.

Can the artistic critique also be reactivated in relation to the project regime? Boltanski and Chiapello believe so (Chiapello 2003: 466–472). The freedom to consume and the so-called freedom of the workplace are often a form of pseudo-freedom. We effectively choose virtually identical products, and freedom in the workplace is often the freedom to work and to allow work to constitute one's entire life world. The drawback of adaptability is stress, which seems to have become a universal ailment. As argued by sociologist Richard Sennett, the great focus on change and

state and market 125

mobility also makes it increasing difficult to maintain a craft (2008). Anyone who attempts to acquire or employ serious skill, e.g. thorough knowledge in a specialised field, is viewed as rigid and immobile. In light of modern pathologies like the stress pandemic, it might therefore be relevant to criticise the extreme commodification of the human form of being. Even its most private aspects are brought into play in order to increase productivity.

chapter 8

Uncertainty
and risk

Bauman and Beck

Zygmunt Bauman (1925–2017) and Ulrich Beck (1944–2015) have contributed enormously to the academic as well as more popular sociological debate from the 1980s until today. Both have written numerous books and articles that attempt to understand and explain the meaning of the most important trends and developments in contemporary society. Bauman became widely known in international sociology when he published *Modernity and the Holocaust* (Bauman 1989). Ulrich Beck gained sociological world fame when his book *Risk Society: Towards a New Modernity* was translated into English in 1992 (German version 1986). Today, both books are international bestsellers translated into many languages and sold in gigantic numbers.

Bauman and Beck started working on their respective analyses of modernity in the 1980s, and both were preoccupied with the question of how modern societies currently change. They hereby continued a discussion within sociology beginning already in the 1970s in the wake of American sociologist Daniel Bell's book *The Coming of Post-Industrial Society* (Bell 1973). Bell argued that our society could no longer be understood as industrial; partly because the majority of people now worked in service jobs and not in the industrial sector. He hereby initiated a discussion about the changing character of contemporary society.

In the late 1970s, the debate about the end of the industrial society was supplemented by a general discussion about modernity and a possible transition to a new, "postmodern" era. French philosopher Jean-François

Lyotard's book *La condition postmoderne* from 1979 (*The Postmodern Condition*, Lyotard 1984) about the status of knowledge in the highly developed societies sparked this discussion. According to Lyotard, scientific knowledge had lost status and did no longer have precedence over other forms of knowledge. Some sociologists therefore suggested that we had entered a new, postmodern era, whereas others pointed out that society's radical changes had to be understood as developments *of* or *within* modernity.

Ulrich Beck clearly belongs to the last group. He introduces the concept of "second modernity" to describe the development of modernity. Bauman is more difficult to place in relation to the two positions. He often speaks of our time as postmodern in his books from the 1990s, but to him, postmodernity is just as much a project; something we should strive for. As we will see below, he points out that modernity has an adverse influence on morality; the weight modernity places on rationality, on rules and procedures, suppresses our moral impulses. Bauman sees this as one of the reasons why the Holocaust – the murder of six million Jews during World War II – was possible. He therefore believes that we should aim for a new, postmodern ethic that will provide space for our moral feelings. In the latter part of his authorship, from the millennium onwards, the concept of postmodernity gradually recedes into the background in favour of a new concept of "liquid modernity", which is equivalent to Beck's concept of second modernity.

The terms "second modernity" and "liquid modernity" are thus diagnostic concepts created by Beck and Bauman to capture the main features of our time. Bauman and Beck are both deeply engaged in understanding the conditions of contemporary society – and understanding them in relation to the general development of modernity. Our presentation of their social theories will therefore focus their critique of modernity and their descriptions of the evolution of a new form of modernity, where individualisation and globalisation become dominant phenomena. We start with Bauman's *Modernity and the Holocaust* (1989).

Bauman's critique of modernity

Bauman begins his academic career at the University of Warsaw in Poland in the 1960s and continues at the University of Leeds in England in the 1970s. Inspired by Marxism, his work revolves around subjects such as social stratification, class and the British labour movement, and from the mid-1980s, he seriously starts addressing the question of modernity. His principal work from this period, and perhaps Bauman's most famous publication in general, is *Modernity and the Holocaust*, published in 1989.

In *Modernity and the Holocaust*, Bauman interprets the Holocaust as a distinctly modern phenomenon made possible because a number of societal factors, key to modernity, have met and reinforced each other. Among these factors are social engineering, bureaucracy, labour, rationality and a shift from a moral to a technical form of responsibility. Let us take a closer look at these factors.

The first crucial prerequisite for the Holocaust is that the world of modernity no longer appears as a preordained condition, but as a changeable entity; as something one can alter. Bauman uses the "gamekeeper" as a metaphor for the premodern understanding of society. It is not the gamekeeper's job to fundamentally change the world, but to maintain and ensure the reproduction of the status quo. To the gamekeeper, and to premodern people in general, society is a "condition". The opposite is the case for the modern approach to the world. According to Bauman this approach may be compared with the gardener's relationship to nature. To the gardener, nature is "mouldable". The gardener follows a plan for how a garden, park, and so on should look, and existing flora accordingly fits into this plan or is classified as weeds that stand in the way of the plan and therefore must be eradicated.

This was also the case with the Jews in Germany in the 1930s and '40s. The Nazis no longer wanted to tolerate their presence in German society. They were seen as "weeds" that did not fit into the plan for the perfect society, a "racially" pure Germany, and therefore had to be removed from German soil. Bauman writes that we must understand the murder of Jews and other unwanted groups in Nazi Germany as "creative work" – as "social engineering" – that according to the perpetrators had to be performed to make room for the perfect society (Bauman 1989: 92) Hitler and the Nazis were not alone in this radical approach to designing the world. In Stalin's Soviet Union, millions died in prisons and labour camps (Gulag) to make room for the "perfect society".

Modern bureaucracy

The "success" of the Holocaust is also a result of modern bureaucracy, and Bauman argues for a functionalist rather than an intentionalist interpretation of this phenomenon. Hitler's original plan did not involve a complete eradication of the Jews. This objective slowly emerged as a bureaucratic response to the task that Hitler had originally given the bureaucrats: to make Germany free of Jews. Before Reinhard Heydrich, Adolf Eichmann and colleagues adopted the Final Solution (the killing of the Jews of Europe) at the Wannsee Conference on January 20, 1942, they had experimented with many other plans. First, they made life in Germany as difficult for Jews as possible, among other things, in the

uncertainty and risk

hope that they would voluntarily emigrate. Then the German Jews were gathered in ghettos and camps, and plans were made to establish permanent reserves for the Jews in Poland. The Nazis even worked with a plan to send all Jews to Madagascar. These plans were abandoned for various reasons, but the bureaucracy kept on working with the task. As Bauman observes in one of many sharp passages:

> It so happened in Germany half a century ago that bureaucracy was given the task of making Germany judenrein – clean of Jews. Bureaucracy started from what bureaucracies start with: the formulation of a precise definition of the object, then registering those who fitted the definition and opening a file for each. It proceeded to segregate those in the files from the rest of the population, to which the received brief did not apply. Finally, it moved to evicting the segregated category from the land of the Aryans which was to be cleansed – by nudging it to emigrate first, and deporting it to non-German territories once such territories found themselves under German control. By that time bureaucracy developed wonderful cleansing skills, not to be wasted and left to rust. Bureaucracy which acquitted itself so well of the task of cleansing Germany made more ambitious tasks feasible, and their choice well-nigh natural. With such a superb cleaning facility, why stop at the Heimat of the Aryans? Why refrain from cleaning the whole of their empire? True, as the empire was now ecumenical, it had no "outside" left where the dumping ground for the Jewish litter could be disposed of. Only one direction of deportation remained; upward, in smoke.
>
> (Bauman 1989: 104–105)

Modernity's functional division of labour also played a part in the Holocaust. When people were willing to take part in this genocide, it was because very few were directly involved in killing Jews; most people either made phone calls, completed paperwork, attended conferences, kept watch, poured chemicals in a tank, and so on (Bauman 1989: 24). As we saw in Chapters 2 and 3, division of labour and specialisation are key to the prosperity of modern society. All tasks are divided into numerous subtasks; no individual makes a product from start to finish, but large numbers of people are involved in the production of even the simplest products. This was also the case for the thousands of people involved in the Holocaust. Some designed the ovens, some drove the trains and some kept watch; some built parts of the camps, engines and trains. They all contributed to the Holocaust even if they did not *directly* kill anyone.

This makes it difficult to assign responsibility for the atrocities. Nazi top official Adolf Eichmann lived in exile in Argentina. In 1960, he was captured by the Israeli intelligence agency, Mossad, and the following year he was brought before a judge in Jerusalem, accused of war crimes, crimes against humanity and crimes against the Jewish people, among other things. His defence was that he had only done his duty and cared about his job as a civil servant. It did not, however, help him. Eichmann was sentenced to death for his crimes.

German-Jewish philosopher Hannah Arendt, who in 1933 fled from Germany to Paris and later New York, covered the Eichmann trial for the magazine *The New Yorker* and published a book about the case in 1963 entitled *Eichmann in Jerusalem: A Report on the Banality of Evil* (Arendt 2006). During the process, Arendt was struck by Eichmann's normality; despite his significant role in the killing of six million Jews he did not appear particularly psychopathic or evil. This gave rise to her concept of "the banality of evil"; of how we all, if we don't use our ability to "think", may end up contributing to atrocities.

Modernity and morals

In *Modernity and the Holocaust* Bauman also discusses how seemingly ordinary people could take part in the killing of six million Jews. How can anyone be a warden in a concentration camp during the day and a loving family father in the evening? Like Arendt, Bauman does not look for an explanation in a sadistic or psychopathic personality. Instead, he argues – based on American social psychologist Stanley Milgram's famous obedience experiments – that most people can be put in a situation where the wrong choice is the easiest choice and where rationality and ethics point in opposite directions (Bauman 1989: 206).

Milgram's experiment shows that most people – decent, ordinary people – can be brought to inflict pain on others if an authority requires it. Milgram showed that it was relatively easy to persuade people to continue, even when they were unsure about whether they wanted to. All it took was an authority (in this case a researcher in a white lab coat), a small amount of money, and telling the doubters that the experiment required that they continue. The fact that it is so easy to get people to act morally wrong may help explain why officials and soldiers in Nazi Germany predominantly obeyed orders – also in relation to the Holocaust. The alternative was most often imprisonment or being shot. Bauman thus interprets the Holocaust in view of Milgram's experiments: "The most frightening news brought about the Holocaust and by what we learned about its perpetrators was not the likelihood that 'this' could be done to us, but the idea that we could do it" (Bauman 1989: 152).

The problem with modernity is, according to Bauman, that due to the division of labour, increased distance between decisions and actions, and

uncertainty and risk

bureaucratic procedures we often come to replace moral responsibility with a purely technical responsibility. Instead of thinking about the children who are killed in some distant war, workers at a weapons factory mainly think about succeeding in their jobs. Instead of thinking about refugees or others who need help as human beings for whom we have a moral responsibility, we think of moral obligations as compliance with certain procedures and rules. But to Bauman it is important that some have the courage to say no and think and act morally. For him, it is crucial that some Germans spoke out against the Nazi regime and their crimes, even if it ended up costing them their lives. As he writes towards the end of the book: "It does not matter how many people chose moral duty over the rationality of self-preservation – what does matter is that some did" (Bauman 1989: 207).

This is why it is important to work towards a new postmodern ethics that embraces the ambivalences of our time present in all moral issues. According to Bauman, it is not possible to establish universal rules on how to act morally. He is sceptical of modern moral philosophy's attempt to find universal rules for morally correct actions. We cannot use reason as a basis for ethics. Instead, we must provide more space for our personal moral impulses. The problem in modernity is that moral impulses too often are suppressed in the name of rationality – with Nazi Germany and Stalin's Soviet Union as horrendous examples. Based on, for instance, Emmanuel Levinas's concept of "the face of the Other" and Knud Ejler Løgstrup's concept of "the ethical demand", Bauman examines the possibilities for ethics to get beyond modernity towards a postmodern ethics in a number of books in the 1990s (for example Bauman 1993).

Modernity and a new existential insecurity

Throughout most of his writings, Bauman had an eye for the dark side of modernity. This is also reflected in the books *Globalization: The Human Consequences* (Bauman 1998) and *Community: Seeking Safety in an Insecure World* (Bauman 2001) which examine the current impact of globalisation and individualisation on peoples' life.

Globalisation means that physical distances lose importance. Information and transportation technologies increasingly blur the distinction between *here* and *there*. With globalisation, mobility becomes an important factor of stratification (Bauman 1998: 9). The more mobile you are, the higher up in the social hierarchy. Indeed, Bauman distinguishes between a new global elite that is free to move around the world and for whom distance means less and less and a new global underclass that is tied to the locality where they live. Mobility also becomes a condition for the lower class, but only as involuntary mobility. Bauman uses "the tourist" and "the vagabond" as metaphors for the winners and losers in the age of globalisation (Bauman 1998: 92–102). The rich global elite can fly from place to place as tourists, constantly on the lookout for new and exciting places to visit. Conversely, mobility for the global underclass only shows itself as an involuntary, forced journey from place to place. As vagabonds the underclass is constantly forced to leave their lives behind and move on to new places; as global migrants or as refugees fleeing war and insecurity.

Bauman claims that capitalism is closely linked to the increasing globalisation. Companies are currently owned by shareholders who are not tied to specific locations, but move their investments to the most profitable businesses anywhere in the world. Driven as they are by the highest possible return, shareholders can also require that a company change location to save on wages and other expenses and to maximise profits.

According to Bauman, companies today feel no responsibility for what they leave behind. They no longer act like the old landlords, who were often absent and lived a life of wealth far away from their manors, but still took care of the local community to a certain extent – the area of the manor – because it was in their own interest (Bauman 1998: 9–11). Today, the interests of corporate shareholders no longer go hand in hand with the interests of the local population. When a company changes location to reduce costs, it no longer feels responsible for the abandoned local community facing unemployment and perhaps environmental clean-up after the company.

In the wake of the emergence of a global market and a global economy follows a "new existential insecurity" for large sections of the population, who risk having destroyed their basis of existence as a result of sudden business closures, restructuring programs and similar phenomena. People's frustrations about such insecurities are, however, rarely directed towards their actual source: the globally operating capitalist system. Instead, there is an increasing preoccupation with law and order (Bauman 1998: 103–122) as people turn the new existential insecurity into something manageable by focusing on the risk of thefts and burglaries.

Bauman also examines the new existential insecurity in *Community: Seeking Safety in an Insecure World* (Bauman 2001), which focuses on the dissolution of traditional communities and the formation of new, more volatile ones. The same development that gave rise to globalisation – the evolution of information technology and capitalism – also dissolves traditional communities. According to Bauman, capitalism has led us into

uncertainty and risk   133

a new period, "the times of disengagement" (Bauman 2001: 39–49), where nothing:

> ... stays the same for long, and nothing endures long enough to be fully taken in, to become familiar and to turn into the cosy, secure and comfortable envelope the community-hungry and home-thirsty selves have sought and hoped for. Gone are the friendly corner grocery shops; if they have managed to withstand the supermarket competition, their owners, managers, the faces behind the counter change much too often for any of them to harbour the permanence no longer to be found in the street. Gone are the friendly local bank or building society branches, replaced by anonymous and impersonal (ever more often electronically synthesised) voices on the other end of the telephone cable or "user friendly", yet infinitely remote, nameless and faceless website icons. Gone is the friendly postman, knocking on the door six days a week and addressing the inhabitants by their names. In are the department stores and high-street chain shops, expected to survive from one friendly merger or hostile takeover to another, but in the meantime changing their staff at a pace which reduces to zero the chances of meeting the same salesperson twice.
>
> (Bauman 2001: 46–47)

The times of disengagement are characterised by resolution, volatility, fast and accelerating pace, flexibility, downsizing, outsourcing, and so on. (cf. Richard Sennett's description of the "new flexible capitalism"; see Chapter 10). The dissolution also affects communities and intimate relationships. With a metaphor from Yvonne Roberts, Bauman says that embarking on a marriage today compares to "taking to the sea on a raft made of blotting paper", and he continues:

> The chances that the family will survive any of its members gets slimmer by year: the life-expectation of the individual mortal body seems an eternity by comparison. An average child has several sets of grandparents and several "family homes" to choose between – each for "time renting", like holiday apartments in fashionable seaside resorts. None of these feels like the true, "one and only" home.
>
> (Bauman 2001: 47)

In the times of disengagement, traditional communities come under pressure because they are not flexible and informal enough. "So far" becomes a key concept in the new era. One stays in a community as long as its social relations are meaningful or satisfactory or until something better turns up (Bauman 2001: 41). Bauman also speaks of aesthetic communities, or "peg-communities", where you can hang your jacket for a short period until you move on. The ties created between members of these new communities arise around a specific interest and are therefore only superficial and ephemeral (Bauman 2001: 70–71).

The tendency towards dissolution has always been part of modernity; but it has gradually led modernity into a new phase marked by radicalised individualisation. Bauman coins this phase "liquid modernity". Today, he says, we live in an individualised and privatised version of modernity, where the individual is forced to create its own life cycle and bear full responsibility for any failures (Bauman 2000: 7). On this point, Bauman's ideas are in line with the writings of Ulrich Beck and Anthony Giddens (see Chapter 9), who also scrutinise the consequences of individualisation in contemporary society.

Beck's understanding of modernity

Ulrich Beck speaks of "second modernity" rather than "liquid modernity". He distinguishes between a first modernity, culminating in the Western industrialised societies, and a second modernity, and new type of society, which he calls "the risk society" (Beck 1992; 2009). Following, we will present Beck's understanding of modernity and look at the transition to second modernity and the risk society. Finally, we will discuss how Beck, like Bauman, understands individualisation and globalisation as key trends of the second modernity.

Beck describes modernity (first modernity) as a historical epoch in which man gradually frees himself from nature's supremacy by means of human reason. In premodern societies we were to a large extent in the hands of nature, but in modernity we gained increasing control over nature through a comprehensive "rationalisation process". This process began during the Enlightenment in the mid-1700s and culminated in the industrial society in the second half of the 1900s. Max Weber was among the first to theorise this process. As touched upon in Chapter 2, he described how the increasing rationalisation pushed back the religious or magical understanding of the world in traditional societies. Rationality led to "disenchantment" ("Entzauberung") of the world, because everything in principle became calculable in modernity (Weber 2002: 488).

Beck endorses Weber's understanding of modernity (first modernity) as a societal period characterised by increased calculability and predictability, and sees rationalisation as an attempt to minimise, and eventually eliminate, the uncertainty, hardship and material misery facing premodern societies. Modernity is also characterised by a huge increase in wealth that enables rapid population growth and a significant increase in the

uncertainty and risk 135

average life expectancy. Life in modernity is thus generally more predictable and less perilous for the individual compared to premodern life.

Side effects and reflexive modernisation

The problem with modernity is that it not only succeeds in producing enormous wealth and unprecedented material security for people in the Western industrialised societies. At the same time, a number of unintended side effects resulting from the process of modernisation and industrialisation start to emerge. In *Risk Society: Towards a New Modernity* (1992) Beck highlights two key developments characterising the progress of the rich Western societies from the 1960s onwards:

> On the one hand, the struggle for one's "daily bread" has lost its urgency as a cardinal problem overshadowing everything else, compared to material subsistence in the first half of this century and to a Third World menaced by hunger. For many people problems of "overweight" take the place of hunger. This development, however, withdraws the legitimizing basis from the modernization process, the struggle against obvious scarcity, for which one was prepared to accept a few (no longer completely) unseen side effects. Parallel to that, the knowledge is spreading that the sources of wealth are "polluted" by growing "hazardous side effects".
>
> (Beck 1992: 20)

The key to understanding these developments lies in the concept of "side effects" (in German: "Nebenfolgen"). If we take energy production as an example, we have been able in modern industrial society to free ourselves from nature by using fossil fuels like oil, gas and coal as cheap and efficient energy sources. We have also succeeded in splitting atoms and utilising this technology in nuclear power plants to generate further energy. However, both developments have unintended side effects, which gradually have come to set the agenda for our society. The burning of fossil fuels does not only offer cheap electricity and heat; it also emits carbon dioxide into the atmosphere, and by all accounts this development causes global warming, which threatens to radically change the conditions of life on Earth. Likewise, nuclear power is more than a smart, new way to provide clean energy to a growing population; it poses new risks to people and nature because of the radioactive waste and potential radioactive emissions.

Paradoxically, our success in overcoming the original problem, i.e. the lack of cheap, efficient and sufficient energy, has created new problems that increasingly set the social and political agenda. This paradox does

136   uncertainty and risk

not just apply to the energy sector. It is a general trend. Beck points out that where a simple modernisation took place in first modernity – because this period was concerned with solving a set of already determined problems such as the lack of electricity and heat – a reflexive modernisation now takes place in second modernity because modernity here meets itself and is forced to deal with itself. The problems we struggle with today are problems that we have produced ourselves; they are the side effects of the first, simple modernity. According to Beck, we are facing a new "manufactured" uncertainty (Beck 1994: 8–13).

Ozone depletion, global warming, radioactive emissions from nuclear power plants and similar phenomena are not natural but products of our industrial way of life. Beck calls such phenomena for "man-made disasters" (Beck 1995: 78) or "new risks" (Beck 1991: 117). They differ from past dangers and risks by being difficult to delineate temporally and geographically. They do not just affect a specific group of people in a specific place during a specific period of time. Their effects may extend over many generations and affect different populations across borders. Hence, new risks are also much harder to calculate than past risks. For example, it is impossible to accurately predict the effects of global warming or the probability of a major radioactive accident.

This is also why we cannot fully insure ourselves against the new risks. Insurances have so far been a key strategy for modern individuals to manage risks and uncertainty. Insurance technology cannot prevent accidents, but it can rationalise our relationship to them by making them calculable and offer financial compensation if accidents occur. With reference to French sociologist François Ewald (1991), Beck describes the modern state as an insurance state that can offer, for example, financial support or free hospitalisation if we become unemployed or ill. But there are no insurance schemes against the new risks and insecurities.

Beck points out that because of the production of such incalculable, new risks – and the growing societal recognition of their existence we no longer live in the industrial society, but in a risk society. Let's have a closer look at the differences between the two societies.

Whereas a key objective in the industrial society is to overcome extensive material shortages, the risk society seeks to tackle the new risks. Previously it was important to achieve something – wealth and better material living conditions. In the risk society it becomes increasingly important to avoid something. Much energy and many resources are invested in preventing future disasters like ozone depletion, radioactive emissions, global warming, terror and global economic crises. Our primary enemy is no longer reality, but the possible dangers awaiting in the future. In industrial society, the focus was on tomorrow's positive opportunities; in the risk society, focus shifts towards the risk of future catastrophes.

uncertainty and risk   137

With a metaphor derived from philosophy, Beck points out that whereas we were spontaneous materialists in the industrial society because being (actually existing poverty and misery) determined our consciousness, we become spontaneous idealists in the risk society, because imagined possible future disasters increasingly determine our being. If we again take global warming as an example, the initial transition to renewable energy can be understood as actions (being) directly related to a new awareness of the possible future disasters that will occur if we continue to burn fossil fuels to the same extent as today. According to Beck, the new global risks therefore also carry with them the potential for major political and social transformations.

Globalisation and cosmopolitanisation

The theory of the manufactured, new global risks and the transition to the risk society also leads Beck into the globalisation debate, which grew prominent in international sociology during the 1990s and early 2000s. According to Beck, globalisation can be understood as a new boundlessness in relation to the economy, information, cultures, the environment, and so on. In *What is Globalization?* he writes that money, technology, commodities, information and toxins currently " 'cross' frontiers as if they did not exist", and he subscribes to Anthony Giddens's definition of globalisation as "acting and living (together) over distances" (Beck 2000: 20).

The current globalisation, which is deeper and more intense than anything we have previously seen, also leads to what Beck terms a "real cosmopolitanisation" of the world (Beck 2005; 2006). A cosmopolitan world order was previously discussed among philosophers and legal experts as a possible future state of society, but reality has overtaken those discussions. Beck and political scientist Edgar Grande write that:

> Global interdependence means that reality is becoming cosmopolitan, though in a thoroughly uncosmopolitan way, one which no philosophical cosmopolitanism or cosmopolitan philosopher anticipated or even thought possible: without publicity, unintentionally, independently of political decisions and programmes, in other words, in a thoroughly deformed way. Real cosmopolitanization – unwanted, unseen, in varying degrees compulsory – is entering through the back door of side effects.
>
> (Beck and Grande 2007: 119)

Again, side effects drive the development. As a by-product of industrial societies' growing trade relationships, increased mobility, use of new information technology, and so on, a new cosmopolitan world order arises behind our backs. This development means that the boundaries between previously separated national societies become blurred, and that a global world (risk) society emerges instead. Interdependency becomes a key concept in this development – it sets new conditions for ordinary people's daily lives for the world order that states and politicians have to manoeuvre in.

Beck's concept of cosmopolitanism is inspired by the ancient Stoics, and with them he points out that man belongs in the world (cosmos) and in a particular place in the world (in a certain polis). We live our lives in specific places in the world, but no matter where on the planet we live, our daily lives are always heavily dependent on developments elsewhere in the world. Beck also calls this phenomenon banal cosmopolitanism, because it includes everyday things like cultural products, clothes and food, which are increasingly the outcome of a global division of labour (Beck 2006: 40–43). If we open our kitchen cabinets, fridges and wardrobes, we see concrete examples of our dependence on conditions elsewhere in the world. Our clothes are typically made in countries with low wages like India, China, the Philippines, Vietnam or Mexico, and due to low transport costs our food comes from all over the world.

This new interdependence between countries and people also includes unemployment, economic growth (or recession), terrorist attacks, forced displacement and global warming. All these phenomena affect our lives, but are to a limited extent influenced by our own decisions. Instead, political and individual decisions made in other countries become increasingly essential to our lives. Likewise, political decisions in our home countries and decisions made in our private lives affect people elsewhere in the world. For example, the price we are willing to pay for our products influences living conditions for the people producing these products.

Globalisation also has implications for the opportunities of nation states to politically regulate the economy. In the industrial era, political actors made direct interventions to regulate the economy. Taxes were levied, rules for working conditions were implemented and environmental laws were gradually passed. But with the diffusion of the global market, new information technologies and highly improved transport technology, today's economic actors can strategically avoid taxes and regulations by moving their production to countries with low wages and their headquarters to countries with low taxes. Although nation states are still tied to a territory and can only regulate the conditions in this territory, businesses and investors are no longer limited to a specific location.

This creates huge problems for the nation states, which are played out against each other by the economic actors and forced into a race to the bottom in terms of company taxes and regulations of the economy. States are still dependent on businesses. As Beck puts it, there is only "one thing worse than being overrun by multinationals, and that is *not* being

uncertainty and risk 139

overrun by multinationals" (Beck 2005: 52). In order to keep and attract jobs and ensure a tax base that can finance the modern welfare states, countries are therefore thrown into fierce competition with each other.

The only way for nation states to regain power in relation to globally operating economic agents is to recognise the new global reality and transform into collaborative transnational states (Beck 2005). Nation states must be willing to give up formal sovereignty in exchange for real sovereignty. For example, during the past years' refugee crisis in Europe, we have seen countries compete to prevent refugees from seeking asylum in their particular country by making conditions for refugees less attractive. At the same time, these countries are competing to make the conditions for international corporations as attractive as possible. But in both cases, the policies are dictated from the outside. Beck therefore wants states to realise that they are facing the same challenges, and he wants them to stop competing and instead engage in new transnational collaborations that let the states regain some of their lost sovereignty. A realisation of Beck's ideas could, for instance, imply that European countries agreed upon a common minimum taxation for companies operating in the European Union, hereby preventing international companies from shopping around between the member states to find the cheapest place to produce and pay taxes. In relation to the refugee crisis, one could imagine a distribution key for the allocation of refugees seeking asylum in Europe agreed upon at the supranational level. This would ease pressure on the countries with the most comprehensive welfare systems, without these countries having to compromise the way they treat asylum seekers and refugees.

It is, however, not only policies and state collaborations that must be reconsidered in light of globalisation. The new global interconnectedness and interdependence also pose new challenges for the social sciences and call for new ways of thinking sociologically. As discussed, societies can no longer be understood as nations, but should instead be comprehended as a world (risk) society. Hence, if social scientists maintain their focus on nation states as the primary framework of explanation, they may end up being guilty of what Beck calls "methodological nationalism" or "zombie science". A zombie is a living dead – someone who is actually dead but lives on in our imagination. If social science uncritically makes the nation state the key focus of its analyses, its conclusions will, in other words, be based on something that no longer exists (Beck 2005: 22–50; 2006: 24–43).

Radicalised individualisation

Like Bauman, Beck sees individualisation as a key feature of our present society. Beck understands individualisation as a process that frees the individual from prior, given and collective identities and opens doors to a life where the individual, to a much larger extent, is forced to pick its own trajectory (Sørensen and Christiansen 2013: 40–59). This development takes place in two waves that hit us respectively in the first and second modernity. In the first wave, the human is liberated from the traditional communities of feudal society. Instead, humans become embedded in new communities (in the industrial society) centred around nationality, social class, the workplace and the nuclear family. The second wave, which we are currently in the midst of, loosens our ties to these surrogate communities and forces us to choose our own life trajectory. Beck describes this second wave as a new, radicalised form of individualisation.

One consequence of this form of individualisation is that the individual, unlike earlier, is responsible for his or her own life. In second modernity, we have to find our own way through the mazes and we are increasingly facing a range of choices that we cannot simply decide on by referring to "what we normally do." The answers are not given in advance, and we are largely left on our own to make the right choices – both with respect to the big questions in life and to the minor everyday decisions. Of course, we can still choose to act in accordance with our friends, parents or neighbours, but it requires an active choice – and this choice is always based on the knowledge that things *could* have been different.

Thus radicalised individualisation does not necessarily make people more happy and satisfied; perhaps the contrary. In his existentialist philosophy, French philosopher Jean-Paul Sartre pointed out that we are "condemned to freedom", because we cannot escape freedom, and because freedom can feel burdensome as a result of all the things we have to deal with – all the choices we have to make. As Beck puts it, we are "condemned to individualisation". Radicalised individualisation makes the individual accountable for his or her own life:

> The normal biography thus becomes the "elective biography", the "reflexive biography", the "do-it-yourself biography". This does not necessarily happen by choice, neither does it necessarily succeed. The do-it-yourself biography is always a "risk-biography", indeed a "tightrope biography", a state of permanent (partly overt, partly concealed) endangerment. The façade of prosperity, consumption, glitter can often mask the nearby precipice. The wrong choice of career or just the wrong field, compounded by the downward spiral of private misfortune, divorce illness, the repossessed home – all this is merely called bad luck. Such cases bring into the open what was always

uncertainty and risk

secretly on the cards: the do-it-yourself biography can swiftly become the breakdown biography.

(Beck and Beck-Gernsheim 2002: 3)

Beck sees modern institutions like the welfare state and the labour market as the main driving forces behind the current wave of individualisation. Its basis is individual rather than collective units. Structural factors in society force individuals to constantly focus on themselves, and this makes it difficult for communities to survive. When institutions pull individual family members in different directions, families come under tremendous pressure. Relationships and marriages also are pulled apart by the parties' often contradictory desires and dreams, which can partly be traced back to institutional requirements and expectations. In a relationship, Beck says, the individualisation of one party very easily hampers the other party's individualisation. This may contribute to explain the high divorce rates in the Western world.

The individual and the community in modernity

As we have seen, Bauman and Beck agree that many of the communities that provided the setting for human life in industrial society today have come under pressure. Intensified globalisation and individualisation force us to constantly be on the move, which makes it difficult to establish and maintain lasting communities around marriages, families or jobs. Beck focuses on institutions such as the education system and the labour market to explain the intensified individualisation, while Bauman refers more broadly to capitalism.

Although both theorists understand individualisation as a societal phenomenon, Bauman is clearly more critical of our way of dealing with this development than Beck. He writes critically and ironically about our volatile communities and continuous individual quest for new "peg communities" (Bauman 2001: 16, 71), where we can hang our jackets for a while before moving on to more interesting communities. According to Bauman, it is crucial that we as human beings always already are connected to and therefore have obligations to others. Individualisation does not change that, although it may make it harder for us to live up to our common human obligations.

Beck also writes about interdependence between people, but focuses primarily on the new interdependence created by globalisation. The real cosmopolitanisation brought about by globalisation has created new communities of destiny across former boundaries such as nation states. The more this cosmopolitanisation manifests itself, the more interdependent we become.

Bauman and Beck draw different implications from this insight. Bauman wants us to move away from modernity's focus on rationality, rules and procedures and in the direction of a new, postmodern ethics, placing the individual at the centre. Beck focuses less on the individual human being. To him, the most important thing is that states and politics act in accordance with the new interdependence. He wants individual countries to realise that their fates are intimately tied together and that it is in their own interest to transform themselves into collaborative transnational states. Only then can they gain political influence. Similarly, sociology and social science must understand that the nation state can no longer contain and enclose a particular society. The nation-state societies have been transformed into a coherent world risk society, and social science must adapt to this reality to avoid making zombie science.

Finally, one can say that Bauman and Beck agree that insecurity is part of everyday life for people in liquid or second modernity. Terror, financial crises and global warming are examples of new risks which – because they affect us all – can potentially bring us closer together in new communities oriented towards finding feasible solutions. But where Beck writes in an optimistic tone and seems to think that the necessity of moving closer together in new cross-border communities will eventually lead to positive change, Bauman has a far more pessimistic view of the future. He emphasises, more than Beck, the major economic differences between people, for example between the global elite and the rest. The global elite will be able to take care of itself also in the face of terror, financial crises and global warming. The situation is different for the vast majority of people. They are still "tied to the place" or involuntarily thrown into a nomadic existence, where they are forced to travel from place to place in search of work or to escape war, terrorism and disasters. Their living conditions do not seem to improve much, and based on Bauman's diagnosis of the times, it is difficult to be optimistic about the future of most people on the planet.

uncertainty and risk

chapter 9

The reflective self

Goffman and Giddens

The majority of the theoretical positions presented in this book conceptualise and analyse society on the macrolevel. This provides an understanding of society's basic organisation and structure and of the potentials for integration between the different spheres. Most macrotheories also reflect on the individual, but they may not constitute the perfect starting point for an exhaustive reflection on what it means to be an individual in modern society. This chapter introduces sociological concepts and analyses that flesh out the microlevel of social interaction. The microlevel is where the individual faces other individuals and comes in direct contact with societal systems and organisations.

A common thread in the microsociological perspectives introduced here is to see the self as being imbued with reflexivity. This does not mean that all aspects of the self are constituted by rational reflection, because a major part of microsociology concerns the unreflected routines of everyday life. In broad terms, reflexivity means that social phenomena – and in this case the self – are not a given. The relationship between the self and the social must be analysed in its own right and as a relationship that is subject to change, which may have to be deciphered via historical analyses or a diagnostic perspective. The reflexive self is thus not just an individual given by nature nor is it a matter of pure individual consciousness; it is also a reflection of the social circumstances surrounding the self.

In sociology, the self is rarely discussed as a psychological object in its own right. Rather, it is understood as a social phenomenon that comes into existence in associations with other individuals or in interactions with societal systems. Such processes are often labelled individualisation. The sociological question of individualisation is not so much about whether every single human being actually leads an entirely individual life, but rather about the social processes creating expectations about individual life courses and autonomous choices. Microsociological analysis is thus not blind to the possibility that phenomena such as individualisation and the reflective self may have macrosociological causes and consequences, as we saw in the previous chapter on Bauman and Beck. However, it sets these macrosociological patterns aside for a while to ask questions about what it means to be an individual under the given set of circumstances.

This chapter first introduces Erving Goffman's (1922–1982) microsociological analyses, which vividly illustrate the presentation of the self in concrete encounters with other people as well as encounters where individuals try to handle weak or imperfect self-presentations. The second part of the chapter focuses on Anthony Giddens's (1938–) theory of the self in reflexive modernity, which emphasises that individuals need a so-called ontological security in order to handle the uncertainty of contemporary life. Both theories focus on the microlevel, but we also aim to show how this level is associated with social order at the macrolevel, although Goffman and Giddens conceptualise this association in very different ways.

Goffman's microsociology

Microsociology is about observing what happens when people interact in their everyday lives; for example observations of the unreflected or implicit routines we constantly reproduce. You may only notice routines when you encounter people who do not abide by these unwritten rules or come from a different social or cultural background with different norms.

If, for example, you meet a person who invades your personal space and talks very close to your face, this will likely disturb the conversation. Because we rarely talk openly about these unwritten rules, it may seem difficult to say to the other person what he or she is doing wrong, or why it is even wrong to invade your personal space. Our perception of the person will almost certainly be affected by details like these because we use conversations and encounters for much more than exchange of words or arguments. We collect information about the other person and use it to interpret who the other person is and how to understand the person's actual message. We also use encounters to present ourselves to others and control how they perceive us. These mechanisms are usually subtle, but microsociological research enables us to find patterns.

the reflective self   145

Goffman is particularly interested in understanding these unspoken everyday interaction forms. Although the processes may be unspoken, they are still reflective processes in his view. When you interpret another person's self-presentation, you reflect on your own presentation. For instance, you may observe the other person in order to evaluate whether you appear in the right way in front of the other, and if not, whether you can improve your performance through small adjustments in tone of voice, facial expression, physical appearance or linguistic style.

Goffman's work grew out of the sociological environment in Chicago where he completed parts of his education. From the start of the 20th century, the Chicago School in sociology constituted a clear alternative to mainstream sociology (see Chapter 4). In contrast with the macrosociological and theoretically more advanced traditions that emerged from the most prestigious universities such as Harvard, Yale and Columbia, the Chicago School was more preoccupied with qualitative studies of concrete human interaction. The approach was formed, among other things, by a profound curiousness about urban life, a relatively recent phenomenon at the time. The early Chicago sociologists simply went into the streets and observed urban life, especially the city's underworld of deviant life forms.

It is quite obvious when you open one of Goffman's books that his approach is unique. It can sometimes be difficult to identify what constitutes the theory and what constitutes his analyses, because the two sides are deeply intertwined (as in Foucault, Bourdieu and Žižek). When Goffman formulates theory in general terms, these are often illustrated with anecdotal examples from his own observations or from popular literature and magazines. What Goffman may lack in theoretical gravity or systematic empirical documentation, he makes up for through extraordinary observations of encounters in everyday life. For most of the postwar generation in sociology, some of the recurrent themes in Goffman's analyses have become synonymous with his particular perspective on the self and social interaction.

The concept of interaction is essential and Goffman is sometimes identified as an "interactionist" or "symbolic interactionist". An underlying claim in his work is that social interaction has its own order. Analysing the interaction order, for instance the patterns of daily interaction, does not fully reveal why individuals act in accordance with these patterns, however. It is characteristic that Goffman describes patterns without searching for a deep, psychological explanation. Instead, he places general labels on individual action patterns, which after all do establish a sort of general explanation of seemingly random events in everyday life.

Goffman's focus on social interaction does not imply that there is only one interaction order that is always the same. The claim is mainly that social

146 the reflective self

interaction is subject to unwritten rules that we may only notice when somebody breaks them. Goffman analyses these unwritten rules by observing what individuals typically do to avoid losing face in encounters with others.

> To study face-saving is to study the traffic rules of social interaction; one learns about the code the person adheres to in his movement across the paths and designs of others, but not where he is going, or why he wants to get there. One does not even learn why he is ready to follow the code.
>
> (Goffman 1967: 12)

As the quote illustrates, Goffman filters out a lot of information in order to establish his particular understanding of the social interaction order, not least what motives individuals may have to act as they do.

In Goffman's analysis, individual autonomy appears to be somewhere between free and enforced actions. On the one hand, the unwritten rules appear to have a forceful and almost ritualistic effect on most people. We cannot choose autonomously how we are perceived by others and which direction the interaction will take. Abiding by the unwritten rules of social interaction can easily become a habit maintained throughout life, for example rituals of civility, greetings in daily encounters or initiating or ending telephone conversations. On the other hand, Goffman also discusses the roles and strategies individuals can choose within this set of social rules. We may be forced to present ourselves in social interaction, but we have some choice in how it is done.

Every time two or more individuals meet and interact, they each try to leave a particular impression, i.e. to form the impression others make of them. This only partially conscious process is also known as "impression management":

> The expressiveness of the individual (and therefore his capacity to give impressions) appears to involve two radically different kinds of sign activity: the expression that he *gives*, and the expression that he *gives off*. The first involves verbal symbols or their substitutes which he uses admittedly and solely to convey the information that he and the others are known to attach to these symbols. This is communication in the traditional and narrow sense. The second involves a wide range of action that others can treat as symptomatic of the actor, the expectation being that the action was performed for reasons other than the information conveyed in this way.
>
> (Goffman 1959: 2)

the reflective self

147

The extra information may for instance be transmitted through looks, facial expressions, odours, ways of talking or other traits of appearance. Other participants in the interaction use these elements to decipher the message and its credibility. They may see the person as trying too hard or as interesting or popular. If a person accidentally smiles while talking about other people's misfortune, the smile will tell others that the person lacks empathy. It is important to establish consistency between an intended message and our appearance, when we deliver the message.

These attempts to manage impressions are usually subconscious and in practice most people have a broader repertoire of ways to appear in front of others in concrete encounters; for example a more formal style in interactions with public authorities, and a more relaxed style in private settings. Individuals perform what Goffman terms "facework" in an effort to be seen in a certain way. If consistent over time, a person may develop a "line" in his or her facework. A line is to some extent the individual's own, but Goffman also claims that individuals draw on a cultural repertoire of legitimate lines.

When individual facework is successful, other people's impression corresponds with the person's line. In this case, a person can be said to "have face" in Goffman's words (1967: 6). In the opposite case, the person loses face. Microsociological analyses of facework typically aim for a nuanced understanding of the different exchanges of impressions and gazes that characterise all social encounters. One example is the specialised literature on system and client encounters, which studies the significance of facework in meetings between individuals and public authorities. This is particularly pertinent for citizens in a weak or fragile social position, because they may have trouble presenting a consistent face to a public authority whose decisions may be critical for their legal situation (see Järvinen, Larsen and Mortensen 2002; Järvinen and Mik-Meyer 2003).

Acts and territories

Goffman is not interested in whether people are sincere when they take a line. The important thing is under which circumstances a person is perceived as being consistent with the line. He also chooses to ignore whether a person is being "himself" or "herself", because he claims that any social interaction is accompanied by a presentation of the self. The self does not constitute a core that exists independently of social interaction; it is a reflexive entity that continuously needs to be presented, negotiated and perhaps even defended in encounters with others.

Social interaction and role exchange are often analysed through a dramaturgical metaphor in Goffman's works. The fact that he characterises human contact as an act has led some critics to call his perspective cynical, because social interaction as such appears fake and strategic. It is probably correct to say that Goffman's perspective is ill equipped to understand what Habermas calls communicative rationality, if the assumption is that all arguments are part of an act and not frank opinions. In addition to looking for conflict between participants in encounters, Goffman goes to great lengths to describe how individuals often cooperate to support each other's lines and thereby ease social interaction (Goffman 1967: 12).

A key factor in individual self-presentation is territories. Goffman argues that the spatial surroundings influence the individual's choice of line, for instance whether a formal or casual presentation is chosen as most appropriate in a given situation. Indeed, not only the exchange of utterances involved in interaction but also the individual's physical performance and how it is interpreted in the eyes of others play an important part in separating a formal from a more casual presentation.

Goffman uses a dramaturgical metaphor to distinguish the two main territories, "front stage" (or "front region") and "back stage" (or "back region") (Goffman 1959: 107–112). Front stage is where a person is "on". The self-presentation is very conscious and controlled, and the self is highly affected by the presence of others. Back stage is where the individual expects to be alone and able to turn "off" his/her self-presentation. As we know, most people act very different at home and in public. Again, Goffman does not portray the front stage presentation as essentially false, or the back stage as representing a person's "real" self. Back stage is simply defined in contrast to the front stage, and Goffman assumes that all individuals need to be able to shift between territories, between turning their performance on and off.

The boundary between territories often follows the traditional differentiation between the public and the private spheres in society. The essential thing is, however, not the legal separation between the spheres, but whether or not the individual is in the public sphere and thereby in the presence of others. The private sphere is also subject to norms about self-presentation, which is perhaps best illustrated by microsociologist Harold Garfinkel (1917–2011), who also inspired Goffman. Garfinkel tried to show the implicit routines that people use in everyday life, but which are often unreflected. For example, he asked his students to go home to their parents and act as if they were tenants, i.e. knock on the door, ask politely for permission to use the bathroom, and so on (Harste and Mortensen 2007: 209). Although one might think that all parents would appreciate this behaviour, it came across as a provocation, because the students broke an unspoken norm to behave informal and relaxed at home.

the reflective self   149

Goffman's interest in acting and territories is developed further in his studies of society's deviants, including the institutions set up to handle them. He is interested in the deviants' own behaviour and in how we interact with them in everyday settings. The key work here is his influential book *Asylums* (1961) on the inner life of a mental institution. Goffman characterised the mental hospital as a "total institution" where patients' selves are violated because they lack any control of territories, not least the possibility to have a back stage. Patients would try to establish private territories such as a hiding place for food. They would sometimes go to great lengths to keep these hiding places secret, even if the hidden objects had little value to them. This confirms the idea that individuals need a back stage where they are not observed and performance can be switched off.

An obvious comparison with Goffman's description of the total institution is Foucault's analysis of the Panopticon (see Chapter 5), because both concern the implications of constant surveillance. Both writers influenced the critical debates in the 1960s and 1970s about anti-psychiatry and the conditions of committed mental patients and prisoners. The two perspectives are quite different, but complement each other.

Whereas Foucault analysed the discourses and technologies of power behind the establishment of permanent surveillance, Goffman describes the implications of surveillance for the individual's facework and the forms of resistance that arise in the underworld of the mental institution. It is nonetheless interesting how two very different theoretical and methodological positions lead to relatively similar conclusions about the effects of constant surveillance.

Another interesting aspect of Goffman's analysis of the total institution is that it extends the scope of a purely microsociological analysis. Some of the described mechanisms are clearly operating on the microlevel, such as the patients' struggle to reclaim their back stage in a total institution. Unlike Goffman's other analyses, *Asylums* involves a clear institutional frame here that sets the terms of microlevel interaction. The focus on the institutional frame constitutes a sort of mesolevel, but Goffman's analysis also points towards a type of macrolevel because it concerns society's approach to handling deviance from the norm.

With *Stigma* (1963), Goffman also contributes to the sociological understanding of deviance. The book describes how normal individuals act when they encounter deviants with "spoiled" identities in everyday situations, especially in face-to-face conversations. A stigma can be defined as a physically visible characteristic that discloses the "spoiled" identity of the individual, that may be hard for others to ignore and will almost certainly affect the conversation.

The first type of stigma Goffman discusses is bodily stigma, which can be any type of physical handicap or abnormality. In the book, a girl born without a nose describes all the awkward ways people try to act normal when they meet and interact with her. The second type is character-based stigma, i.e. physical marks that may be interpreted as signs of a poor character. For instance, a very red nose may be interpreted as a sign of alcoholism, and obesity as a sign of laziness. The third type is tribal stigma, which comprises all physical signs of ethnic, religious or linguistic background (Goffman 1963: 14). What constitutes a stigma differs greatly over time and space for all three types. Dark skin, a French accent or dirty clothes may constitute stigma in some social settings, but not in others.

Goffman claims that it is very hard not to make an implicit devaluation of a stigmatised person's intelligence or moral status if the person's looks are highly deviant. So-called normal people do not necessarily reject stigmatised individuals, but may unwillingly patronise or victimise them. People with physical disabilities often experience being treated or talked to as if they were children or less intelligent. Goffman is not out to blame us for this awkwardness. He reads it as an indication of the unspoken social order regulating everyday interaction. The analysis further demonstrates how people with stigma are often expected to play along and defer from commenting on people's awkwardness (Goffman 1963: 147).

To sum up, Goffman's microsociological perspective gives him a unique insight into the unreflected processes of face-to-face interaction. It is far from being a complete sociological theory about the self and individualisation, but it undoubtedly provides a particular microsociological insight that abstract macro theories tend to overlook. It is essential to add that Goffman's interest in individual microlevel interaction does not imply that he sees microbehaviour as completely autonomous or different from person to person. There are patterns and rituals in individual self-presentation and facework, so interaction may be more compulsive than it initially seems. The compulsiveness points to a general social interaction order that takes place between the concrete encounters of everyday life. This interaction order cannot be reduced to macrosocial systems in Goffman's view, but it nevertheless reaches beyond each individual encounter.

Giddens's theory of reflexive modernity

Whereas Goffman's theory appears relatively ahistorical – concepts such as line, presentation, stigma or back stage are not limited to one historical era – Giddens aims to establish a diagnosis of contemporary society as the basis for microsociological observations. We will therefore attempt to place Giddens's theory of the self within the framework of what he terms "reflexive modern" society, a term used in a slightly different way by Beck (see Chapter 8).

Foucault and Goffman both described a period where the disciplinary logic was dominant. Identities were fixed because they were bound to a series of well-defined institutions. You were either inside or outside these institutions and could be identified as normal or sick, friend or foe, superior or subordinate. Modern society is not significantly different from traditional society in this respect. Both are organised through "solids" (see Chapter 1). But in modern society these solids are no longer seen as given by nature or by a deity, but as created by humans. Instead of natural law, i.e. objective legal principles given independently of human conventions, we develop positive law, created by human beings. Like traditional society, modern society is a place where comfort, security and regularity reign. The basis for this may have changed, but modern society is able to replace what was immediately lost in the passage from tradition to modernity. Take for example Durkheim's idea about the change from mechanic to organic solidarity (see Chapter 3). Most commentators emphasise the change-aspect of this development, but we might as well point to the establishment of two different organisation forms fulfilling the same purpose: solidarity. It may be that with modernity, a deity is replaced by a human construction, but again this construction should not blind us to the persistence of a social order in a conventional sense. This is an order that limits individual behaviour if we formulate it negatively, or that gives individuals opportunities if we choose the positive formulation.

In reflexive modernity, many of the underlying principles of modernity are challenged. Instead of a focus on proximity there is now a focus on the ability to operate over large distances. Networks grow more important and become the general principle of governing and production instead of hierarchy. Control increasingly replaces discipline. The family is under pressure from serial monogamy. Contingency rather than order becomes the point of departure, and finally the distribution of risk becomes the main concern instead of the provision of security and goods. Despite comprehensive changes, Giddens still understands these tendencies as belonging to the modern epoch. As he observes, all the classic institutions of modernity do not disappear with the strike of a magic wand. These new tendencies were already present in seed form at the dawn of modernity. We are still in modernity, but now in a reflexive form.

Giddens emphasises how the ability to transcend time and space makes possible a new type of society. In the reflexive modern society, interaction does not require actors to be in the same place at the same time. Again, this is not completely new, but it is the pace, scope and institutions of this change that make possible a great and unprecedented dislocation (Giddens 1990: 6). Modernity gives us the empty clock time and thereby the idea that different activities can be properly located at various times of the day and the year. They no longer follow a predetermined rhythm. Space is dislocated from physical places in a similar fashion. Where activities were previously bound to, for instance, a village, they can now increasingly take place anywhere, especially with the communication technology. When you call for computer support from your home in Europe, you may reach a person in India.

Our ability to transcend time and space stems to a large extent from symbolic signs such as money. Giddens is close to Luhmann's understanding of symbolically generalised communication media here (see Chapter 6), so we will not describe this in detail. Another contributing factor to the dislocation of time and space are expert systems (Giddens 1990: 17ff.). Experts ease communication and choices because the individual can lean on professional evaluations and expertise. Professions are thus surrounded by what Giddens terms abstract trust. You no longer have to know the doctor who treats you personally. As long as you believe that he or she has a medical degree, this guarantees the quality of the treatment, at least to some extent. Symbolic signs also require trust in order to function; for instance that a $100 bill is in fact worth $100. We can distinguish between credibility and trust in both situations. Where credibility may depend on a physical encounter or specific knowledge about another person, trust is abstract and unbound by time and place. The passage from early to late modernity is characterised by a parallel passage from a society based on credibility to one based on trust.

Giddens explains this point through Goffman's theory of facework and the distinction between front and back stage. Most people encounter experts on a daily basis and may sometimes appear as experts when asked about their work. In our capacity as experts, we play a role. There is a significant difference between how you appear on the private back stage and on the front stage, where you meet customers or clients. A judge is expected to appear serious and listen. A doctor is perhaps expected to appear calm and distanced, and a flight attendant is expected to act polite and calm to put travellers at ease. On stage we encounter a specific type of facework designed to make us trust the expert system in question (Giddens 1990: 83–87). Here, Giddens would argue that Goffman's theory is really a theory of the self in modern society. In contrast to a premodern individual who to a larger extent always played the same role, the modern individual is expected to be able to understand itself in different roles, not least in regard to the separation between a private and a public self.

the reflective self   153

Finally, the dislocation of social activities and our ability to distinguish between different roles makes it possible for us to distance ourselves from these roles and reflect on them – thus the term reflexive modernity. A continuous stream of knowledge and the critical distance established to this knowledge enables us to critically reflect on society and our own behaviour. Reflexive modernity is fundamentally sociological in this way (Giddens 1990: 43). The starting point is that everything could be different. We can manipulate nature, the social and our identities to an extent previously unheard of. This also implies that we are more likely than ever to create problems for ourselves.

The self in reflexive modernity

We have now described reflexive modernisation "from above" so to speak, but what if we reverse the perspective and observe modernity "from below", i.e. from the perspective of the individual?

Giddens has also tried to characterise the position of the self in reflexive modernity. He emphasises that modernity is increasingly dominated by "pure relationships". This means that individuals encounter each other with less baggage than before. Marriage is a good example. Earlier, it was conditioned on the family's wishes or economic ability, but now we are free to choose partners as we wish, for instance based on love. Offhand, this looks like a liberation, and it is. However, it is also a colossal challenge, because everything is up for discussion in a pure relationship. Everything depends on whether this specific interaction is deemed valuable by those involved, and this becomes increasingly difficult due to our high standards for success in reflexive modernity.

Another difficulty is that we are often unable to process the high degree of contingency in reflexive modernity. Everything is potentially up for discussion, but not everything can be discussed or be subject to reflection simultaneously. Like Bourdieu, Giddens emphasises that much of the individual's behaviour must be preconscious if the individual is not to burn out. Giddens adds a new, psychological level to his understanding of the individual and claims that a healthy child must necessarily develop a high degree of basic trust in his or her surroundings (Giddens 1991: 38ff.). Not trust in a specific person, but a basic trust in the world or, perhaps more accurately, in our environment in the broadest possible sense of the term.

There are three levels of consciousness: the unconscious or nonconscious, practical or bodily consciousness (like a password memorised in the fingers), and the things we are fully conscious of and reflective about. In abstract terms, the individual needs a certain degree of ontological security. It is a relief if problems or situations can be transferred from the reflexive to the practical level of consciousness, so that our entire being and identity are not constantly challenged. The individual requires a routinisation of social relations, which is hard to accomplish in reflexive modernity.

For the individual to feel secure, its trust in its surroundings, the symbolic signs and expert systems must be unabated. Further, the individual must be able to connect various life events into relatively coherent self-narratives. It needs to feel in charge of its own life, and not like a pawn in someone else's game. To protect itself from the pressure of its surroundings and facilitate a coherent self-narrative, the individual develops what Giddens calls a protective cocoon (Giddens 1991: 40). This enables the individual to be selective and to filter different forces and impressions.

Giddens locates a fundamental conflict in the relationship between reflexive modernity and the self, which can only handle reflexivity in metered doses. The problem is that reflexive modernisation does not offer ontological security as such, but rather the opposite: existential fear or ontological insecurity, if you will. The distinction between anxiety and fear is instructive in this regard. Inspired by Søren Kierkegaard, Giddens understands fear as being related to a concrete object or event, whereas anxiety does not have a specific object. Similar to basic trust, anxiety is abstract and undetermined. Existence is not only about accepting the world as it is (basic trust), but also about creating an ontological basis for oneself in a world that is constantly moving. What we have is thus a "struggle of being against non-being" (Giddens 1991: 49), or in more simple terms: the conflict between the individual's desire for security on the one hand, and the insecurities circumscribing its existence, on the other hand. To fully capture the new conditions for the individual, we should perhaps – instead of Beck's concept of risk society (see Chapter 8) – rather talk about an anxiety society (that replaces a society of fear).

In classic modernity, freedom was typically understood as the freedom from government intervention or as a freedom from the trammels of tradition. Psychoanalyst Sigmund Freud's discussion of the burden of culture is classically modern in this respect. In Freud's time, culture was associated with the permanent conflict between individual instincts (the principle of enjoyment) and the different demands of a modern, social order (the principle of reality). Culture created predictable and safe surroundings at the expense of individual freedom. Freud consequently wanted to ease the symptoms of the individual's difficult encounter with culture and in a broader sense with the social.

the reflective self 155

The anxiety of contemporary individuals is radically different from the one described by Freud. The characteristic discomfort of reflexive modernity is at its root a symptom of excessive rather than insufficient freedom, and it comes at the expense of increased insecurity. Giddens claims that feelings of shame are intimately connected with reflexive modernity (1991: 64ff.). Where guilt can be attached to collectives, shame sticks with the individual. One may feel shame for not having optimised one's career, for not generating enough revenue to one's employer, for having an unfaithful partner or for being poor. When shame rather than anger becomes the primary response when something goes wrong, problems are turned inward. They are no longer seen as structurally given, but as the individual's own fault.

We noted earlier that reflexive modernity is "sociological". It means that reflexive modernisation comes with an awareness that social conditions are not given by nature, but created by human beings and thus amenable to change. If we look at the individual, it is worth noting how little sociology is left when individualisation takes over. It becomes increasingly difficult to argue that something is "society's fault".

To be critical of reflexive modernity, one can thus point to the individualisation of societal risks. A manufacturing defect at a car factory may lead to a series of car crashes. The response to stress, sleeplessness or other pathologies of reflexive modernity may be individual therapy rather than social critique. Being sick often becomes a question of the relationship to oneself or of an unhealthy lifestyle. Disease is thus rarely associated with its social causes.

The anxiety generated in reflexive modernity stems from the loss of social authorities. The individual tries to follow all recommendations – be healthy, exercise, enjoy life, and so on – but always aims too high or too low. No matter what you do, there is a rankling fear that your choice was not right. The problem is that reflexive modernity meets us with two demands – on the one hand, we seek security and comfort, and on the other hand we seek freedom. These two demands are often impossible to bridge. You cannot have your cake and eat it too – in this case harvest the advantages of both tradition and modernity.

In reflexive modernity, authority no longer commands clear, undisputed rules for the individual to follow. The types of enjoyment that say "you can" are transformed into commands for enjoyment saying "you must!" (Žižek 2000: 133, see Chapter 12). Be healthy, take care of your body, exercise often, eat this and certainly not that, and so on. The fall of authority thus leads to the development of more sophisticated and camouflaged forms of social force, which are no less "real". We are faced with the paradox of reflexive individuality. On the one hand, we are supposed to be ourselves and realise our creative potential. On the other hand, these attempts result in the exact opposite, the experience of all actions as insufficient and inauthentic. No actions or consumer goods can render our existence more authentic. Increased freedom thus often leads to increased dissatisfaction with one's ability and identity.

Anorexia is an obvious example of the troubles facing the reflexive self (Giddens 1991: 105). The disease was largely unknown until it became a mass phenomenon from the 1970s and onward. In Giddens's terms, anorexia can be viewed as a reflexive project that requires a high degree of consciousness about one's behaviour. It is an extreme expression of how the self relates to the body in reflexive modernity. You "are" not simply in your own body, because the body is an object of manipulation. Anorexia is a desperate attempt to establish some form of ontological security. It is a means to create control in an otherwise uncontrollable and confusing world.

For patients with anorexia, the liberation associated with reflexive modernity becomes an inner compulsion. Classic modernity offered a set of clearly defined ideals, but the lack of clear rules and rooted traditions in reflexive modernity means that nothing is ever good enough. You are always too fat. As endless as the starving project may appear, it is nevertheless a project. Similar to bulimia, anorexia can be seen as an attempt to eliminate ambivalence. Anorexia is an expression of what Bauman has called the "North Korean solution" (2008: 112); the border is sealed and the result is complete starvation of the inhabitants. Bulimia is the opposite – a strategy without any limitations whatsoever. Both disorders show how hard it is to maintain the relationship between the self and its environment. For the anorectic, the cocoon is sealed shut; for the bulimic it is nonexisting.

Finally, the example shows that individualisation does not make every individual unique. The question of the status and character of the individual therefore becomes the key focus of the sociological analysis. As mentioned, consumerism can be viewed as an example of an institution that gathers what reflexive modernisation spreads in the form of individualised life projects. Anorexia is of course not without relation to the beauty ideals projected in the media. Again, a focus on individualisation does not make the social disappear. The way we become individualised is often remarkably similar, which makes it essential to connect individualisation tendencies with broader, structural changes, and in Giddens's case, with reflexive modernity.

In this regard it is relevant to highlight Giddens's general concept of structuration, which concerns the more general relationship between

the reflective self 157

individual agency and social structures. The concept builds on the classic debate between structure- and agency-based theories in sociology, i.e. a debate about whether individual agency has some degree of autonomy or whether it is mainly determined by structural factors such as economy. Like Bourdieu, Giddens prefers not to choose between structure and agency in sociological analysis, but seeks instead to understand the dynamic between them.

The core idea of structuration is that individual action is structured by society, but that structures only reproduce through individual actions. Language is perhaps the most obvious example. When we use language to communicate with others, we have no choice but to use the built-in structures of the existing language, for instance regarding the meaning of words or grammatical rules. But while we make use of linguistic structures and rules, we also reproduce them. Similar recursive processes can undoubtedly be found in some of Goffman's examples of ritualised social interaction. The rituals for appropriate behaviour only reproduce as long as actors continue to act in accordance with them.

Compared with structure-based theories, Giddens (1984) ascribes greater importance to individual agency because there is room for intentional individual action. However, it is not the intentions of the agent that reproduce structure because the reproduction of structures is an "unintended consequence" of the agent's intentional action:

> Acts have unintended consequences; and ... may systematically feed back to be the unacknowledged conditions of further acts. Thus one of the regular consequences of my speaking or writing English in a correct way is to contribute to the reproduction of the English language as a whole. My speaking English correctly in intentional; the contribution I make to the reproduction of the language is not.
>
> (Giddens 1984: 8)

Similar to Goffman, Giddens here describes processes at the microlevel that reach above this level. The reproduction of social structures, whether it is language or social norms, is not pure microphenomena, but they only continue to function as long as agents act in accordance with them on the microlevel. Language, for example, changes when individuals begin to use it differently. The ritualised forms of courtesy Goffman analyses may similarly change if groups of individuals develop new conceptions of where to draw the line between acceptable and unacceptable behaviour in social interaction. The new structures similarly create a framework that new actors are bound to use as the basis of their actions.

Norm and exception

If we draw a broader comparison between Goffman and Giddens, both obviously try to answer the question of what it means to be a self in society. Both of their answers to this question require an analysis of a series of regulated and institutional contexts. They both mainly focus on the microlevel as a level that needs to be analysed in its own right, but societal or social structures do not disappear for that reason. Giddens employs the broadest possible perspective and understands the behaviour of the self against the backdrop of reflexive modernity and structuration more broadly. Goffman connects the self and the microlevel with a mesolevel analysis that includes organisations and institutions (e.g. the asylum).

A major difference between them is that Goffman tries to describe how the self interacts with disciplinary institutions whereas Giddens seeks to understand a new situation where the problem is excessive freedom, and not how institutions pressure individuals. However, their accounts of what it means to be a self are surprisingly similar. Both, for instance, underline the significance of a practical consciousness, i.e. routines we normally do not reflect on.

When norm and exception are connected in Goffman's and Giddens's work, this gives us two analytical strategies. Goffman takes his point of departure in routinised behaviour and attempts to illuminate the practical consciousness through breaches of social conventions. The analytical strategy is to provoke exceptions or study deviations in order to reach a fuller understanding of the norm. Giddens takes the opposite route and starts from freedom, insecurity and the fall of authority to explain how the self establishes coherence, security and trust. The exception is the norm, one could say, but the existence of a continuous life narrative is what should be analysed and explained.

Finally, it is worth noticing that both sociologists take an interest in the distinction between the public and the private self. This is most obvious in Goffman's distinction between front stage and back stage as well as between the different types of behaviour that correspond to each territory. Goffman seems to accept the idea of a disciplinary modernity regulated through clear boundaries and distinct territories. When Garfinkel encouraged his students to act as guests in their own home, the distinction between private and public collapsed because measured politeness was not expected among family members. Under normal circumstances, then, behaviour can be clearly assigned to each territory, to the home or to the public space.

Giddens's critique of reflexive modernity is based on a similar blurring of the distinction between public and private, as the distinction appears

the reflective self

159

in the public debate. Due to individualisation, political problems are no longer seen as something that requires a collective solution. In reflexive modernity it is no longer society's, but the individual's fault. Thereby we obviously overlook the social background behind the self's sufferings, as exemplified in the discussion of anorexia. One of the main points of analysing reflexive modernity is to "re-politicise" these allegedly private forms of suffering and individualisation, and to do so through an analysis of structural relationships in society.

chapter 10

Family and work

Sennett and Hochschild

In the preceding chapters, we have presented some of the most agenda-setting diagnostics of an era in sociological thinking, which can be summarised under the notions "liquid modernity", "second modernity" or "late modernity". In this chapter, we look at the fundamental transformations characterising work and family life during this period.

In their respective writings, Richard Sennett (1942–) and Arlie Hochschild (1940–) have tried to pinpoint the societal and individual consequences of the last 20–30 years' intensification and flexibilisation of the organisation, form and content of work life. This chapter gives an introduction to their different, yet often complementary perspectives on these consequences. In particular, we focus on the new conditions for family life under flexible capitalism and the instable foundations on which individuals are expected to create and maintain a consistent, meaningful life narrative in a volatile work sphere structured around temporary goals and relationships.

The first part of the chapter briefly discusses how the social practices and activities we associate with work can be analysed sociologically. The second part introduces Sennett's analysis of life under flexible capitalism and his famous diagnosis of the personal consequences of work life in a society that orients its activities towards short-term objectives and encounters. The third part describes and discusses Hochschild's detailed and eye-opening interactionist study of everyday life in the large US company "Amerco", which, despite a declared mission to be a family-friendly workplace puts its employees under increasing time pressure and promotes a cultural reversal of the norms and values that we usually associate with work and family.

Work as an analytical prism

Imagine yourself at a dinner party. Across from you sits a couple you have just met for the first time. As is usually the case in such situations, your conversation quickly turns to the question: "What do you do for a living?" With polite caution, each of you responds with a brief career description, and you acquire a basic understanding of each other's educational background, occupation and social stance. From that moment, job experiences will be a recurring topic of conversation throughout the evening.

Understanding work through a sociological lens is not merely a question of analysing society's economic basis and overarching organisation forms. Work is an important identity marker. It ascribes meaning and value to our existence; not only for ourselves, but also for our fellow human beings, who, like the couple at the dinner table, are interested in understanding who we are and what we stand for.

Ever since the beginning, work has been a central theme in sociological theory development. The founding fathers, Marx, Weber and Durkheim, were all immersed in understanding and describing the work-related processes leading to (and the consequences of) industrialisation and modernisation. Indeed, as touched upon in Chapters 2 and 3, work constituted the analytical starting point for more comprehensive investigations of the prevalent development trends characterising society in the transitional phase from premodern to industrial modernity. Studying work practices during this period became an analytical starting point for more wide-ranging sociological diagnostics of a society undergoing rapid transformations.

What is undergoing transformation is often easier to catch sight of than what is stable. And due to its transformative and multifaceted nature, work is a useful analytical prism for discovering broader trends with long-term societal impacts. Marx, Durkheim and Weber all developed their theories in a transition period epitomised by rapid industrialisation, occupational differentiation and the emergence of new and more rationalised forms of bureaucracy. Sennett and Hochschild provide an updated view by studying changes in work life in the transition from a "solid" to a more "liquid" form of modernity.

As we shall illustrate in the following, this transition involves an ideal-typical shift in the meaning and value ascribed to work activities. Whereas workers in the early industrial modernity "worked to exist", workers in flexible capitalism increasingly "exist to work". Work now assumes a

162   family and work

more ambiguous form. It opens new opportunities for employees but also erodes core aspects of their character and social relationships.

As touched upon in Chapter 7, even the most private aspects of human existence are now activated to increase work productivity. We are moving from a "heavy" to a "lighter" form of capitalism (Bauman 2000), or as Polanyi (2001) says, from a society with islands of market life to a market with islands of society (cf. Hochschild 2005). This Janus-like nature of work life under flexible capitalism represents the shared starting point for Sennett's and Hochschild's sociological contributions.

The authors also share an affinity to the philosophical and sociological tradition known as American pragmatism (see Chapter 4). In short, this tradition seeks to move philosophical and social scientific thinking out of the armchair and into social reality with the purpose of developing concrete and applicable concepts and theories with practical relevance for the context under investigation. As Sennett formulates it, an abstract idea "has to bear the weight of concrete experience or else it becomes a mere abstraction" (Sennett 1998: 11).

Both Hochschild and Sennett place the actors' personal experiences and life narratives in the foreground of their analyses. This leads to richer and more detailed accounts of the practical implications of work and family life in late modernity than what we usually see in sociological diagnostics of contemporary society (see for example Giddens, Bauman and Beck).

Through detailed everyday and biographical descriptions, the authors bring the lived experiences of human beings to the forefront of the sociology of work, hereby continuing the famous ambition of American sociologist, Charles Wright Mills (1916–1962): to explore interactions between the public and private by making the intersection between the individual biography and society's cultural and structural formations the core subject matter for sociology (Mills 2000).

Whereas the structure-oriented macrosociology sketches the coordinates of society's cultural and structural landscape, Hochschild and Sennett invite us on a journey into this landscape. Through personal and perceptive travelogues, they deepen our understanding of how this landscape appears to the travellers (cf. Garey and Hansen 2011: 4). This approach gives the reader a "bottom-up" perspective on the dialectics of work. The employees are here, more or less, analysed as cocreators of the same social world that influences and forms their day-to-day activities.

Richard Sennett on flexible capitalism

In the *Manifesto of the Communist Party* from 1849, Marx and Engels, with almost prophetic clear-sightedness, formulated a diagnostic description of the "zeitgeist" of industrial modernity. Today, more than 150 years later, this formulation seems more succinct and topical than ever. According to Marx and Engels, the industrial society diverged from earlier historical periods in that "all fixed, fast-frozen relations, with their train of ancient and venerable prejudices and opinions, are swept away, all new-formed ones become antiquated before they can ossify" (1969). In the same breath, the authors conceived their famous depiction of modern society as the place where "All that is solid melts into air" (see Chapter 1). As mentioned earlier, this depiction shares an affinity with Bauman's concept of "liquid modernity" (see Chapter 8). However, their depiction also captures core aspects of Sennett's diagnosis of work life under flexible capitalism in *The Corrosion of Character* (1998) and *The Culture of the New Capitalism* (2006).

Sennett's concept of "new capitalism" or "flexible capitalism" stands out most clearly in contrast to the so-called social or long-term capitalism that gained foothold in Western societies from the late 1940s to the early 1970s (Sennett 2006: 6). As Sennett observes, capitalism in the 19th century seesawed from one recession to another as a result of irrational corporate investments. These financial insecurities were gradually harnessed in the postwar period, where "strong unions, guarantees of the welfare state, and large-scale corporations combined to produce an era of relative stability" (Sennett 1998: 24).

Drawing on Weber's classic analysis of modernity and bureaucratic development, Sennett highlights the societal shift towards a military-inspired organisation model, as one of the central characteristics of work life during this period. The military model was based on long-term strategic planning and heavy hierarchical organisation structures. Everyone was assigned a position in the hierarchical system, and each position had a specified function. Large government institutions operated as counterweight to the volatile fluctuations of private markets and workers joined forces with private corporations, through their unions, to ensure long-term planning, financial stability and secure employment (Sennett 2006: 20–23).

A pivotal aspect of this period's long-term, strategic planning, according to Sennett, lay in a new and more rationalised organisation of time:

> Time lay at the center of this military, social capitalism: long-term and incremental and above all predictable time. This bureaucratic imposition affected individuals as much as institutional regulations. Rationalized time enabled people to think about their lives as narratives – narratives not so much of what necessarily will happen as of how things should happen. It became possible, for instance, to define what the stages of a career ought to be like, to correlate long-term service in a firm to specific steps of increased wealth.
>
> (Sennett 2006: 23)

To restate, rationalised time provided both institutions and individuals with more stable and long-lasting foundations for developing coherent career trajectories and greater certainty about their future than the 19th century's volatile financial markets and insecure jobs. As Sennett observes, social capitalism's "time-motor" was driven by the Weberian principle of "delayed gratification", i.e. a postponement of the immediate rewards of work with a view to more long-standing objectives. Workers obeyed orders and accepted their irrevocable positions in the hope of breaking away from these positions in the long run. Delayed gratification required self-discipline and a certain form of allegiance between employer and employee, which has since become superfluous under flexible capitalism (Sennett 2006: 76–77).

With the oil crisis and the collapse of the Bretton Woods system in the early 1970s (Bretton Woods was an international monetary cooperation established in the wake of World War II; this cooperation regulated international flows of capital to ensure financial stability), Western corporations were unbridled to pursue new global opportunities and adapt their businesses to an emerging clientele of international investors and venture capitalists, which in Sennett's words "were more intent on short-term profits in share prices than long-term profits in dividends" (Sennett 2006: 6). This entailed an acceleration in the exchange of commodities and services across national borders, further sustained by new communication technologies, which as illustrated by Giddens made possible an unprecedented separation of time and space (see Chapter 9).

Gradually, a more flexible, short-term capitalism rose from the ashes of the industrial era's pyramid hierarchies. In the *Corrosion of Character*, Sennett summarises this form of capitalism in three core characteristics: mobility, speed and deregulation. The ideal-typical company under flexible capitalism is characterised by a flatter, more network-based organisation structure. It is lighter on its feet and "more readily decomposable or redefinable than the fixed assets of hierarchies" (Powell and Smith-Doerr 1994; cf. Sennett 1998: 23). Flexible organisations are therefore better at adapting and pursuing new opportunities for returns on a rapidly changing market epitomised by "impatient capital".

As we shall see, this form of organisation requires employees who are capable of moving in and out of contexts and pursuing new opportunities before existing projects die out. This adaptability also implies that hiring and firing to a decreasing extent follow formalised procedures, and that work portfolios are becoming more volatile and unclear in form and content.

New organisation forms also lead to new ways of organising time. Sennett emphasises the increasing prevalence of temporary appointments and short-term contracts under flexible capitalism; a development he sees

family and work   165

as a break with the coherent, long-term perspective of the typical social capitalist career trajectory.

Changing work and the corrosion of character

Based on these characteristics, Sennett, in *The Corrosion of Character*, formulates three central questions about the individual consequences of work life under flexible capitalism:

> How do we decide what is of lasting value in ourselves in a society which is impatient, which focuses on the immediate moment? How can long-term goals be pursued in an economy devoted to the short term? How can mutual loyalties and commitments be sustained in institutions which are constantly breaking apart or continually being redesigned?
>
> (Sennett 1998: 10)

In addressing these questions, Sennett entwines social theories, economic data, historical developments, informal interviews and participant observations in an essayistic representation combining theoretical ideas with individual life experiences (Sennett 1998: 11). The methodological qualifications of his writings are, however, limited. In most cases, the interviews and observations function as anecdotal eye-openers putting a human face on the theoretical discussions, rather than as empirical foundations for methodologically stringent inferences.

In the first chapter of *The Corrosion of Character*, Sennett unfolds a compelling narrative about an Italian-American janitor, Enrico, and his son Rico, whose biographies represent ideal-typical examples of work life under social and flexible capitalism. Sennett first met Enrico when he was conducting fieldwork for *The Hidden Injuries of Class* (1972). At that point, Enrico was in his 20th year as a unionised janitor cleaning toilets and floors in a Boston office building. His long-term objective was to provide for his family and enable his son to establish a better life with a more respectable career than his own. As Sennett observes, Enrico saw his work as an investment in the future. The union protected his rights and the government pension ensured a reasonable life after retirement. These circumstances created a coherent life narrative characterised by linearity and predictability.

The career progression of Rico, a 39-year-old electrical engineer with a master's degree from one of New York's prestigious business schools, stands in clear contrast to his father's more linear and cumulative narrative. During the 14 years elapsed since Rico's graduation, he and his wife, Jeanette, have moved four times to maintain progression in their careers, and despite well-paid jobs, they both live in constant fear of losing control of the future.

When Sennett meets Rico, he has recently settled down as an independent consultant in Manhattan's tech industry. As a consultant, Rico is required to constantly adapt to changing requests of a volatile customer base; and despite his young age, he feels outdated as an engineer. It is no longer possible for Rico to keep up with the latest developments in his field, and he often finds himself outpaced by younger colleagues with more up-to-date qualifications.

Compared to his father, Rico lacks clear routines and predictable work tasks. Whereas Enrico, as a result of his long-term dedication to the laborious occupation as a janitor, accumulated a positive and meaningful life narrative that gave self-respect, Rico has become a victim of flexible capitalism's break with the principle of delayed gratification. He devotes most of his waking hours to a production regime where enduring relations are replaced by loose professional associations, and strong social ties characterised by loyalty and mutual commitment have become superfluous.

Rico therefore lacks stable principles of guidance in his life. Moving from one place to another has made it difficult for him to maintain close friendships, and the emotional relationship to his two kids has come under increasing pressure due to high levels of work-family conflict.

With reference to Habermas (see Chapter 6) one could say that work (the system) in Rico's situation has colonised the life world. The pervasive requirements in flexible capitalism refrains him from establishing long-lasting social ties and well-functioning affective bonds. Unlike his father, Rico is not struggling to create a better life for himself and his family in the long run. His struggle takes on a more existential character. He lacks enduring perspectives and reference points that can ascribe meaning to his life and function as guiding examples in the rearing of his children.

In Sennett's words, short-term capitalism threatens to corrode Rico's character, "particularly those qualities of character which bind human beings to one another and furnishes each with a sense of sustainable self" (1998: 27). Indeed, as displayed in Table 10.1, the contradiction between the requirements of the flexible employee and Sennett's conception of the qualities of the good human character is the central theoretical contribution in *The Corrosion of Character*.

Sennett's main argument can be summarised as follows: The emergence of new and more flexible forms of organisation detaches work from its traditional temporal and geographical fixations and replaces enduring social ties with looser forms of association. This weakens the individual's opportunities to acquire experiences that take time and impedes the establishment of social relations of a deeper and more long-lasting nature.

family and work

Table 10.1 The conflict between the requirements of flexible capitalism and the good human character

Requirements of the successful employee under flexible capitalism	Foundations for the good human character
Flexibility	Stability
Adaptability/willingness to take risks	Continuity
Mobility	Solidity
Large networks, weak social ties	Loyalty and mutual commitment
Volatile and unclear work tasks	Determination and decisiveness
Seeking new opportunities	Delayed gratification with a view to long-term goals and rewards
Independence of rules and procedures	Repetitions and routines

Note: Inspired by Pedersen (2007).

The flexible work regime hereby risks corroding the human character, i.e. "the personal traits which we value in ourselves and for which we seek to be valued by others" (Sennett 1998: 10). The quintessence of this character, according to Sennett, lies in loyalty, mutual commitment and the pursuit of long-term goals. It represents our linkage to the social world by making us dependent on one another.

Borrowing a concept from Giddens, one could say that flexible capitalism is undermining the ontological security of modern employees (see Chapter 9; Sennett 2006: 144–145). Increasing demands for mobility and constant changes in work tasks, customers and collaborators make it difficult for the modern employee to reconcile personal values and beliefs with the conditions and values characterising a volatile work life; and this incongruence, combined with a fundamental uncertainty about the future, can paralyse even the most resilient and adventurous employee.

This point is best illustrated in Sennett's story about Rose, a middle-aged woman who after many years as a bar owner in New York's SoHo district made a career shift to Manhattan's volatile realm of advertising.

Rose's story offers an outsider's view on an industry where middle-aged employees are seen as "dying trees" and lifelong experiences appear useless. In Manhattan's world of advertising, work activities are oriented towards short-term financial gains and the fickle impulses of the present. Consequently, success in advertising does not necessarily imply hard work and ambition. Instead, success is determined by the ability to nourish one's professional network and leave dying projects and catastrophic ideas as quickly as possible. As Rose formulates it, the advertising industry suffers from an egregious short-term memory: "you are always starting over, you have to prove yourself every day" (Sennett 1998: 84).

Rose ran a risk when she changed careers, but she was not aware that this risk would become a defining tenet of her new occupation in an industry where routines erode and work activities are played out in unpredictable network constellations. In advertising, Sennett recounts, employees are evaluated on unclear and volatile criteria, and these conditions ended up riddling Rose's work life with worries and permanent feelings of uncertainty (Sennett 1998: 85–86).

Sennett's story about Rose reminds us that the flexible work culture's break with the more restrictive and repetitive work routines of social capitalism does not necessarily set the modern employee free. Quite the opposite in Rose's case. Flexible capitalism paralysed her adventurous spirit to the extent that the intrinsic rewards associated with work became deflated.

To avoid this paralysis and become a successful employee in the work culture of flexible capitalism, one has to be an unusual human being, Sennett asserts. One should be willing to set aside many years of life experience, refrain from establishing a consistent and long-lasting self-narrative and give up any ambition to become good at something specific (Sennett 2006: 5). As these requirements correspond poorly with the preferences and ambitions of most human beings, life under flexible capitalism gives rise to simmering feelings of ontological uncertainty and a permanent confusion about the basic question: Who in society needs me? (Sennett 1998: 146).

Escaping the iron grip

As described, Sennett deplores flexible capitalism's volatile change imperative. In his view, this work culture obliterates the spiritual meaning ascribed to work and impedes its intrinsic potentials for self-realisation. Much like Marx's idea about the alienation of labour, his main argument is based on a normative conception of the modernisation process as a movement away from authentic and meaningful forms of production. In *The Corrosion of Character*, he concludes that a regime that takes away the human character and hereby our reasons to care about each other will not be capable of preserving its legitimacy in the long run (Sennett 1998: 148). For human existence to be bearable, the common "we" and the mutual dependence of individuals have to be reinstalled in the culture of work. This requires a restoration of three basic human values: narrative, usefulness and craftsmanship (Sennett 2006: 147–161).

As illustrated in the stories about Enrico and Rico, the idea of the linear, cumulative life narrative is a core tenet in Sennett's conceptualisation of the good human character. In *The Culture of the New Capitalism*, he proposes a number of ways to restore such a life narrative. Among other things, he highlights a promising potential in a burgeoning British-American development towards new and more community-oriented, union-like "parallel institutions" that actively seek to re-establish and nurture the experiences of continuity and sustainability that are missing in the flexible work regime.

"Usefulness" concerns the experience of making a valuable contribution to others. This value is best exemplified in the story about Rose, who lost her sense of usefulness in an industry epitomised by unpredictable and volatile performance criteria. Sennett claims that public service work is associated with higher levels of symbolic recognition, status and legitimacy than work in the private sector, and he suggests that a pullback of public sector responsibilities that have been outsourced to private companies could contribute to restoring a feeling of usefulness in parts of society.

Last but not least, Sennett emphasises the value of craftsmanship, i.e. becoming immersed in doing something for its own sake and practicing until you excel at what you are doing. For Sennett, this value represents a possible means to escape the alienating downsides of flexible capitalism. In contrast to the ideal-typical characteristics of the flexible employee, the craftsman's work ethics is characterised by higher levels of engagement, commitment and pride in one's work. Craftsmanship requires immersion and repetition, which means that the horizon of alternative opportunities is narrowed down for the sake of devoting full attention to one task or activity. In his book *The Craftsman* (2008), Sennett provides a more elaborate discussion of this particular value.

Against the backdrop of these potential "escape routes" out of flexible capitalism's iron grip, we will now introduce Arlie Hochschild's sociology; especially her contributions to the sociology of work and family, which both complement and challenge central arguments in Sennett's work.

Arlie Hochschild on the cultural reversal of work and family life

A frequently overlooked point in Sennett's diagnosis is that the front-runner companies forming the basis of his analysis employ relatively few employees in most Western countries. Despite the general discursive emphasis on the emergence of a project-based work regime requiring mobile and adaptable employees (see Chapter 7), the day-to-day work activities of most employees across the globe are still characterised by too little rather than too much flexibility (Sennett in Lykkeberg 2007).

Hochschild's in-depth case study of employee life on the shop floor and in the management corridors of the large American company *Amerco* (pseudonym), illustrates this point quite clearly. Amerco is proactively pursuing a global competitive edge by introducing new and more flexible management forms. Yet, the company's employee turnover is limited. Most employees spend large parts of their careers at Amerco and establish close and long-lasting ties to their colleagues. Indeed, the typical career trajectory in the company has more in common with the Weberian principle of "delayed gratification" than with the short-term and hypermobile job commitments of flexible capitalism.

The human consequences of work assume different and more paradoxical forms in Hochschild's analyses than what we have touched upon in the preceding sections. Although the typical career at Amerco tends to be long term, everyday life has become a "time struggle" for many employees, who constantly leap from one ice floe to another to reconcile the daily conflicts between work and family life. Before we delve deeper into Hochschild's compelling portrait of the time-starved Amerco employees, let us briefly introduce her earlier writings and distinct analytical strategy.

Microsociological perspectives on work and family life

Hochschild's sociology is largely inspired by symbolic interactionism; especially Goffman's work, to which she adds an innovative account of the subtle, emotional underpinnings of social life. The analytical emphasis on feelings is most pronounced in *The Managed Heart* (1983), in which she explores the exhaustive "emotional labour" carried out by American flight attendants between take-off and landing. Through in-depth observations, this pioneer book illustrates how modern service employees are expected to harness even the most intimate emotions and relations in their daily work activities. The book contributes numerous analytical concepts to the sociology of emotions (including "emotional labour", "feeling management" and "feeling norms") and raises important questions about the human consequences of a work life situated on the border between the private and the public self; questions that have since proven quintessential to most of her writings (Bloch 1998).

In her follow-up book, *The Second Shift* (1989), Hochschild shifts focus from work to family. More specifically, she sets out to investigate the gender strategies and feeling dynamics in 50 two-career families' daily struggles to make ends meet at home. Through interviews and participant observations, she identifies three dominant cultural ideals (or "gender

family and work   171

ideologies") about appropriate marital roles: the "traditional ideal", where women's responsibilities are oriented towards the family and men's towards work; the "egalitarian ideal", where women's and men's work and family responsibilities are equally shared; and the "transitional ideal", which combines gender role conceptions from the two other ideals. *The Second Shift* contributes with important sociological insights on the often class-related underpinnings of these cultural ideals (working-class couples tend to be oriented towards the traditional ideal and middle-class couples towards the egalitarian). Moreover, it reminds us that mothers, despite women's continuous inroads into the labour market, are carrying by far the biggest burden in terms of child-rearing and domestic responsibilities (i.e. the second shift). Hochschild summarises this paradox with the concept of the "stalled gender revolution".

A distinct quality in Hochschild's writings lies in her ability to step down from the academic ivory tower and into the work settings and living rooms of "regular people". Through curious microsociological endeavours her analyses give voice to destinies and life stories that are otherwise left unnoticed in the abstract conceptualisations and statistical models of the mainstream sociological literature. Indeed, her sense for detail sometimes enables her to reveal distinct social patterns and trends in the most unexpected and unusual places.

This point is perhaps best illustrated in this excerpt from *The Time Bind*, where the content and spatial location of family portraits becomes a proxy for identifying gender and class-related social patterns in the world views and life priorities of Amerco employees:

> A family photo on an office wall is like a handshake: it introduces us to a person. ... Men at the top like Bill Denton tended to have large individual color photos showing the children in studio poses, or in shots taken at important ceremonial moments. ... Such photos, mounted like degrees, were usually placed behind the executive (like football trophies ...). At the banks of desks in windowless inner spaces where women answered phones and typed reports for managers and professionals, one could see small, unframed photos discreetly placed beside word processors or telephones, or taped to walls where working mothers could see them. ... These photos seemed like personal mementos, informal reminders of other lives. ... Women managers – especially in male-dominated divisions – were caught between cultures. They tended to display neither larger trophy photos, nor intimate snapshots of recent events. Instead, credentials – such as diplomas – and awards often hung on the walls behind them.
>
> (Hochschild 1997: 85–86)

In an almost Durkheimian sense, family portraits are here conceived as social facts, crystallising underlying social patterns. They represent stories about the social hierarchies that structure work behaviours at Amerco and offer insights on the microstrategies adopted by employees to bridge (or separate) their commitments inside and outside the workplace. Family portraits, in other words, become symbols of the employees' willingness and leeway to bring personal aspects of their identity into their jobs.

The time bind

In *The Time Bind*, Hochschild synthesises the analytical approaches to family and work put forth in her preceding books. More specifically, she explores the human consequences of an emerging work culture that reverses the values associated with work and family life with specific focus on the time dimension as a qualitative dynamic in everyday interactions (Bloch 1998).

The book is based on intensive field studies carried out between 1990 and 1993 in the American Fortune 500 company Amerco (pseudonym), which at that point was ranked among the most family-friendly workplaces in the United States. Hochschild has conducted 130 interviews with top managers, HR consultants, factory workers, psychologists, nursery teachers and life-partners of Amerco employees. She has participated in business meetings, conferences and leisure activities and been a "fly on the wall" in six Amerco families' daily routines and activities. Finally, she draws on internal work-climate surveys, national reports and existing academic research on work-life dynamics, to complement her qualitative explorations with insights on broader quantitative patterns.

In the introductory chapters of *The Time Bind*, Hochschild carves out an interesting puzzle: Amerco has made considerable efforts to introduce family-friendly personnel policies offering part-time positions, job sharing, flex-time and options to work from home. Yet, with the exception of flex-time, very few employees (approximately 1 per cent) take advantage of these opportunities. In fact, the average weekly work hours have increased in parallel with the implementation of a new, more family-friendly corporate culture.

Even more surprising, employees with toddlers, as reflected in the company's statistics, spend more time at work than their colleagues without children. Indeed, a large share of employees work overtime and take extra shifts on weekends and nights, and the company's childcare facilities, which un-freeze extra hours for undisturbed work, are very popular in the organisation. As Hochschild sums up, "working parents are voting with their feet, and the workplace is winning" (1997: 199).

family and work 173

To tease out the social dynamics of this time paradox, she investigates a number of well-known, potentially relevant explanatory factors, including the financial necessity of full- and overtime work and the fear of being laid off. She finds that part-time work and long-term leave are incompatible with the financial situation of many Amerco families; but this does not explain why a majority of employees abstain from fully using all paid vacation days. Further, the best-paid Amerco employees tend to show lower interest in part-time positions and job sharing than their lower-earning colleagues, and national surveys reflect a similar pattern: "Money matters, but other things do too" (Hochschild 1997: 29).

The fear of being laid off does not fully explain Amerco's time paradox either. Despite some resistance to job sharing and part-time positions among the company's mid-level managers, the limited use of these options in the vast majority of cases is due to a lack of demand among the employees rather than fear of being laid off. Moreover, labour unions are relatively strong at Amerco, which complicates illegitimate firing of employees on such grounds.

Hence, Hochschild proposes another, more surprising explanation of the time paradox: Amerco promotes a cultural reversal of the social values associated with home and work, and the family tends to lose in the process. She argues that the daily hours spent at the workplace have become a harmonic and predictable alternative to the unresolved quarrels and dirty laundry at home. Indeed, for some employee groups, the workplace becomes an almost family-like, supporting environment, where employees can vent their frustrations about a hectic and unrewarding life at home. The traditional conception of family life as a "safe haven" guarding the employee from the cold-hearted and instrumental realm of work is, in other words, reversing (Hochschild 1997: 37).

A key factor prompting this development lies in Amerco's orientation towards a softer, less hierarchical, corporate culture. To increase work motivation and competitiveness in a globalised world, the company has introduced Total Quality Management (TQM), a system that promotes a corporate culture based on self-managing teams, "enriched" jobs, and flatter organisation structures. It resembles Sennett's description of flexible capitalism's break with heavy pyramid hierarchies and bureaucratic control schemes.

TQM's declared goal, Hochschild asserts, is to create more committed and independent employees who identify with Amerco's overarching visions and take part in their fulfilment. Through participant-based management techniques, employees are trained to make autonomous decisions, and employee recognition has become an important strategy for increasing work motivation. The quarterly company magazine, *Amerco World*, communicates positive stories about exceptional job accomplishments, and employees are frequently encouraged to invest positive feelings in their work. Amerco organises "casual Fridays", company picnics, holiday parties, celebratory company gatherings and recognition ceremonies. Employees are no longer reduced to cogwheels in the company's complex, bureaucratic clockwork. They have become "believers" and they devote most of their waking hours to the values and visions of the "Amerco family" (Hochschild 1997: 206).

Much like Boltanski's and Chiapello's point about the ability of capitalism to reinvent itself and co-opt the cultural trends and critiques impeding its function, these examples illustrate how feelings and values normally associated with the family are nourished in the workplace to boost employee motivation and productivity.

In contrast, the weekly hours spent at home take on a more "industrial tone". Indeed, family life is being exposed to the same efficiency logic that formerly structured the work arrangements of industrial capitalism. While long work days foster new forms of inefficient and non-work-related socialisation among colleagues, the far fewer hours spent at home become streamlined and optimised in any way possible. This point is best illustrated in Hochschild's descriptions of John and Gwen Bell's daily struggles to make ends meet at home:

> Even if they didn't intend to, Gwen and John regularly applied principles of efficiency to their family. For them, as for so many other Amerco parents, saving time was becoming the sort of virtue at home it had long been at work. Gwen regularly squeezed one activity between two others, narrowing the "time frame" around each. ... Whenever she could get a lot done at home in less time, Gwen congratulated herself for solving a time problem. ... Numerous activities formerly done at home now go on outside the house as a result of domestic "outsourcing". Long ago, the basic functions of education, medical care, and economic production, once based in the home, moved out. Gradually, other realms of activity followed. For middle-class children, for instance, piano lessons, psychological counselling, tutoring, entertainment, and eating now often take place outside the home.
>
> (Hochschild 1997: 49–50)

The growing focus on optimising and systematising time use in the family has paved the way for what Hochschild describes as a "third shift", i.e. parents' intensive efforts to win "quality time" with their kids and compensate for the temporal deficit caused by their increasing work commitments. Indeed, the complications associated with this third shift make up a central theme in many of the life stories and empirical examples in *The Time Bind*.

family and work

We are introduced to Linda, a shift supervisor at one of Amerco's plants, who feels far more appreciated at work than at home. We meet the senior manager, Bill, who mainly evaluates the work efforts of his employees based on their hours spent in the office. Bill himself has ultralong work days and a stay-at-home wife taking care of house and children. We follow Vicki, another senior manager, who in contrast to Bill cannot leave domestic responsibilities to a homemaking partner and struggles to make ends meet in the family. We also meet Vicki's husband, the dentist Kevin, who matches the work and family commitments of his successful wife by the minute to remain even in the eyes of the community and to avoid feeling subservient in his marriage. We follow Becky and Sue, two single-mom, production line workers, whose friendships and social ties at work provide a sense of continuity and predictability that is missing in their complicated private lives with divorces and unstable family relationships. Finally, we meet the plant worker Mario, who is working as much overtime as he can to get away from his family and earn more than his wife, Deb, who is also working double and weekend shifts to force Mario to stay home with his kids (Bloch 1998; Hochschild 1997).

The Time Bind, as illustrated by these examples, is more than a micro-sociological study of the multifaceted qualitative dynamics of the time paradox and the "exogenous shocks" absorbed by family life. The book sketches an edifying portrait of the gender- and class-related status dynamics that reinforce or weaken the personal consequences of a time-starved work culture, revealing Hochschild's implicit links to the Marxist and feminist research traditions.

In accordance with her pragmatic starting point, Hochschild wraps up *The Time Bind* with a list of practical suggestions on how to resist the time paradox and establish better, more balanced family lives. She identifies three individual microstrategies adopted by Amerco parents to cope with their growing "time debt".

Some parents ease their bad conscience with "emotional abstinence". They convince themselves that not being present at home has little influence on their children's well-being, and that children, in general, become more independent by having "alone time". Others, like John and Gwen Bell, outsource their caring responsibilities to a rapidly expanding American industry of time-saving business offers including phone services for home-alone children who need an adult to talk to and event planners specialising in children's birthday parties. A third group devalue their ever-increasing time debt by building imaginary future alternatives for a better and more family-friendly life.

These coping strategies may help the "time-poor" Amerco parents postpone or ease the disheartening consequences of their conflicting work-family commitments, but they are not long-term solutions. As a more enduring alternative, Hochschild therefore calls for mobilising a collective "time movement", anchored in civil society, lobbying for more balanced work-life arrangements through public dialogue and joint action. Today, approximately 20 years after the *The Time Bind* was first published, such a movement is yet to be realised, and the promotion of family-friendly work-life arrangements is predominantly biased towards corporate interests.

The hidden dangers of contemporary capitalism

In this chapter, we have described and discussed how two of the leading theorists in contemporary American sociology, Sennett and Hochschild, theorise and make sense of the complex and sometimes paradoxical work-family dynamics of late modernity. In this concluding section, we will summarise similarities and differences in their viewpoints and point to limitations in the range and scope of their theoretical claims.

Both adopt a pragmatic, empirically driven approach to the sociology of work and family. Personal experiences and life narratives are at the foreground in their analyses, which produces richer, more detailed descriptions than we usually see in the sociological literature. Sennett's historical, socioeconomic framing gives his writings a slightly more macro-oriented emphasis than Hochschild's, who is more consistent in her microsociological, interactionist endeavours.

As regards the differences in the two authors' subject matter, Sennett confines his focus to a relatively narrow, but growing segment of flexible, front-runner companies, whereas the work forms analysed by Hochschild appear more widespread and common in an Anglo-American context. Her finding that Amerco's employee turnover is low despite the company's orientation towards new and more flexible organisation forms thus does not necessarily contradict Sennett's basic idea.

Sennett and Hochschild share a fundamentally pessimistic view on the logic and change dynamics of contemporary capitalism. We might even say that their theoretical contributions can be read as extensions or "updates" of the 19th century's bleak sociological diagnoses of modern work life, with Marx's concept of alienation and Durkheim's concept of anomie constantly lurking in the background.

In view of the positive, general developments in the form, content and physical demands of work activities over the last 30–40 years, however, one could question the one-sidedness of these mainly pessimistic portrayals (Jacobsen 2007). With respect to Hochschild's analysis, one could ask whether the paradigmatic efforts made by modern corporations to render work activities more attractive only have negative consequences for

family and work

working parents, or if there is a more positive side to the story as well. Likewise, it remains somewhat unclear in Sennett's writings exactly why continuity and a long-term career perspective are core elements in acquiring a good and healthy human character.

Both theoretical contributions are, in other words, based on implicit ideas about the true, naturally given conditions of human existence. In Hochschild's work this is reflected in a wish to reinstate the cultural boundary between the social values of work and family and to preserve family life as the primary sphere of meaningful human actualisation. In Sennett's writings, we find this implicit normative foundation in the idea of capitalism's development as a movement away from authentic and meaningful production forms.

Whether one buys into these implicit normative premises or not, Sennett and Hochschild provide important observations and reminders of the hidden dangers and adverse effects of a flexible and limitless work culture. Indeed, as rapid technological advancements dissolve the spatial boundaries between work and private life, these reminders seem more topical than ever.

chapter 11

Gender, body and identity

Butler and Haraway

Since the dawn of sociology, the question of gender has occupied sociologists and, as an analytical category, the concept has changed and developed dynamically over time, along with society and our conceptions of family and work. Gender runs as a thematic thread through many micro- and macrosociological theories and sociological frameworks, including those outlined in this book. Though early sociology held a largely functionalist view of gender and gender roles (Durkheim and later Luhmann), postwar sociologists, for instance, sought a thematic understanding of sexuality as a matter of subject-related categories of normality and abnormality (Foucault), or conceived notions of gender and body according to power and dominance relations (Bourdieu). Elsewhere, gender and sexuality have served as thematic prisms for sociological reflections on the challenges and requirements for identity and social relations in late modern society (Giddens, Bauman and Beck).

Since the 1970s, however, gender has held a place in sociology as a specific, albeit cross-disciplinarily grounded field of study, not least due to significant theoretical contributions from Judith Butler (1956–) and Donna Haraway (1944–). They are both highly interdisciplinary in their work, and neither comes, or works, from a strictly sociological background. Butler's educational background and training is in philosophy, Haraway's in zoology, philosophy and biology; but both have produced theoretical works on gender studies of high sociological impact and, in

gender, body and identity

Haraway's case, of great influence on the philosophy of sociological science and history.

The first part of this chapter presents Butler's postmodern, anti-essentialist theory of gender as a social construct and her view of gender as something "one does" rather than something "one is". This is followed by a presentation of Haraway's highly influential cyborg figuration and her theoretical notion of "situated knowledge" (Haraway 1988). Finally, we juxtapose Butler's social constructivism with Haraway's transgression of it.

Butler and Haraway have developed their theoretical apparatuses more or less concurrently since the 1980s with the shared ambition to transgress the nature/culture dichotomy (materiality/discourse) and the division between biological and sociocultural gender. Both are occupied with the processes of conceptual origin, both aim to deconstruct social categorisations that may otherwise lead to exclusionary positions and practices, and both do so based on a fundamental assumption that change is both desirable and indeed possible.

Butler: "doing" gender

> What continues to concern me most is the following kinds of questions: what will and will not constitute an intelligible life, and how do presumptions about normative gender and sexuality determine in advance what will qualify as the "human" and the "livable"? In other words, how do normative gender presumptions work to delimit the very field of description that we have for the human? What is the means by which we come to see this delimiting power, and what are the means by which we transform it?
>
> (Butler 1999: xxii)

These questions, posed by Judith Butler in *Gender Trouble*, are among her hallmark reflections on gender, sexuality and identity. They play a prominent part in her most renowned books which, along with *Gender Trouble* (1999), include *Bodies That Matter* (1993) and *Undoing Gender* (2004b). Butler has written extensively on other topics such as kin, race, identity, politics and violence, but we will focus on these keystone works and on gender, body and performativity. Throughout her writings, Butler consistently raises more questions than answers. This is in line with her theoretical point and methodology: just as we must understand the creation of gender, identity and subject as "an ongoing discursive practice [which is] open to intervention and resignification" (Butler 1999: 43), we must consider our analyses and our questions to be fundamentally processual. Our analyses and our questions are not means to achieve ultimate "truths"

180   gender, body and identity

about ourselves, society or reality, but rather methods for challenging and deconstructing such fixed "truths" that support extant, dominant power structures.

In this, Butler follows Hegel's dialectical approach: Every thesis must be countered by an antithesis in order to reach new, "truer" understandings of the world. Butler, so to speak, forms dialectic "syntheses" only to immediately counter each synthesis with a new antithesis, in a continuous loop. Final truths are not merely unattainable; they are, says Butler, undemocratic. The point is exactly that fixed truths often result in ideological certainty and are used as justification for undermining certain categories of identity, e.g. homosexuality. Butler challenges established gender categories. Drawing theoretically on Foucault, she utilises his genealogical method of analysis to investigate how dominant conceptions of gender are formed and how they change over time in a continual, circular process. This process may also uncover other discursive conceptualisations of gender (Butler 1999; Salih 2002).

The genealogical method, in the Foucauldian sense, is a historical, interpretive method of analysis that breaks with the traditional idea of history as an ongoing progression of acts of rationality. The method aims to uncover relations of power and arrive at a historical understanding of who we are. According to Foucault, the discourses of a society create individuals, rather than the other way around (Foucault 1984). Foucault's work has a strong influence on Butler, which reflects in her conceptual point that gender, along with other marks of identity, are always produced through discourse. In fact, says Butler, "it becomes impossible to separate out 'gender' from the political and cultural intersections in which it is invariably produced and maintained" (Butler 1999: 6).

Butler is fundamentally inspired by poststructuralist thought in philosophy and psychoanalysis, and she draws theoretically from Jacques Lacan, Jacques Derrida, Louis Althusser and feminist thinkers such as Julia Kristeva, Simone de Beauvoir, Monique Wittig and Luce Irigaray. It is from within this eclectic theoretical framework that Butler finds her own unique theoretical positions.

In order to understand Butler's main thesis about gender as a construction and performative concept (Butler 1993; 1999; 2004a), we must begin with the following questions: What constitutes or creates gender? How can we understand biological gender (*sex*) versus socio-cultural gender (*gender*)? What does Butler mean when she says that "gender is always a doing, though not a doing by a subject who might be said to preexist the deed"? (Butler 1999: 33).

Let us consider an example: Nina Lykke describes how arguments in the 19th century against women's enrolment in universities tended to focus almost exclusively on the biological nature of women. If a woman

gender, body and identity

were to partake in academic pursuits, the argument went, it would result in barrenness and infertility for the woman, because her precious and limited energy would be redirected from her uterus to her brain. By using her brain, she would dry out her womb. Such examples of "biological determinism" show how biological arguments can come to naturalise and fix "the" female nature and how biology may be used to legitimise gender differences and exclusionary practices. One's biological sex, in other words, can be used to define one's sociocultural gender and thus one's place in "the hierarchical gender order of society". Early feminism sought a way out of such deterministic and gender conservative frameworks by calling for the necessary distinction between biological and sociocultural gender. Or simply put, feminism called for the separation of nature and culture to do away with oppression of women and the notion of "biology-is-destiny" (Butler 1999: 9; Lykke 2010: 22–25).

Butler criticises such classic – and here somewhat simplified – variants of feminism and argues that they only maintain the notion of biological gender as a prediscursive and naturally established fact that only leaves us with "two biological genders, of which social genders are interpretations" (Stormhøj 1999: 57). Butler rejects this sex-gender tradition and criticises classic feminism's focus on "women" and its use of the term as a joint term of identity that takes all women to be alike (Stormhøj 1999: 56–57). In *Gender Trouble* (1999), Butler makes a significant critical argument against feminist views of the "woman" as a universal subject that were championed by political feminists throughout the 1980s. These views were also strongly criticised by black, gay, queer and postcolonial feminists, many of whom argued that traditional feminism, by taking the "woman" as its archetypical "oppressed subjected", ignored differences between women and thus (oppressive) categories like ethnicity, class and race (Lykke 2010: 32–33).

When classic feminism uses the category of the "woman" as a unitary political subject, says Butler, the ironic consequence may be that it offers little more than a misrepresentation. The effect of this categorisation is reproduction of extant conditions for women rather than liberation and diversity. The central point here is that identity categories such as gender are always the result rather than the cause of discourses, institutions and practices. While Butler is critical of the predefined categories of identity politics, she is not convinced that they can be avoided, any more than we are able to stand outside the field of power. Any theoretical criticism must start from what Marx called the "historical present" (Marx quoted in Butler 1999: 44) and must investigate and address, through genealogical analysis, those power structures that retain exclusionary practices through fixed identity categories (Butler 1999).

Butler poses the following rhetorical question: Does feminism not, through its adherence to normalising identity categories, serve to objectify and reify gender within "the heterosexual matrix" (Butler 1999: 9) in exactly such a way as to defeat its own purpose of liberation? In an interview with *Radical Philosophy* (1994: 32), Butler says of *Gender Trouble* that it is primarily addressed to feminists and that its main purpose is a fundamental critique of feminism's dominant focus on implicit and obligatory heterosexuality in research. Butler, in her own words, seeks to cause "gender trouble" in order to problematise exactly the (re)production of gender categories as stable and universal entities and the heterosexual matrix. This matrix covers the dominant, cultural understanding of gender as the biological categories man and woman that governs the socially stable genders, the masculine man and the feminine woman (Butler 1999). This binary distinction maintains the heteronormative idea that men desire women and women desire men, which, as Butler writes in her 1999 introduction to *Gender Trouble*, may cause sexual "minority practices", e.g. homosexuality, to be seen as "unthinkable" and even "illegitimate" (1999: viii).

Gender Trouble is thus a normative statement that aims to expand our possibilities and ability to perform gender and sexuality, without suggesting normative practices or frameworks for how to do so (Butler 1999). Indeed, Butler's work has been criticised for being strongly deconstructive and for failing or neglecting to offer new theory or suggestions in place of what is removed and rejected. However, Butler raises a fundamental, post-structural point against this criticism: Normative judgments are themselves malleable and subject to change; we are not able to produce ultimate, unchangeable or final lists of criteria and requirements for how to resist and undermine dominant cultural forces of oppression; any attempt to fix or dictate specific criteria for normative subversion will – and always should be bound to – fail (Butler 1999: xxi). Butler does not posit criteria for doing gender, for that would defeat the purpose.

As mentioned earlier, Butler draws on the theoretical work of Simone de Beauvoir (1908–1986), who in *The Second Sex* (1949) outlines her view of gender as a construction: "one is not born a woman, but, rather, becomes one" (as quoted in Butler 1999: 8). The view of gender as something we do, rather than something we are, says Butler, is also a view of the body as "a historical situation" and of gender identity as something that is not fixed or given, but rather created through a "stylized repetition of acts" (Butler 1988: 519). Simone de Beauvoir focuses on sociocultural gender and its discursive aspects, and Butler expands her theory in two key areas. First, she is interested not just in sociocultural gender but, along with it, the notion of biological gender or sex

gender, body and identity   183

and its materiality. Second, she rejects Beauvoir's thesis that doing gender is an action that can only be undertaken by a subject that already exists. In *Gender Trouble*, Butler argues that Beauvoir's account of sociocultural gender does not actually require that the individual who becomes woman by doing gender be of the female sex; nor, says Butler, does Beauvoir's account show that such doings of gender should be considered the results of biology or biological predispositions. Butler rejects the notion of biology as a prediscursive and stable "fact" of gender. Biology, she says, is not a fixed entity and it is not clear whether we are to interpret it as something "natural, anatomical, chromosomal or hormonal" (Butler 1999: 10).

Biological gender, says Butler, cannot simply be defined as a binary, oppositional pair, as is evident for example in the case of transgendered and agendered persons. In her view, it would "make no sense, then, to define gender as the cultural interpretation of sex, if sex itself is a gendered category", which is produced, delimited and kept in its sociocultural place as a binary, oppositional pair (Højgaard 2012: 284). The gendered body, in other words, is not a stable or predetermined structure. Rather, it is a sign of the sedimentation of gender norms over time, through regulating practices (Butler 1993).

Gender Trouble, and Butler's attempt to transgress the sex-gender distinction and the gap between materiality and discourse, was taken by many as a negation of bodily materiality in favour of gender as a performative and active choice, which would allow for identity to be constructed and deconstructed at will. According to Butler, *Bodies That Matter* (1993) was a reaction to this reading and an attempt to revisit exactly the notion of biological gender and the topic of body materiality (Butler 1994). This leads us to Simone de Beauvoir's thesis that gender requires an acting subject. Butler rejects this view and calls for a way to "formulate a project that preserves gender practices as sites for critical agency" (1993: x) that does not take gender to be a choice but rather something that is constituted through the materialisation of regulating norms. Butler's own proposition for such a project is outlined in her performative theory of gender.

Gender and performativity

Since her earliest writings, Butler has worked towards a theory for the performative construction of gender and the performative constitution of cultural norms which both inhibit and facilitate our actions and our doing of gender (Butler 2004a). Her theory is already presented in the article "Performative Acts and Gender Constitution" (Butler 1988) and refined in later works such as *Bodies That Matter* (1993).

Performativity must be understood not as a singular or deliberate "act", but, rather, as the reiterative and citational practice by which discourse produces the effects that it names.

(Butler 1993: 2)

We are all, says Butler, perpetually performing gender through dominant gender norms, just as we perform everything else through the gestures and stylistics of our bodies (Butler 2004a: 344). She invokes the performative element of the theatre metaphor to illustrate how we present ourselves dramaturgically to others and why we act as we do (see Goffman 1959, and Chapter 9 of this book). To grasp the performative theory of gender, we must follow Butler in distinguishing between performativity and performance – the latter is to be understood as an important aspect of performativity, but the very notion of performing one's gender may lead us to think, wrongly, that performing gender is tied to the actions of particular individuals, who are simply deciding on or selecting their own gender through their act. But performativity is exactly the notion that dominant discourses and gender norms provide both the conditions and limitations of those very processes that create and cement gender. A theatre play, Butler reminds us, is not simply free performance or freely chosen actions but rather interpretations, the performance, of clearly designated stage instructions, roles and lines. It requires an existing manuscript as well as an interpretation by individual performers to properly perform the play (Butler 1988; 2004a).

Performativity, then, is not to be understood as a series of isolated actions and events performed by individuals, but rather as an ongoing praxis of citation wherein gender becomes "an effect of culturally regulated, discursive practices which, by the very process of regulation, create that which they regulate" (Højgaard 2012: 288). In order to understand how discourses create what they address, Butler draws on Foucault's idea that (productive) power constitutes bodies, as well as Derrida's revision of Austin's speech act theory. According to Austin, any performative utterance must be the cause of a direct effect or action. An example is the wedding ceremony and the statement "I now pronounce you ...", where the statement is also that action that joins the couple in marriage. To Derrida, however, the new situation is not brought about due to the intentions of the individual performing the speech act, but rather due to the very citation of extant authorities (Butler 1993; Stormhøj 1999). Butler illustrates this point with the legal system and the judge, whose speech acts carry direct, observable and binding effects, but not due to the will of the individual judge as a person, but rather because judges are verbal invocations of the written law (Butler 1993: 225).

gender, body and identity

185

Similarly, Butler views gender as something that is created by a repeated practice of citation of established gender norms in a way that mirrors Althusser's notion of interpellation (see Chapter 6). Butler uses the idea of being "called on" to adopt certain subject positions to illustrate how biological sex and bodies are not irreducible entities, but materialise in and are shaped by discourse. As an example of medicinal interpellation, Butler mentions those calls for subject positions that we often make when a child is born: "It's a girl!", "It's a boy!" Such interpellations, says Butler, serve performatively to posit a binary, gendered categorisation of gender; they are repeated continuously over time by multiple authorities as a way "to reinforce or contest this naturalized effect" (Butler 1993: 8; Salih 2002).

If this process of materialisation is indeed established over time, and if it does indeed result in the ongoing consolidation of cultural norms within the heterosexual matrix, how can we imagine that change or action is possible at all? How can we broaden our conceptual field of how to perform, and think about, gender and other categories of identity? Such questions, to Butler, are matters of subjectivation and the processes that drive it. They are also questions of "resignification" – the reassignment of new meanings to concepts and discourses. The continual, performative citation of so many concurrent and coexisting norms and discourses is bound to result in mistakes, errors and failed attempts at repetition and citation. The numerous existing discourses and norms are the perpetual subjects of a continual flow of new variations, of "stylised repetitions" (Butler 1988: 520) and parody, which seek to bring about resignification, potential subversion and reconstructions of identity (Butler 1999; Højgaard 2012). In *Bodies that Matter*, Butler draws on the concept of *queer*, which collective opposition has changed from a derogatory term for "pathologised sexuality" (1993: 223) into a positive and affirming category of identity.

As mentioned, Butler thinks that "gender is always a doing, though not a doing by a subject who might be said to preexist the deed" (Butler 1999: 33), and she strives, with her performative theory of gender, to approach an understanding of how change is brought about. But given that Butler holds that there is no such thing as an "I" or an "us" who can be held responsible for performing gender, how can we maintain a sense of critical action that does not merely end up as a form of cultural determinism? (Butler 1993). This, we will look at next.

Butler's constructivist approach to gender is an attempt at finding a theoretical path between the constituted and constitutive subject, between determinism and autonomy and between structure and agency.

As a public action and performative act, gender is not a radical choice or project that reflects a merely individual choice, but neither is it imposed or inscribed upon the individual, as some post-structuralist displacements of the subject would contend.

(Butler 1988: 526)

Starting from Foucault's theories of subjectivation and productive power, Butler sets out to show how we as individuals are both constituted and constitute our own selves, as subjects locked in a continual process of becoming, within a specific historical and discursive framework. This process of constitution is double-sided. On the one hand, we are subjected to – and the subjects of – dominant cultural discourses and norms that define our cultural conceptions of gender and gender identity constructions. On the other hand, we come into being as subjects exactly by challenging and negotiating our way through possible subject positions within the framework. It is a central aspect of Butler's critical position that it spans the deconstruction of apparently essential identity constructs and the subject's subversion of them (Butler 1999; Højgaard 2012). It is this double-sided process that is encompassed within Butler's performative theory of gender.

Haraway: "organisms are not born, but they are made" – between fact and fiction

I am neither a naturalist, nor a social constructivist. Neither-nor. This is not social constructionism, and it is not technoscientific, or biological determinism. It is not nature. It is not culture. It is truly about a serious historical effort to get elsewhere.

(Haraway 2004a: 330)

With her interdisciplinary approach to the history of feminist science and criticism, Donna Haraway is not an easy theoretician to pin down as a thinker. She seeks to break with established categories and existing boundaries between social constructs (culture/discourse) and natural objects (nature/materiality) and, like Butler, she is concerned with the boundary between sociocultural gender and biological sex. But while Butler's main focus is on discursive practices rather than biological sex, Haraway's background in biology and natural sciences lends her a different perspective and a stronger focus on the material aspects of gender, which do not occupy Butler to the same extent. Haraway does not wish to neglect or reject the physical body as a prediscursive fact in her theoretical work. Her position is one of body materialism, which takes body and subject as concepts that must always be considered together – biology is not simply a "blank page for social inscriptions", nor is it a matter of (or cause for) pure biological determinism (Haraway 1988: 591; Lykke 2010).

gender, body and identity

187

In a play on Simone de Beauvoir's words about women not being born as women, Haraway suggests that "organisms are not born, but they are made" (2004c: 67); organisms, she says, are made both by human and nonhuman actors, through technoscientific and discursive practices, in different places and at different times, and nature is created both as fiction and as fact (semiotics and materiality) in a singular transgression of the nature/culture dichotomy. Although objects of knowledge are continuously formed and created in a process of technological and social implosion which may be subject to scientific enquiry, biological organisms continuously materialise in their embodied forms as material facts that we do not fully control. Haraway uses the term "material-semiotic actor" (Haraway 2004c: 67) to refer to the ontological duality embedded in these processes, and in the intertwinement and interdependence of technocultural discourse and biological materiality (Haraway 2000; 2004c). She is concerned with the material/semiotic dichotomy and what she calls "the apparatus of bodily production" (2004c: 67) – the body as an object of scientific enquiry which is created through dominant discursive practices. But the body is also created in an interplay between discursive practices and technoscientific intervention and is, simultaneously, a material matter that we can never fully control (Haraway 2004c). Haraway's ambition to transgress extant dichotomies in order to "get somewhere else" is reflected in her epistemological view of scientific knowledge as being situated.

Situated knowledge

> Relativism and totalization are both "god tricks" promising vision from everywhere and nowhere equally and fully, common myths in rhetorics surrounding Science. But it is precisely in the politics and epistemology of partial perspectives that the possibility of sustained, rational, objective inquiry rests. So with many other feminists, I want to argue for a doctrine and practice of objectivity that privileges contestation, deconstruction, webbed connections, and hope for transformation of systems of knowledge and ways of seeing. But not just any partial perspective will do; we must be hostile to easy relativisms and holisms built out of summing and subsuming parts.
>
> (Haraway 1988: 584–585)

The above excerpt appears in "Situated Knowledges: the Science Question in Feminism and the Privilege of Partial Perspective" (1988), one of Haraway's most influential works. Originally a reply to feminist philosopher of science Sandra Harding, whose book *The Science Question in*

Feminism (1986) strongly problematised feminist scientific criticism, "Situated Knowledges" offers a thematic discussion of our concepts of scientific objectivity and knowledge. Haraway joins a broader discussion between proponents of realist and constructivist theories of science that extend far beyond feminist literature: the former claim that reality is objectively and exhaustively describable, whereas the latter hold that reality (realities) are merely social constructs (Hastrup 1992: 55). The question – and possibility – of objective knowledge is a fundamental theme of cultural and scientific history, and it has always been a special theme for feminist philosophers of science.

In "Situated Knowledges" Haraway sketches the thematic divide between the realist and constructivist paradigm as a matter of "feminist critical empiricism" on the one side versus "radical constructivism" on the other (Haraway 1988: 580). Feminist critical empiricism insists that it is possible, through extant empirical practices, to produce objective descriptions of reality that are indeed legitimate and true. The feminist critical empiricist, for example, holds that it is a true fact that by increasing the number of women that hold research positions and positions of academia and science, it is possible to infuse academia and science with a fundamental female perspective and experience and thus, objectively, reduce the degree of scientific androcentrism in the fields. Against this view, radical constructivism argues that we must always reject universalising and essentialist narratives about e.g. the "woman" (see e.g. this chapter's introduction on Butler) and that we must turn away from purportedly "objective" descriptions and final "truths" if we wish to effect change. This position has been criticised for being relativistic in the sense that all stories, narratives and interpretations of reality are equally allowable and, in principle, all equally good or bad.

Haraway sees both relativism and totalisation as examples of what she calls the "god trick" – the illusion that there is a neutral and objective scientific view that resides "nowhere and everywhere". Haraway erects a new doctrine for objectivity, which she believes to be better able to account for the "radical historical contingency" and create "a critical practice for recognising our own 'semiotic technologies' for making meanings" and which is obligated to deliver "faithful accounts of a 'real' world" (Haraway 1988: 579).

In other words, Haraway's goal is to redefine the concept of objectivity, so as to produce trustworthy and obligating stories about real, problematic circumstances without ending up in the morass of total relativism and without being reduced to power games and "positivist arrogance"; her ambition is to allow for all such stories of science to be told, be they concerned with social classes, elementary particles or race or anything

gender, body and identity 189

else (Haraway 1988: 579–580; Markussen and Gad 2007). To Haraway, science itself is a practice of story-telling practice" and she also considers herself to be a theoretical and scientific storyteller. As a storyteller, the scientist is never "outside of" her field of research – she is not observing it from some distant vantage point of supreme objectivity and clarity which allows her to produce fitting meta-narratives of what goes on "inside" the field she is describing. Rather, she is always a situated part of her own field and story; she is engaged in and part of the story created within her field, just as we are perpetually situated within certain material and discursive (power) relations. The scientist, her view, perspective and knowledge, then, is always a situated and particular one. It is only by acknowledging our own situation, says Haraway, that we can achieve even a partially objective view of reality, by becoming aware of our own position and place within it (Haraway 1988; Haraway and Williams 2010).

Haraway insists on wrestling the scientific view from its metaphoric vantage point of "everywhere and nowhere" and returning it to a situated position, turning it into "views from somewhere" (1988: 590). The situated view, the view from somewhere, is not meant to denote simply a particular physical location any more than situated knowledge is meant to denote a particular subject or identity position. It is not a matter of being in, or seeing from, a particular physical location; nor is it a matter of being, or seeing as, a particular physical person or identity. We are not, says Haraway, "immediately present to ourselves" (1988: 585). Nor is the situated view neutral, or innocent or immune to interpretations. The very matter of "seeing" is always, fundamentally, also a matter of having "the power to see" (1988: 585): By occupying or assuming certain positions, we exclude or marginalise other positions in turn. Haraway often explores such positions of otherness in her works, by drawing on metaphorical and figurative representatives of "others". For example, "The Promises of Monsters: a Regenerative Politics for Inappropriate/d Others" assigns the position of the excluded or marginalised "other" to actual monsters (Haraway 2004c; Højgaard 2007).

Haraway draws on feminist thinker Trinh Minh-Ha's notion of "inappropriate/d others" in a way that adopts the intended double meaning of the term: She wishes to talk both about those who are deemed inappropriate because they will not submit to dominant categories of identity, and those who are unappropriated because they do not belong to any specific "taxon" but remain in critical opposition to dominant hierarchies. Haraway draws on the term to challenge uniformity and create new stories through a process she refers to as diffraction.

Diffraction is an optical metaphor that Haraway seeks to put in place of metaphorical reflection. Reflection is the production of patterns of light that are shifted from, but identical to, the source of light; diffraction turns

190   gender, body and identity

a source of light into new and different patterns and produces interference. In physics, diffraction is the process that takes place when waves of light pass through narrow openings and break into different patterns of interference. Haraway uses diffraction as a metaphor for critical awareness; she seeks to discover new, complex patterns and connections of reality by diffracting its objects, its sources of light. Her ambition is to effect change by "making visible those things that are lost in the object" (Haraway 2000: 101–105; 2004c).

With regard to the situated view, Haraway proposes a doctrine for objectivity which, as mentioned, is fuelled by deconstruction, passionate construction and new intertwinements; she seeks better scientific practices and, ultimately, a better description of reality. Rational knowledge, she holds, can only be attained by a scientific process that is entirely open to continual, ongoing criticism and interpretation. Such a scientific practice must be open to multiple, partial views, vantage points and positions; if it is, it may allow a new and broadened understanding of science and reality. Situated knowledge, to Haraway, is not an individual exercise but a collective effort to obtain "objectivity as positioned rationality" (Haraway 1988: 590).

Haraway's approach to the concept of situated knowledge is apparent in her works, such as "The Promises of Monsters" where she, through extensive analysis of the artefactuality of the technoscientific world, seeks to map out what we mean by, and take to be, the concept of "nature". She does so in an attempt to get to "somewhere else", to somewhere where nature is not objectified and retained as a conceptual "otherness" as viewed through the lens of colonialism, racism and class domination, for instance (2004c). By seeing the world as consisting of material-semiotic actors, Haraway avoids seeing objects as passive entities waiting to be subjected to "the view from nowhere" (1988: 581) and is able to approach them as active agents. A recurrent ambition in Haraway's work is to explore the possibility of getting elsewhere and challenging existing, dominant histories of creation and identity categories. Her aim and purpose is to propose a continual, ongoing, contrasted, complex and ambiguous exploration of being and the potential for new, and other, stories (Haraway 2004a).

Through her criticism of science and culture, Haraway investigates how we may bring about change. She does so primarily by challenging and deconstructing established dichotomies such as nature/culture, nature/society and subject/object and questioning rational discourses and Western cultural understandings of e.g. race, gender and class.

Haraway uses biology as a lens for exploring the question of what counts as nature, what counts as culture and what draws and defines the borders between the two. She does not see biology as an isolated field,

gender, body and identity

but as a discipline that is deeply intertwined with political and semiotic practices and closely tied to literature, history and anthropology. She is concerned, always, with fact and fiction and her work addresses cultural phenomena and technoscientific interventions such as gene technology (Haraway 1997), the immune system (1991), embryos (2004b) and dog breeding (2008). Among her many cultural and technological metaphors for her theoretical work, none is more known or more renowned than her cyborg figuration, which we will look at below.

The cyborg as a feminist figuration

To Haraway, a figuration is a narrative figure or metaphor which is used as a tool for the analytic deconstruction of established conceptual pairs such as nature/culture, man/machine and self/other. A figuration is neither culture nor nature, but is situated somewhere between what is real and what is imagined, between fact and fiction. Crucially, figurations serve both as criticism of current situations and as vision for alternative identities that may be realised. They are embedded in current societal structures of power and hierarchy and serve as indications of potential opposition.

Among Haraway's figurations we find the cyborg, the coyote, the OncoMouse™ (a patented, genetically modified laboratory mouse), the Female-Man and other nonhuman primates. The primate, for example, is used to open the categories of animal/man, the cyborg is used against the dichotomy of machine/organism and OncoMouse is used to explore the conceptual pair of nature/work. Trinh Minh-Ha's "inappropriate/d others" and Judith Butler's "queer" are other examples of feminist figurations. All Haraway's figurations serve as ironic confusions of our existing sense of logic and the world. Their purpose is to illustrate that concepts such as gender, body, nature and culture are not universal or naturally decided facts but constructs that can be changed and influenced (Haraway 2000; 2004a; Lykke 2010). In a certain sense, such figurations serve the same purpose as Goffman's use of metaphors; his metaphor of the theatre gives us a method to abolish those common-sense understandings of how and what reality is that usually guide our thinking. Its purpose is to allow for a new way of thinking and thus for a new way of sensing and seeing connections (see Chapter 9). Haraway uses figurations as similar tools of thought, although she holds that they are not merely metaphors but also products of our lived, material reality (Haraway 1991: 150).

Tasked with the deconstruction of categories and classifications on the one hand, and with avoiding a total reduction of meaning on the other, we are, says Haraway, locked in a constant methodological dilemma.

First of all, categories are never entirely "frozen" or static, and the world and its goings-on are much more complex than we imagine. Second, we cannot simply begin to disrupt, disturb and define existing categories without paying very close attention to the categories that we use as tools to do so; choosing one category as a tool over any other, after all, is itself a material act that also involves choosing one sense of meaning over any other. Third, Haraway is not in the business of using categories – what she refers to as "thinking technologies", e.g. diffraction – to bring about theoretical clarity or reduce complexity. Rather, her aim is to highlight the complexity of relations, connections and processes of creation to produce "thick descriptions" of the many necessary conditions for the existence and creation of biological and technoscientific phenomena (Haraway 2004a).

Haraway has repeatedly emphasised that she prefers verbs over nouns in her theoretical vocabulary; she seeks to avoid unnecessary naming and fixation of the phenomena she investigates, because giving processes and entities a name is in a sense a step on the way to fixating and delimiting that which is investigated. This is true whether we speak of nouns such as "the human", "the animal" or "the social", with the latter often being interpreted only under the terms and conditions of the former (Latour is a noteworthy exception, see Chapter 12). The use of nouns, says Haraway, may cause us to ignore complex interactions and networks in our biogenetic and technological age and may blind us to interactions between the human and the nonhuman, between organisms and technology. In short, Haraway prefers verbs, words of action and doing, over nouns and names because she seeks to describe "doing worlds" (Haraway 2000; 2004a; Haraway and Gane 2006: 143).

The cyborg is a classic example of transgressing dichotomies such as human/nonhumans and organism/machine, for which progress and development in biology, evolutionary theory, micro-electronics, information technology and biotechnology have paved the way. But it has also provided the very foundation for our systems of power and modern technoscience in general: A cyborg is a cybernetic organism or a hybrid between organism and machine. Body and technology have come to be so intertwined that it no longer makes sense to pretend that there is a meaningful distinction between natural and artificial or, ultimately, between nature and culture (Haraway 1991).

The cyborg appears for the first time in Haraway's celebrated 1985 essay "A Cyborg Manifesto: Science, Technology and Socialist-Feminism in the Late Twentieth Century". In 1983, following the presidency of Ronald Reagan and the declining influence of the political left, *The Socialist Review* invited Haraway and other feminist thinkers to give their

gender, body and identity

views on the future of socialist feminism. Haraway produced the Cyborg Manifesto, but The Socialist Review East Coast Collective considered it too controversial and declined to publish it. It was well received by The Berkeley Socialist Review Collective, which published it in 1985. The cyborg is not an ahistoric artefact; it is a product of, and embedded in, a reality marked by certain historical conditions and grand concepts, such as militarisation, Big Science, patriarchy, information technology and post-WW2 theoretical attempts at understanding these new and complex sociotechnological interactions and their effect on women, in particular (Haraway 2000; 2004a).

The Cyborg Manifesto presents two central arguments: First, it rejects all forms of purportedly universal theory, e.g. classic feminism's categorisation of "woman" as a universal subject (see Butler above), as unsatisfactory descriptions of reality in all its complexity. Haraway seeks to do away with politics and categories of identity that are based on essential units and properties rather than affinity.

Second, the Cyborg Manifesto is an argument for critical consideration of sociotechnological interactions, as only deliberate and critical consideration can make possible the deconstruction (and reconstruction) of extant, dominant and oppressive boundaries and structures.

Although the cyborg is always a product of its time, it has theoretical potential in other contexts. It has served as concrete reference for feminist thought, to show that things may be different than previously assumed (Lykke 2010); and it serves as a starting point for investigating the fusion of body and technology and its implications for our view of gender and identity (Haraway 2004a). Such fusions are seen, quite concretely, in assisted reproduction (artificial insemination), where reproductive technologies now make it impossible to distinguish between the personal, political and technological and, ultimately, between nature and culture. Identity, body, specific reproductive technologies for fertility treatment and specific political and judicial measures to decide what treatments can and cannot be offered, and to whom, are all fused together in this new process of turning particular individuals into parents. Reproductive technologies disrupt and change our understanding of how we are made, and of categories such as family and kin. The parent category, for example, can now be extended to account for the fact that any one child may have up to five parents: the egg donor (the genetic mother), the sperm donor (the genetic father), a surrogate mother who gestates the child, and the social parents who are considered to be mum and dad (Golombok 2005: 9). Such possibilities change and redefine our way of thinking and doing family as well as categories that we thought were natural and fixed (see Thompson 2005).

Discourse and materiality

As illustrated in this chapter, the theoretical works of Judith Butler and Donna Haraway are shaped by different scientific backgrounds and different theoretical sources of inspiration and tradition. Their different "situations" have shaped the theoretical lenses through which they view feminist themes such as gender, body, science and identity. But their shared focus is on processes of becoming and both are concerned with the question of how certain categories and phenomena come to be constituted and stabilised in our conceptualisation of reality and how to challenge our idea that certain things are essential, naturally given or "fixed". Both seek to deconstruct ready-made and solidified binary distinctions between prevalent conceptual pairs, and both reject the distinction between sociocultural gender and biological gender.

Butler's *Gender Trouble* and Haraway's "Cyborg Manifesto" criticise classic feminism and its focus on woman as a singular subject and identity politics that emphasise similarities over differences in a way that brings about exclusive categorisations and practices. Their theoretical approaches share an implicit desire and vision for change and an ambition to break established and universal categories such as gender, class and race when they cause inequality and exclusion.

Butler is strongly influenced by poststructuralist thinkers and is against creating or establishing new normative frameworks and criteria for subversion. She does not wish to end up in the very position that she rejects, and she believes that normative frameworks and criteria are themselves subject to change; she seeks to expand, not regulate, our potential field for how to think and do gender. Haraway is somewhat more critical and seeks to offer clearer and more sharply drawn alternatives for how to define human and nonhuman agents and the conditions of their existence. She presents a doctrine for feminist objectivity in the shape of "situated knowledge", which offers a way to commit to descriptions of real, problematic circumstances and affairs through the use of feminist figurations such as the cyborg. Such figurations are, as described, "objective materialities" but also serve as visions or propositions of an imagined reality and alternative identity categories.

This intertwinement of fact and fiction, of the material and the semiotic, is a consistent theme in Haraway's body of work; it is a fusion that serves to disrupt and deconstruct extant boundaries between what we conceive as nature/culture, man/machine and self/other. Where Butler's approach to the discursive practices that establish gender remains essentially social-constructivist as she does not specifically address the "agency of bodily matter" (Lykke 2010: 120), Haraway sees the body as a material, living

gender, body and identity 195

fact – a matter of agency of bodily matter that is never passive or static and never in our complete control.

Despite their differences, Butler and Haraway seem to share an ontological foundation in the idea that objects of science are always products of both material and discursive processes of creation. Gender is not something "one is", but something "one does", just as "organisms are not born, but made". This is the common ground, the shared point of departure, in the theoretical works of Butler and Haraway: Gender and other identity categories are products of material and discursive processes in different cultural and historical contexts.

chapter 12

Factish and fetish

Latour and Žižek

In the attempt to explain the social, sociology has always emphasised the significance of distinctions and breaks. In the beginning, Auguste Comte (1798–1857) was concerned with creating a social science that broke with the religious world picture. To him, sociology was a purely scientific investigation of the common. This did not only represent an epistemological break in which a scientific horizon was staged as a possible replacement of a cosmic or religious horizon. The break also had an ontological character: Sociology was born as people started to acknowledge that they form their own world. But it was not only the loss of faith in an intervening and creative God that gave place to sociology. Our increasing independence of nature, both the inner and the outer, also played an important role. These breaks rendered visible the key object of sociology: society.

The sociological conception of society also brought along new distinctions – between nature and culture, subject and object, the material and the conceptual, past and future, active and passive, knowledge and superstition – that all contributed to distil and delimit the social and thereby also society. Regardless of whether the social is conceived of as what explains or what needs explaining, the idea is that the social exists in its own right. Therefore, it is distinctively different from material objects, from nature, and from that which is attributed entirely to the individual.

The invention of the concept of the social and society has made it possible for us to understand ourselves, think and function in new ways. But if we ask the theorists introduced in this chapter, Bruno Latour and Slavoj Žižek, such concepts are not without problems. They might help us understand how we think about the social and society and perhaps also modernity. However, they hide as much as they reveal. By using such concepts, we risk reifying the social, and we lose sight of how the social is supported by and interacts with what we might identify as the "nonsocial" – it becomes a thing existing "out there".

For more than thirty years, the conception of pure sociality has been strongly criticised within sociology. Scholars have defined this form of critique as "the material turn" (Pierides and Woodman 2012). The material turn does not refer to a sociology of things (material objects and nature-like types of dwelling, conveying systems or landscapes), but rather to a form of sociology that allows things and non-things, human and nonhuman actors, to interact in networks without having their relation reduced to distinctions between things (subject and object, matter and idea, the active and the passive).

In this chapter, we will discuss this material turn from two perspectives. First, we introduce French sociologist Bruno Latour, who attempts to make room for the object and the material in his sociology. Latour is the most significant exponent of the so-called actor network theory (ANT), which represents an entirely new way of thinking about the social and society. Slovenian thinker Slavoj Žižek, like Latour, undermines the empire of subject and society, but from the "inside". Society does not exist, and we are so to speak not masters of our own houses. This leaves us with an endless dialectic between subject and the societal, and these two factors are held together by the conception of the unconscious and desire. In our discussion of Latour and Žižek, we link the field of sociology to the domain of material objects (science) and the domain of desire (psychoanalysis). In both cases, the result is a radical break with the sociological concept of society.

Although classic sociology is based on distinctions (see preceding), Latour and Žižek are interested in dissolving these distinctions. Both consider the indistinct rather than the distinct as fundamental. The main focus of this chapter is the object (i.e. the social or society) that sociology has occupied itself with for generations; but through a discussion of Latour and Žižek, we will attempt to relate this object to the domains of subjects and things. Latour's concept "factish" refers to a fusion or an indistinction between societal and material objects. Žižek's concept "fetish" refers to a fusion or an indistinction between the societal and investments based on the subject's desire. The social does not exist independently of neither material things nor subjects. As Žižek expresses it (1991b), we must "look awry": The object of sociology can never be comprehended directly. It interweaves with something that distorts and displaces it. In other words, we want to investigate what could be called an impure sociology.

Latour: actants and network

Latour has, more or less, dedicated his whole career to criticising the idea of society as an independent domain. The great villain in his framework is Durkheim (cf. Chapter 3). According to Latour, sociology is Durkheimian, and this is definitely not meant as a compliment. An important, but often forgotten debate in classic sociology took place between Durkheim and French sociologist Gabriel Tarde (1843–1904). While Durkheim insisted that the social exists as a special domain, Tarde claimed that everything is social. And whereas Durkheim conceived of the social as something that transcends the individual, Tarde saw it as immanent, i.e. as nothing but constant interactions between people (Latour 2002).

Tarde represents a movement in philosophy and societal thinking known as "vitalism". This movement focuses on change as opposed to objects and essences. Individuals or material objects are here conceived of as connections between movements and order must be understood as a partial and temporary stabilisation of these movements. Latour (2005) concurs with this perspective:

> The world is not a solid continent of facts sprinkled by a few lakes of uncertainties, by a few islands of calibrated and stabilized forms.
> (Latour 2005: 245)

Instead of seeing society as a special order, Latour focuses on a row of small, hybrid and constantly changeable orders. These temporary stabilisations are described as networks. This perspective paves the way for a new form of sociology that is concerned with connections between what Latour describes as actants. Actants can be anything – material objects, human beings or phenomena. What determines whether something is an actant or not is whether it takes position in a network. This means that an object – human or nonhuman – can become part of different networks and hereby gain different meanings or roles.

Latour's source of inspiration lies in structuralism. In structural linguistics, the value of the individual elements of meaning is determined by their position in a certain structure. Or as it is later described in poststructuralism: a discourse (for instance, the sign "woman" holds a different value in a patriarchal and a feminist discourse). More specifically, the concept of actants is taken from Algirdas J. Greimas (1917–1992), who uses it to analyse folktales. According to Greimas, the plot of a folktale must expand between six structural positions, which he describes as actants: an object that is passed from a sender to a recipient, and a subject facing a helper and an opponent. These positions can be populated by actual people, material objects or phenomena. In criticising the

factish and fetish

sociological tradition, Latour draws heavily on this conception. In contrast to most sociological theory, he sees things as contributing to action and change.

Society is not the explanation, as Durkheim and his successors would claim it to be. Society is that which needs explaining (Latour 2000: 113). Thus, Latour prefers to talk about collectives (or associations), which can be uncovered by thoroughly following the connections between that which cannot yet be described as parts; because the idea of parts presumes a preexisting whole. The social is the web spun between the actants, but the actants are nothing more than positions in a network. Hence, the task of sociology is not to formulate general regularities – this is impossible, according to Latour. Instead, sociologists should seek to describe the composition and development of these networks. Latour expresses the task of the actor network theory as follows:

> Using a slogan from ANT, you have "to follow the actors themselves", that is try to catch up with their often wild innovations in order to learn from them what the collective existence has become in their hands, which methods they have elaborated to make it fit together, which accounts best define the new associations that they have been forced to established.
>
> (Latour 2005: 12)

Drawing on the ANT framework, Latour formulates three fundamental critiques of sociology (Blok and Jensen 2011: 104ff.). First, the concept of the social is both too narrow and too wide. Too narrow because it is easily associated with the nation state. Too wide because there are societies without human beings; for instance biotopes, organisms consisting of a society of cells and, perhaps most obviously, societies of animals. The term society does not encircle that which is special for human societies – or even better: This distinction between human and nonhuman societies is problematic. As mentioned, Latour's solution is to discuss networks.

The second point of criticism is that sociology understands unities and especially the society as cohesive and given, and the significance of displacement of scale is therefore often disregarded. Something local develops towards global and vice versa. Networks are constantly transformed and their span is therefore not easily defined. Latour is not the only sociologist to voice this criticism. But unlike most others, he does not make this point a question about whether a global sociology should replace a national (or local). Instead, he points to the porosity and changeability of any spatial and geographical demarcation. The conception of "society" is easily associated with a constantly stable and spatially delimited unity. According to Latour, such unities do not exist.

Finally, the third point of criticism is that the use of the term society easily leads us to believe that society only consists of human beings. However, societies can also contain material objects, organisms, germs, opinions, landscapes, houses and so on. More specifically, society is the connection between these factors. We typically think about human societies and especially modern societies as endlessly complex. Sociology contains many of these stories. But at the same time these societies are stabilised through different arrangements that reduce the complexity. For instance, Luhmann refers to the symbolic generalised media, whereas Latour points to the meaning of material objects. Consider, for instance, the network of an educational setting – the building, the placement of desks and other furniture contribute to a stabilisation of a network (a temporary order) that also contains teachers, students, parents, books, knowledge, and so on.

It is possible to distinguish between the complex and the complicated (Blok and Jensen 2011: 79ff.). Complexity increases as different actants in the network constantly adjust their behaviour to one another. A society of baboons is, for instance, highly complex. Relations between group-members are constantly tested and negotiated. The group seeks stabilisation through hierarchy, but as this type of order takes form as "pure" sociality it appears almost endlessly fragile. The human society can be considered far less complex, because it is stabilised by objects, by things.

In turn, human societies are very complicated. Stabilisation through objects allows advanced operations to take place. For instance, different test procedures can be used and connected to different reporting mechanisms in a laboratory. At first, each operation appears simple but when the operations are combined everything becomes very complicated. Or another example; a computer is complicated, not complex. It consists of simple distinctions between zeros and ones, which can be combined in nearly endless ways whereby something very complicated appears.

Several of Latour's books include detailed studies of networks and how they change and stabilise. His main focus has been scientific networks, and this is not a coincidence. If there is one sector that bases its judgments on a clear distinction between human and nonhuman, between subject and object between theory and reality, it is science, and especially the natural sciences. Put simply, the idea looks like this: A brilliant scientist gets an idea, which he or she tests on an external reality. But in reality, things are quite different. Latour claims that scientific facts are "fabricated" and that this is overlooked by conventional theory of science. He bases this claim on observational studies carried out in a neuroendocrinological laboratory at the Salk Institute for Biological Studies in California (Latour and Woolgar 1979), on historical analyses of Louis Pasteur's development of the theory of pasteurisation (Latour 1988) and on Rudolf Diesel's development of the diesel engine. We will use the latter as a quick illustration, but first we have to introduce a new concept: translation.

The concept of translation (in other contexts replaced with terms such as hybridisation, mediation, circulation or association) is used to describe the processes behind the fabrication of facts, which draws on machines, texts, statements, laboratory animals, researchers, materials and resources. Blok and Jensen describe the process as follows:

> First, imagine a state of disorder. Then imagine that certain actors – let us call them scientists – mobilize a variety of resources and materials that gradually allow them to establish, register and repeat a number of orderly patterns. Finally, imagine that such locally constructed orders are distributed and stabilized in other contexts, through the active participation of numerous actors and tools. Each step along the way requires work, resources and participants, who must all be enrolled one way or another. Facts are orders that are forced onto a world that is not always receptive. Facts exist only in and through networks of actors and material objects; just as electricity, gas, mail services and parking regulations in a big city only exist in and through complex and well-ordered networks.
>
> (Blok and Jensen 2011: 27)

The production of the diesel engine is a good example of the translation process, which Latour notices with great precision (Latour 1987: 104ff.).

In 1887, Rudolf Diesel introduces the idea of an engine functioning by ignition without increase of temperature. This requires a special fuel injection method, which is based on Carnot's thermodynamic principles. In the first translation, Diesel's invention thus builds on an existing idea. Next, Diesel patents his invention and hereby translates it into ownership. The third translation takes place as Diesel contacts MAN, a large producer of machines, and convinces them to start working on a prototype. The process from patent to prototype is a translation, and not just from one medium to another (from idea to product). The machine changes character as part of the process; the leading principle is no longer injection by constant temperature but injection by constant pressure.

Diesel presents the machine to the public in 1897, and it is now possible for companies to buy a licence and produce diesel engines on their own. But as the machine tends to stop, this doesn't really work. The translation is unsuccessful, and Diesel therefore faces economic problems. He ends up bankrupted with a nervous breakdown. The network around the machine appears to be dissolving. However, MAN continues to work on the machine and when Diesel's patent expires in 1912, they market it with great success. Here we see yet another translation, and this time the network is expanded immensely. Diesel feels double-crossed and claims that he owns the invention, but MAN insists that their engine only has a vague similarity to Diesel's original machine. Diesel commits suicide in 1913.

Translation is a process where something is changed via its position in a complex and dynamic network. This "something" is not a material object or an idea that is realised – something that is already there and unfolds over time. "Something" is passed on and changed in the same process. As shown in the example, there is another central aspect – power. It is crucial for the fact-builder to be in control of the process. Diesel wasn't. Pasteur was; he managed to spread the method of pasteurisation to the entire world. Latour's study of translations shows how new actants are included or excluded from the network and how the product, in this case the diesel engine, is transformed in the process. Relations and power relationships play a crucial role, but become invisible when we think about the diesel engine as a fixed and stable entity. Finally, networks are capable of growing and shrinking by themselves. The conception of a well-defined object, which is constant in time and space, is in other words problematic. This has implications for the analysis of objects and networks, but it is also significant for our self-understanding and especially for our understanding of being modern.

Latour and the modern

Latour's analysis of networks is bound to provoke. It breaks with common modern conceptions of how knowledge is produced and with nearly all basic distinctions in our understanding of the modern. Latour goes as far as to claim that we have never been modern, which is also the title of his famous book from 1993. Nature and culture, knowledge and power, subject and object have never been separated as radically as modern sociology tends to assume. So why do we carry on this conception? And which status does it hold?

Latour speaks of "the modern constitution" as a certain way of relating to the world (1993: 13ff.). The term "constitution" emphasises the idea of a matrix, a sort of fundamental law. But in opposition to the constitution that underlies our political community, the modern constitution stipulates guidelines for our entire "society". It makes the realm of chaotic possibilities something of the past and makes the hybrid appear as something entirely different.

The modern constitution consists of two key aspects (Latour 1987: 10ff.). The first is to keep categories separated – especially human/non-human. Latour describes this as purification work. The second consists

factish and fetish   203 of communicating the translations and hybridisations described in the previous section, the so-called translation work. The modern constitution guards the distinction between systems, unities, periods, logic, and so on. and between the two types of work (purification work and translation work). These must be kept apart in order to function:

> How did the modern manage to specify and cancel out the work of mediation both at once? By conceiving every hybrid as a mixture of two pure forms. The modern explanations consisted in splitting the mixture apart in order to extract from them what came from the subject (or the social) and what came from the object. Next they multiplied the intermediaries in order to reconstruct the unity they had broken and wanted nonetheless to retrieve through blends of pure forms.
>
> (Latour 1987: 78)

The "modern" trick is to look at the hybrids as mixtures of pure forms. We can relate politically to the economy, artistically to the political, religiously to the aesthetic, scientifically to the religious, and so on. Certainly, the modern as described by sociology exists, but only as a partial and temporary stabilisation of something that will always be in motion and therefore hybrid. The modern constitution makes it possible to "pretend". Hybridity is a fundamental condition, but we pretend that it is not. If we accepted this idea, the conceptions and systems of modernity would fall apart.

The modern constitution functions in two dimensions: in a "here and now" where hybrid phenomena, e.g. human and nonhuman, are separated, and in a temporal perspective where past, present and future are kept apart. The modern constitution can thus be said to underpin sociology. It draws a distinction between a modern world (characterised by industrialisation, secularisation, urbanisation, individualisation, scientification, etc.) and a premodern and traditional world characterised by the absence of such processes. Anthropology's distinction between primitive and modern communities and between superstition and genuine religion can likewise be seen as an expression of the modern constitution.

The modern constitution also enables a distinction between people who live in accordance with nature and people who create their own nature in independent societies. Finally, the modern constitution paves the way for science and the scientific way of predicting and controlling nature. The constitution, in this sense, prescribes a distinct temporality: First we get to know nature, then we learn how to master it and finally, we construct it.

In the same way as networks are always hybrid orders, our modern orders always rely on the past and point to the future. As we saw in the development of Diesel's engine, the past is always a part of the present. However, past and present must be separated for incidents, elements and relations to be sorted. Based on this separation, they can be reconnected in narratives, innovations and other forms of stabilisations – the mediation work (Latour 1987: 74).

In *We Have Never Been Modern* (1993), Latour thematises the modern constitution through a discussion of Robert Boyles (1626–1691) and Thomas Hobbes (1588–1679). Both were writing in a time when the modern constitution was consolidating. Indeed, one could argue that Hobbes and Boyle *write* the modern constitution. But because they are in the process of writing, the hybrid is still visible to them. They are trying to establish distinctions but hereby expose that these distinctions are not natural or given.

It is characteristic that both Boyle and Hobbes strive to separate and establish nature, culture, religion, state and science as independent domains. This will be clarified in a moment. However, the discussion between the two also shows something else: Hobbes attempts to ascribe authority to the political domain, Boyle to the scientific. They hereby become each other's obvious critics. They disagree on whether priority should be given to either the political or scientific domain, but they both bring with them a premodern conception of authority and seek to pass it on to the modern world, and this involves a refusal of the possibility of plural interpretation centres.

Hobbes establishes the authority of the state via the contract argument: Before the state was established, individuals were left to fend for themselves in a presocial natural state where mutual fighting was necessary in order to provide the most basic necessities of life. There was no law in force, and there was no agreement on the meaning of concepts like trade, science, and so on. Tired of fighting, the individuals realised the rationality of giving up their weapons, and established a sovereign to regulate their interaction. The modern state was born and along with it the role of the citizen. In return of guaranteeing peace and safety, the state demands unconditional obedience. To Latour, the central point is the idea of representation. The sovereign represents the citizens and is therefore able to speak for them. Hobbes's contract argument resembles mathematic evidence. It is compelling. As everyone loves life and wants to stay alive, the contract argument must convince everyone. Hereby, any governmental action is legitimated as the state will always be better than the inferno of the state of nature (Latour 1987: 27).

For the chemist Boyle, it is about scientific authority. While Hobbes uses compelling arguments, Boyle seeks to convince through scientific experiments. Boyle constructed an air pump that could generate a vacuum, which made it possible to conduct chemical experiments. To convince

factish and fetish

the public about his knowledge, Boyle invited members of The Royal Society to visit him. In this way, Boyle constructed a laboratory that could be used in the fabrication of facts.

Whereas Hobbes's logical reasoning allows him to speak on behalf of the public, Boyle's scientific experiments make him capable of speaking on behalf of nature. These two modes of representation enable a mutual separation of nature and politics and hereby leads to dispute between the two. Because Boyle's experiments can be executed by anyone and thereby allow experts and authorities to challenge the authoritarian state's monopoly of definition, he is a threat to Hobbes. And for Boyle, Hobbes represents a prescientific approach to truth. For Hobbes, authority becomes power, and it is precisely the effect of this power that Boyle seeks to eliminate through his experiments.

In both cases, their purification work depends on the mobilisation of a large number of actants. Hobbes's authoritarian state does not only depend on a contract argument but also on the establishment of multiple governmental authorities. Without a state apparatus, the contract has no power: "Covenants, without the Sword, are but Words, and of no strength to secure a man at all" (Hobbes 1991: 117). Likewise, the mobilisation of Boyle's experiments depends on instruments, resources, chemical mixtures and witnesses.

Finally, two conditions left unaddressed in Latour's own writings, illustrate the continued relevance and function of the modern constitution. First, the modern constitution enables a certain kind of criticism that seeks to detach us from prejudice. In this case, criticism is about facilitating autonomy, and both Hobbes and Boyle can be considered critical in this particular sense of the term. Both seek to enlighten with the purpose of establishing something more solid – Hobbes the foundation of the state; Boyle the legitimation and promotion of scientific reasoning. Second, the modern constitution is also present in ideological criticism. Indeed, purification work enables a criticism of mixtures. Ever since the Enlightenment, the conception of an independent nature has created opportunities to criticise all kinds of distortions, e.g. the distinction between the scientific and the unscientific. Compared to society, nature can be understood as something transcendental and in this way constitute an independent standard; something that society can be compared to. At the same time, society can be conceived as something immanent, something that we create ourselves, and in this case people can be criticised for underestimating this condition. In both cases, the distinction between culture and nature is fundamental (Latour 1991: 35).

Now we have the basis for construing Latour's conception of factish (Latour 2015), which he develops in his sociology of religion, but based on insights expressed in *We Have Never Been Modern*. The modern constitution distinguishes between superstition and faith, and in the criticism of the so-called primitive religion the fetish becomes of central importance. A fetish is an object that is invested in and gets its religious value exclusively from this process (e.g. a stone, a piece of wood or a bone). Modern people consider primitive people to "fetishise" objects. They actively and deliberately produce sacred objects (they carve figures and make amulets). Their religion is completely immanent and therefore superstition, while our Christian religion refers to something outside this world, something transcendental.

The modern constitution allows us to distinguish between that which is a question of faith and therefore refers to another world (the transcendental) and that which is related to this world (the fabricated and therefore immanent). However, such a distinction is not meaningful to "primitive people". But according to Latour's "symmetrical" anthropology, we do exactly like them. Is a crucifix less fabricated than an amulet, he asks polemically (Latour 2015: 45)? Both objects are produced, made, and both appear as actants in a network. They are material (therefore "fact"), but they are also products of our practical and affectively investigating intercourse with them (therefore fetish). Latour combines these two concepts into one: factish.

As we will see, the intention behind Žižek's relaunch of the concept fetish is approximately the same, although he discusses the other part of the equation, so to speak. He also criticises the modern constitution, but on the basis of the conception that we invest in objects in exactly the same way as "primitive people" do. In contrast to Latour, his manoeuvre is not to show that the primitives also deal with their objects in a factish way, but inversely that we "fetishise" objects just as the "primitives". We too have our fetishes. Unsurprisingly, this point relies on psychoanalysis. But before we get to the conception of the fetish or what Žižek describes as the sublime object of ideology, we must discuss his conception of the social and the unconscious.

Žižek: the unconscious and the social

The notion of the unconscious as some sort of ghost-like or hidden substance has caused many to liken psychoanalysis to mysticism. It seems natural to claim that psychoanalysis does not meet the standards of scientific enquiry. How can we scientifically investigate an object that lacks any positively given substance? We may speak fruitfully of the nonconscious: that about which we know nothing; we may speak of the preconscious, namely that which we do know, but of which we are not currently conscious (most people know that the capital of Spain is Madrid, even though they seldom think about it). We may speak of the prereflexive: knee-jerk reactions to situations with which we are so familiar that we no longer need to reflect on them. That is to say, a kind of practical consciousness – and one might even speak of a sort of bodily intelligence, muscle memory, for instance how a phone number may be stored in one's fingertips, as it were. The unconscious, however, is none of the above (Hyldgaard 1998: 38f).

The unconscious is a type of knowledge, but it is not knowledge as we usually understand the word, nor is it knowledge that belongs in some spiritual beyond. It is, to briefly recapitulate the key point of the previous section, what we do not know that we already know; i.e. a way we act or position ourselves in the world without being aware of the implications. The unconscious is articulated like a language, as Lacan says, but it is not yet articulated *for* the analyte *as* a comprehensible message. It is the contexts and relations of meaning in which we take part without being conscious of it. In other words, the unconscious consists of the individual's lack of overview of his/her own situation, the inner workings of the world and the relationship between his/her own speech and the greater context. A symptom is therefore an immediately incomprehensible message that must be interpreted for it to make sense. It must be inserted into a context of meaning that has not yet been articulated, but which the analyte – with the interrogative help of the analyst – possesses the necessary tools to elucidate. The question is: What are the connections, contexts or positions of which the analyte is not (yet) conscious, i.e. what position in the symbolic order does the subject occupy when speaking or acting in some particular manner?

The sequence of analysis is meant to establish how the analyte "lives his world" (Žižek 1997: 29). One could say that the theme of analysis is precisely the individual's unacknowledged relations to society or others. The thesis of the unconscious is therefore the very thing that ties together the poles of the individual and society. It is on account of the individual's perpetual state of incompletion and lack of mastery in its own house that it must identify with socially given roles and values. The unconscious refers to a constitutive lack of being, which on the one hand continuously forces the individual into acts of identification, but which on the other hand means that such acts always miss the mark. The psychoanalyst listens to the ways in which the analyte cultivates this constitutive void.

However, the traffic between the psychological and the social may also be analysed from the opposite angle. As the subject is driven towards the social, the social is driven towards its subjects. Society, too, is constituted by a void. "There is", in the words of Margaret Thatcher, "no such thing

208   factish and fetish

as society." Any regime needs to secure support and legitimacy, which is usually done not only though the corporeal exercise of power, which would, in the long run, be a self-subversive strategy, but also – perhaps primarily – through ideology. The function of ideology is to make it possible for the individual to project its own image onto society and view itself as, for instance, a faithful son of the nation. But why does ideology work?

The critique of ideology has found support in psychoanalysis because the latter provides a theory of the constitution of "the psyche" and an explanation of why people, contrary to their own interests, identify with ideologies and allow them to direct their actions. Thatcher's rejection of the existence of society can be said to find a parallel in Lacan's famous description of "the big Other": It does not exist, and yet it functions. There is no unambiguous, legible conspiracy (a mastermind) behind, say, the overall effect of ideology upon its subjects, at least not necessarily, and yet it continues to function. And yet the subjects continue to find their bearings by virtue of, and through the notion of, a coherent force behind actual events in society. There *is* no society, and yet it continues to function.

One may thus focus either on the pressure exerted by society on the individual or on the individual's way of dealing with this pressure. The latter is the primary task of clinical psychoanalysis, whereas the former task is carried out by psychoanalytically founded social theory. Whereas clinical psychoanalysis is stimulated by the propositions of the individual patient, psychoanalytically founded social theory is stimulated by social phenomena. In other words, something is always bracketed: "the social" in clinical psychoanalysis and "the individual" in psychoanalytically founded social theory.

It is often held that psychoanalysis is irrelevant because it deals with individuals and the individual's motivation for acting the way it does. This may be worth investigating for psychiatrists, psychologists and psychoanalysts, but social science happens to be concerned with society. Likewise, psychoanalysis has been charged with biologism, pansexualism, naturalism or determinism with reference to its conception of the individual as shaped by presocial forces (Žižek 1997: 8). Freud, it follows, was blind to the intersubjective and linguistic context within which the individual unfolds itself. This critique, however, knocks on an open door. The forces that transect the subject are precisely socially mediated.

For instance, a singular, isolated subject cannot fantasise about obtaining a particular object of desire. The question is, as Žižek says in *The Plague of Fantasies*, how the subject knows in the first place that it desires this particular object. How has it learned what an object is and

factish and fetish

that this object in particular is desirable? According to Žižek the "independent" subject does not recognise an object in the world as the possible means of satisfying a corresponding pre-linguistic desire. Rather it *learns* to view certain things as desirable or interesting because it already takes part in a socially articulated interplay of desire.

A central example is Žižek's reading of why Freud's young daughter Anna fantasised about strawberries one night when she was rambling about sweet things to eat (Freud 1999: 135). Žižek explains this fantasy against an intersubjective background: The daughter had discovered that her parents enjoyed watching her eat strawberry cake. This notion of doing something that fulfilled her parents' desire to see their child in a certain way gave rise to a strong partiality in little Anna for strawberry cake. She learned to desire strawberry cake because that way she succeeded in becoming the object of the others' (the parents') desire – she became the joyfully indulging little girl whom they loved (to observe) (Žižek 1997: 9). This account illustrates how desire, in the words of Lacan, is always already the other's desire: What I desire is first and foremost to be desired by the other, which means becoming or doing that which the other will find desirable. Even the most "immediate", private wish is thus already mediated by some kind of consciousness or embeddedness in a relationship to the other or others. In a fundamental sense, there is no psychological private language. However, the subject of psychoanalysis is more than a product of its linguistic and social moulding.

Žižek's blend of philosophy and psychoanalysis has its unique advantages in the analysis and critique of ideology. Although Žižek is a philosopher, his ambition is not to develop a positive philosophical theory of, say, justice in the traditional sense, but rather to make explicit the unacknowledged means and instruments that accompany official political rhetoric and action. It is out of such analysis that the "positive" is meant to emerge, i.e. as the creation of new possibilities for understanding what is socially possible. In this sense Žižek is a Hegelian: It is the "determinate negation" that brings about the possibility of a new form of society or consciousness. It is in the analysis of the contemporary that one may create or find the opening that points forward.

The sublime object of ideology

The use of psychoanalytic insights in the traditions of Marxism and critical theory is primarily due to the possibility of analysing not only the distribution of value – who gets what and when? – but also how such decisions are legitimised. As opposed to "bourgeois/liberal" theory, the traditions of Marxism and critical theory view legitimation as a political process. An important component of many attempts to understand the legitimation of political decisions has been the concept of ideology. The task of psychoanalysis in such matters has been to explain the role of ideology in the psychological life of the subject.

Traditionally, ideologies have been identified as systems of ideas, which communicate incorrect representations of reality: an imagined state of affairs or, if we emphasise the systematic coherence of the elements of an ideology, a system of beliefs that did not match the actual state of affairs. It was accordingly seen as the task of the critique of ideology to correct these false representations by way of enlightenment. No matter how intensely this representationalist approach has been criticised, it has proven remarkably tenacious. When ideologies are often taken, in public discourse, to be outdated, rigid and naïve, such notions should be seen in this context: as a continuation of the conviction that ideologies are misrepresentations of a reality that may be described simply through common sense and a nonideological approach. However, it has long been clear that "false" ideas (false in their objective content) are not necessarily ideological, just as "true" ideas might very well be ideological in a fundamental sense (Žižek 1993: 230–231).

Ideologies were later taken to be false because of the position from which they were enunciated. Ideologies were "false" if they were functional in the creation and legitimation of relations of social dominance and exploitation. The critique of ideology in this perspective was typically Marxist and attempted to analyse and uncover the relations of dominance that were hidden by hegemonic systems of ideas. The thesis was that this ideological effort must remain hidden in order to function and that it would thus be impossible to maintain once openly displayed (Žižek 1994: 8).

The struggle was therefore no longer against ideas that were scientifically untrue, but against a false consciousness of the social world. Enlightenment now aimed at enlightening workers about social reality, i.e. capitalist exploitation, in order to unite them in a common struggle. The criticisms of this perspective are numerous: Its focus on consciousness misses the point that ideologies are manifested in social practices; the representationalist approach presupposes a nonideological layer of reality behind the ideological; it is difficult to trace emancipatory potential when false consciousness prevails; and finally it is precisely in claiming to speak objectively and neutrally – in an attempt to become immune to critique – that one performs an ideological operation.

However, the most important critique is that the ethical foundation for seeing ideology as false consciousness consists in the notion of irreversible emancipation through enlightenment – and thus the hope of creating ever more enlightened and rational subjects who may ultimately escape ideology as such. The critique of ideology would thus, if successful, render itself superfluous. The problem is, among other things, that this

factish and fetish

form of enlightenment has merely paved the way for an even more subtle form of ideology that takes an ironic approach to its own truth value. The problem now is not false consciousness, but enlightened false consciousness. We know very well that we are commodity fetishists. That God is dead, that nations are political constructions and so on, all these things we know but we nonetheless insist on these ideas in our everyday practice as if they were final and true. This criticism paves the way for a new type of critique of ideology, proceeding from the fact that we are ironic with regard to the messages of ideology, and that it therefore takes something other than bedazzlement to explain our (unconscious) support for the dogmas of ideology. It is this insight, or claim, if you will, that forms the point of departure for Žižek's critique of ideology.

The three approaches to the critique of ideology outlined in the preceding represent three different conceptions of the relation between reality and its reflection and may be categorised via the triad of realism, modernism and postmodernism (Žižek 1996: 233, n. 16). In realism, reality has a structure and nature of its own, independently of our reflection and experience of it. This conviction can be found in classic pre-Marxist conceptions of ideology, which saw it as their task to fight unscientific ideas. Modernism (as represented for instance by Marxist György Lukács) entails belief in the liberating power of reflection and its ability to change its object (consciousness). This is the foundation of the Marxist paradigm, according to which enlightenment will make possible a change in consciousness and thereby work for the abolition of the existing structures of dominance. Postmodernism, in Žižek's variety, takes another step, claiming that ideologies are maintained precisely through a reflective distance, and that it is through our nonidentification with the configurations of ideology that we make them possible.

Žižek's critique of ideology is about the disclosure of the cynical, reflective distance from ideology as a hidden or unspoken approval of it. By ironically dismantling our relation to ideology (state, party, market), we allow it to function in practice. We *claim* not to believe in ideology, that our everyday masks are only that: masks, a provisional, necessary charade – but we still *act* in accordance with it. Or in Lacanese: At the level of the enunciated we are "unideological", but when it comes to our position of enunciation, we are (all the more) ideological. The result, according to Žižek, is that ideology ends up functioning in exactly the opposite way that traditional critique imagined:

> Ideology is not a dreamlike illusion that we build to escape insupportable reality; in its basic dimension it is a fantasy-construction which serves as a support for our "reality" itself.
>
> (Žižek 1989: 45)

We must "be realistic" – the realities of life demand that we play our roles, even though of course we "really" want a different and more just society. In other words, the critique of ideology reveals that any given ideological construction is based on the antagonistic nature of society. The task is therefore not to show that ideologies misrepresent reality, which is the modernist gesture, but to show how the very idea of a reality behind the ideological mask is an illusion. Ideologies are not representations, but the anchor of social reality. The very idea of moving beyond ideologies by "being conscious of them" therefore actually shows our submission to them. We always remain within ideology. This realisation is paradoxically the necessary condition for moving beyond.

> There is more truth in a mask than in what is hidden beneath it: a mask is never simply "just a mask" since it determines the actual place we occupy in the intersubjective symbolic network; what is effectively false and null is our "inner distance" from the mask we wear (the "social role" we play), our "true self" hidden beneath it. The performative dimension at work here consists of the symbolic efficiency of the "mask": wearing a mask actually *makes us* what we feign to be.
>
> (Žižek 1992a: 34)

The true illusion is the very idea of a difference between the mask and the true self behind it. By insisting that our inner kernel is something apart from the mask we wear in everyday life, we may convince ourselves that we hold ideology at arm's length, but therein resides the illusion. We know very well that we participate in objective mechanisms that structure the design of our political world, but we are not *really* involved in it because it is not our personal, conscious goal to support the precise concrete consequences that follow from our social structures.

Hans Christian Andersen's fairy tale *The Emperor's New Clothes* paradigmatically illustrates the problem concerning the sublime object of ideology and the constitutive, cynical denial of ideology that are the precondition for the "functioning" and "cohesion" of modern society. The emperor is fooled by a couple of make-believe tailors into having them make him a costume. It is to be a suit so lavish that only people of special intelligence will be able to see it. The emperor in his naiveté and vanity refuses to admit that he himself cannot see this wonderful garment. According to Lacan, a madman who thinks he is king, emperor, Christ, and so on, is no madder than a king who thinks he is king, i.e. a king who identifies directly with his symbolic mandate (Žižek 1989: 25). The emperor in *The Emperor's New Clothes* is a fool because he believes that as emperor he must be the smartest, the most beautiful, most distinguished,

factish and fetish

213

and so on. He thought he was intelligent, handsome, sophisticated, and therefore emperor, whereas the inverse is obviously true. The very instant when his subjects cease to treat him as emperor, he will appear as a mere human among many others. The emperor alone believes that he is wearing something; everybody else knows that he is not. The story about *The Emperor's New Clothes* sees the day when the emperor presents his new attire to the people. The emperor, as we know, is naked. The silence is total, however, until a little boy yells out the unthinkable: "But he's not wearing any clothes." From this moment the emperor has the appearance of a complete fool, or more precisely, he no longer appears to be emperor.

The classic ideology-critical reading interprets this act as a divesting of power. The emperor is a mere human being once stripped of the attributes of power. This reading is too simple, however, because it merely discloses the emperor as a product of his positioning within a social and political order. The real matter of interest is not why the little boy symbolically divests the emperor, but rather why everybody else fails to do so. They all see that the emperor is naked. When they all view the emperor as emperor, whether or not he wears clothes, the reason is of course that they look at him "askew". They view the emperor as incarnating a special sublime object that makes him more than a mere human. In doing so they obviously overlook the fact that the emperor only becomes emperor the moment they treat him as such, that the ritual by which the emperor's body is made to appear as something sublime constitutes the very social reality, and that the emperor was nothing prior to and outside of this ritual practice (Žižek 1997: 146f).

In a study of medieval political theology, historian Ernst Kantorowicz develops the thesis of the king's two bodies – one sublime and one earthly. As monarchy incarnate the king is immortal (which awards him a sublime body), but as a concrete person he is of course mortal (which awards him an "earthly" body.) When the audience fails to divest the emperor in Andersen's fairy tale, this is precisely because the emperor possesses two bodies: one earthly and one sublime. The sublime body appears as a phantasmatic object of identification, casting a unique light upon the king's actual charisma. Details that we would deem quite ordinary in other families suddenly become special because they pertain to a royal family. Through the emperor's "earthly" body, his subjects gain access to the sublime. There is something more than the emperor in him, which means that what makes the emperor "emperor" is not the attributes of power – his position within a social structure – but rather the emperor's function as sublime ideological object.

The Emperor's New Clothes is a story about the problem of cynicism. Whereas Marx in his theory of commodity fetishism writes that they do not know it, but still do it, thus conceiving of fetishism within the confines of a classic modernist distinction between essence and representation – between practice (commodity fetishism) and consciousness – Hans Christian Andersen's version must be this: They know very well (that the emperor is not wearing anything), and yet they do it (treat him as emperor). In Lacanian terms we know very well that the big Other does not exist, that the symbolic order is fictitious, and yet we obey. They only thing the cynic believes in is enjoyment, and the symbolic order is thus accepted only by virtue of serving as the precondition for enjoyment and because it thereby gives direction to desire.

However, it is important to emphasise that such identification with the emperor is no private matter. In identifying with the emperor, we identify first and foremost with others who likewise identify with the emperor. The catastrophic consequences of the little boy's exclamation are not so much due to his disclosure of the emperor (the Other) as a mere product of the subjects' libidinal investments, but more so to the fact that the desublimation of the emperor's body disintegrates the bond that ties his subjects together: respect for the empire and the positions guaranteed by this social structure. When we refrain from divesting the emperor, it is because his nakedness would abandon us to our own nakedness. Underneath our clothes, we are all naked.

To recapitulate, we may ascertain that the ideological phantasm functions only so long as the object actually appears as sublime. The object must be discovered, conquered, bought, and so on. It cannot have the appearance of mere conjecture. The belief must prevail that the fascination with the object derives from the object itself. The object must therefore be kept at a distance. If we get too close to it, as in *The Emperor's New Clothes*, it will become apparent that it is just an ordinary object. Lacan thus defines anxiety not as the condition of fearing the loss of the object, but rather as the result of excessive proximity with the object (Žižek 1991a: 8). But at the same time: We do know that the emperor is not wearing anything, and yet we cynically uphold the power structure in which he is embedded. There must be some underlying reason, and this is precisely Žižek's point.

The two sides of the social bond

It may therefore be analytically fruitful to claim that "the law" and the social have two sides – surface and reverse. A surface consisting of written or explicitly stated prohibitions (norms, conventions, rules, positions, etc.) and a reverse permeated by enjoyment; a domain of transgression. Whereas the surface of law prohibits enjoyment, the law's reverse communicates the opposite imperative: Enjoy! The true master is unconscious; it is he (qua superego) who commands enjoyment. No hegemony without an undercurrent of phantasmatic enjoyment. There are thus two masters – a public symbolic authority and a "hidden", spectral master.

Transgression is thus constitutive for social life, rather than negating it. Nazism may be the best illustration. The nightly pogroms and assaults on political opponents were not destructive to the idyllic popular community. One could say that the condition for idyllic community was a brotherhood of guilt. Transgression in Nazism was not an individual, but a socially constructed and ideologically valorised phenomenon. Or to return to an earlier example: What bound the emperor's subjects together in a community was not their positions as subjects to the emperor, but rather the fact that they all shared the same dirty secret of the emperor's nudity.

> The deepest identification which "holds a community together" is not so much identification with the Law which regulates its "normal" everyday circuit as, rather, *identification with the specific form of transgression of the Law, of its suspension* (in psychological terms, with the specific form of enjoyment.
>
> (Žižek 1992b: 225)

Žižek is fond of telling military anecdotes to illustrate this point: Is not the repressed homosexuality in the army the best example? We often find here an explicit prohibition against homosexuality, and simultaneously an entire jargon and a set of rituals structured around the transgression of this absolute prohibition. A recurring dirty practical joke during Žižek's conscripted time in the Yugoslavian army was to stick one's finger up the anus of the soldier ahead of oneself in the line for food in the mess hall, and then quickly turn away in order for the "molested" party not to spot the culprit. The perverted recurrence of homosexuality in stupid "practical jokes" actually undergirded the explicit prohibition.

We are now able to further specify the problem of cynicism and with it the ideological deadlock of our time. Cynicism "disregards" the surface of the law. It produces a distance to the symbolic mandates (the subject positions) articulated by the law. But the very same cynicism leaves the law's reverse side intact. The very same subjects who take a cynical stance with regard to the message of public ideology, participate without batting an eye in paranoid fantasies about the excessive enjoyment of the others, for example Jews or immigrants (Žižek 1996: 142). Such cynicism does not mean that the public ritual is without significance, that the ideological call is ineffective, but rather that it makes possible the appropriation of enjoyment.

The insight into the structuring of power provides oppositional forces with opportunities to take power at its word. The realisation that power is structured "inconsistently" around a fundamental inscrutability, and that it rests upon the fragile balance of "civilisational" and "barbaric" elements, may be turned against power itself (Žižek 1997: 3). The strategies available to counter ideological phantasms vary from one situation to another. One thing remains clear, however: The classic strategy of disclosure and enlightenment often proves impotent in the face of an ideology legitimated through a cynical practice. The strategy of enlightenment focuses solely on the surface of the social bond – on the level of discourse – whereas the critique of cynicism focuses on the reverse, and with it, enjoyment.

Alternative strategies to that of enlightenment might be to state explicitly the unwritten rules, thereby forcing a system to openly acknowledge their existence. Articulating these hidden rules would force a system to react with either concessions or violence – and either way, it loses (Helmer and Žižek 1995: 14ff.). Žižek often speaks with admiration of the rock and punk band Laibach and its prudence in this very regard. Laibach's strategy was to identify excessively with the obscene reverse side of the social bond and mixed totalitarian symbols and paroles with an apparently perverse stage act. The purpose, naturally, was to subvert dominant social phantasms by making them explicit:

[Laibach's strategy] *"frustrates" the system (the ruling ideology) precisely in so far as it is not its ironic imitation, but overidentification with it* – by bringing to light the obscene superego underside of the system, overidentification suspends its efficiency. The ultimate expedient of Laibach is their deft manipulation of transference: their public (especially intellectuals) is obsessed with the "desire of the Other" – What is Laibach's actual position? Are they truly totalitarians or not? – that is, they ask Laibach a question and expect an answer from them, failing to notice that Laibach themselves *function not as an answer but as a question.*

(Žižek 1994: 72)

"Functioning as the question rather than the answer" is also the task of the analyst in analytic practice. Laibach's strategy is analogous to what Lacan called "traversing the phantasm" (Nicol 2001). The task of the critique of ideology, in other words, may consist in conducting therapy in this sense: forcing us to traverse the phantasm and thus to realise that some of our most libidinously invested notions are precisely projections of our wish for the fulfilment of desire into a particular object – either as its actual fulfilment (the emperor, the teen idol) or as that which prevents fulfilment (the Jew, the Muslim, the unemployed, the criminal, etc.). To identify with the symptom is to see one's own gaze in the image of the other. In any case the question is redirected back at the subject. The analysis concludes with the fall of the big Other, i.e. the abandonment of any notion of an ultimate founding of meaning or identity.

Conclusion: an impure sociology

Do the social and society exist? Both Latour and Žižek will answer in the affirmative but add that this sociality is always given in complex interaction with something that the conception of a "pure" sociality will not be able to catch. For Latour, it is of central importance to emphasise the interaction between human and nonhuman actants in complex networks. And the social is a process rather than a thing (a social fact). Žižek also criticises this objectification of society. The social exists in our investments based on desire, and ideology functions as a significant frame for these. It is impossible to separate the two "things". Whereas Latour uses the concept of translation in an attempt to capture the constant change and hybridisation of networks, Žižek considers the conception of the unconscious and of desire to hold together different actants in a complex and dynamic unity. Both are vitalists: They start from the movements and consider the stabilisations to be temporary and fragile constructions.

And what is it that creates these temporary stabilisations? Žižek's answer will be the ideologies as they direct the course of our desire. The ideology creates a distance between the subject and a desired object and thus constitutes something we can aim for, but never achieve. Žižek defines fear as the condition caused by the realisation that the sublime object is only an object, as we get too close to it. There is nothing more desublimating than having one's desire fulfilled. Latour points to the modern constitution as a description of how distinctions do not merge and how purification work and mediation work can be separated. In both cases, a contracting instance (the modern constitution, ideology) regulates the relation to the fluid and hybrid.

In both cases, a form of cynicism must inevitably be said to play a role. Our practice takes place in a complex interplay with objects and with other subjects. But at the same time, it must be denied in order to ensure that our horizons do not collapse. In both cases something non-thought and non-thematised is at work and it is these "holes" that our practices actively and constantly deny. Žižek refers to this "hole" as the unconscious, whereas Latour emphasises how hybridity is constantly denied.

For this reason, the critical practice unfolds as a kind of demonstration that operates in two moves, to both Žižek and Latour. Our cognitive schemes and the distinctions that support them are contrasted with a vitalistic understanding of the fundamental ontological constitution of the world. Consequently, the criticism becomes immanent and not transcendent. It points out the present but denied premises for our actions: hybridity and desire. Both Latour and Žižek find it to be of central importance to move beyond the form of criticism of classic modern and Enlightenment philosophy. Criticism is no longer a matter of unmasking. Instead, it must take place immanently. To Žižek, this is the requisite for breaking down the distinction between practice and consciousness, and for Latour it is about seeing and following the relations between subjects and objects in complex networks. For both it is of central importance to understand the social as something that is constituted and challenged by something "nonsocial".

factish and fetish

219

chapter 13

Sociology as an analytic praxis

In the previous chapters, we have outlined key theoretical movements and problems in the sociological literature to illustrate the many ways in which the common question of our social existence can be raised and addressed. In this chapter, we will engage in a broader discussion of the contemporary challenges facing sociology. One reservation should be made in advance: There is, of course, more than one form of sociology and therefore the different sociological perspectives will be challenged to varying degrees. In this chapter, we have decided to keep our discussion at a general level and hereby make it possible to relate sociology to something outside the discipline itself. In practice, sociological theory is challenged by stakeholders both inside and outside the discipline. So far, we have delimited our focus to discussions within the discipline, such as Habermas's criticism of Luhmann's systems theory, and now it seems appropriate to make room for an external view.

We will begin with a brief discussion of the anatomy of the sociological analysis. How are the emergent properties of the social brought to the fore? In this case, we conceive of the social as something not immediately apparent to the naked eye. The social is something more and something else than we typically assume. Drawing on the writings of Hegel, we will argue that a sociological understanding requires an account for the societal totality. To analyse sociologically is to be aware of society's many constituent parts. We move between the whole and its parts to reveal patterns and relationships that would not otherwise be visible.

Indeed, many other disciplines adopt a similar approach. But sociologists raise different questions than physicists, theologians, biologists and psychologists and therefore also reveal patterns and relationships of a fundamentally different nature.

Some might claim that the theoretical branch of sociology is far too general in its descriptions of societal life and that its concepts and ideas are too abstract and complex to be verified empirically. Indeed, almost all sociological theories use abstract concepts to capture significant characteristics of modern society and this operation is not unproblematic. This chapter begins with a critical discussion of sociology and argues that sociology and diagnosis of the times should not be separated entirely.

On the one hand, sociology can be criticised for being too abstract and too distanced from the day-to-day practices of human beings. On the other hand, the discipline is sometimes criticised for being too involved. Indeed, sociology has its shortcomings when it comes to describing the freedom and ethical position of the individual. Yet, sociological analyses often give an impression of being capable of explaining any aspect of individual action in sociological terms. This tendency is discussed in the second part of the chapter, in which we grapple critically with the question of determinism. The third part of the chapter discusses the tendency in sociology to generalise its own view to a broader context and the possible problems caused by this form of scholastic reasoning.

A story of a murder

Sociology does not limit its focus to the immediately observable. As we have seen, sociologists attempt to parcel out the distinct object given for sociology: the social. They separate this object into several elements – institutions, expectations, incidents, interests, resources, and so on – and place them in a new context. It is this respecified totality that we refer to as the social and that we wish to elicit through our analyses. Elicit, as the social is not something that can be "made up". It exists out there, but it can only be approached through a certain sociological analytical strategy. Let us have a closer look at this idea.

The social can be said to have emergent characteristics. This object – the social – only appears through the sociological analysis. It emerges through a particular view, and if this view is not adopted, the social slips through our fingers. Of course, a society can also be broken into elements that enable a psychological, an economic and perhaps even a biological description of its totality. Although a psychologist seeks to understand the individual by detecting meaningful patterns in his/her actions, experiences and identifications, and a biologist parcels out an organism in its organic components, the sociologist understands the social as relations between classes, as systems of norms and identifications or as mutual affective investments, among other factors.

sociology as an analytic praxis   221

Thus, the sociologist subscribes to a perspective of unity, but this unity can be constructed in various ways. Perhaps several sociologies can be said to exist simultaneously, exactly as many as there are sociological analytical strategies.

Unlike many other scientific disciplines, sociology, as a practice and tradition, is characterised by a fundamental disagreement on the nature of the object of analysis, and thereby also what its components or smallest unities consist of. In other disciplines, such as biology or economy, there is considerably broader agreement on the building blocks of analysis. This is not the case in sociology; sociological theories are not necessarily competing explanations of *the same*. Here, this fundamental disagreement on what characterises the object of the discipline is not considered a weakness; rather the opposite. Few disciplines equal sociology in the production of innovative estimates about what the social consists of and what characterises and shapes us as social beings. This means that the discipline has not been stabilised as a cumulative normal science (which some people lament), but there is a great sense of creativity and innovation.

One reason for the volatility of the discipline is doubtlessly the scope of what sociologists attempt to analyse. As we have seen, there is almost no limit to what can be implicated as relevant in the understanding of the stabilisation and change of the social. In this way, the distinct thing about sociology is not that a matter is parcelled out into a series of elements that are afterwards used to describe a (new) pattern between the parts. The special thing about sociology is the ambition that lies behind this practice. Putting it in a Hegelian way, sociology can be claimed to be a form of holistic science.

We are often affected by the conception that an explanation and analysis becomes more true and irrefutable when an object of study is reduced to increasingly smaller parts. The exact science is "concrete" and "specific". The scientific logic, which is often aspired to, is the microscope and the magnifying glass. Sociology is not a science of everything that exists, but it shares the criticism of such a particularism. In fact, this leads to an overly abstract and vague analysis. In this case, sociology avoids the tunnel vision of other sciences. Our behaviour is also written into a complex net of social determinants, and if this fact is ignored we end up with poor descriptions of the phenomena that we observe. In some cases, there is not only talk about reductionist conceptions, but also about false and ideological conceptions.

Paradoxically, one of the best outlines of this ambition is found in a text written by a theorist who considered himself a philosopher rather than a sociologist. The theorist is Georg Wilhelm Friedrich Hegel, and his text from 1808 is called "Who thinks abstractly?" (1991). In the text

222   sociology as an analytic praxis

he uses the concept "judge of character" and this is exactly how the sociologist can also be described. Such judges of character can also be found in other disciplines, but in this case we will focus on Hegel's example:

> A murderer is led to the place of execution. For the common populace he is nothing but a murderer. Ladies perhaps remark that he is a strong, handsome, interesting man. The populace finds this remark terrible: What? A murderer handsome? How can one think so wickedly and call a murderer handsome; no doubt, you yourselves are something not much better! This is the corruption of morals that is prevalent in the upper classes, a priest may add, knowing the bottom of things and human hearts.
>
> One who knows men traces the development of the criminal's mind: he finds in his history, in his education, a bad family relationship between his father and mother, some tremendous harshness after this human being had done some minor wrong, so he became embittered against the social order – a first reaction to this that in effect expelled him and henceforth did not make it possible for him to preserve himself except through crime. – There may be people who will say when they hear such things: he wants to excuse this murderer! After all I remember how in my youth I heard a mayor lament that writers of books were going too far and sought to extirpate Christianity and righteousness altogether; somebody had written a defense of suicide; terrible, really too terrible! – Further questions revealed that *The Sufferings of Werther* were meant.
>
> This is abstract thinking: to see nothing in the murderer except the abstract fact that he is a murderer, and to annul all other human essence in him with this simple quality.
>
> (Hegel 2016)

Hegel asks what it means to think abstractly and who thinks abstractly. For most people, philosophers think abstractly. The next suggestion will often be theologians and the third will probably be scientists in general. We think abstractly, as we leave this world in its concrete appearance and the air becomes increasingly thinner. Philosophers practice the pure thought and shun any form of disturbing and intrusive reality. Theologians are concerned with the other world, that which we cannot grasp empirically: God and the divine. And scientists sit in their ivory tower, which might offer a nice view but at the same time induces them to look at everything from a distance.

To Hegel, the opposite is the case. The people who still happily criticise philosophy for being abstract and vague are exactly that way too. (Good)

sociology as an analytic praxis

philosophy is, unlike what most people and many philosophers think, concrete thinking. It might be added that this also applies to good sociology. Why is that? Hegel gives an example. Imagine a murderer! If the person or the case appears mean, common people, priests and judges usually meet the murderer with condemnation and contempt, whereas they might meet an attractive, vulnerable or repentant murderer with forbearance and maybe even sympathy. Such a focus on the immediate appearance of the person and on the murder as an isolated incident, which is at most explained in the light of psychological dispositions – *that* is abstract thinking. In contrast, (good) philosophy – and sociology – is concrete thinking, as it does not focus on the incident as an isolated action and on the individual as solitary and self-reliant.

A concrete and, one can say, sociological way of thinking pursues the history of the murderer: Which vexations that could later lead to violent actions has the person been exposed to? Concrete – and sociological – thinking relates to the action as something conditioned and situated. It asks: How and under which circumstances did such a thing as a murder make sense? Finally, concrete and sociological thinking looks at everything as social processes, conditional on the way individuals stand in relation to each other – a son's relation to his parents, for instance.

A "holistic" explanation like the one just outlined, an explanation that seeks to understand a phenomenon in relation to its social setting, is concrete – an isolated explanation, or perhaps just an isolated observation, feeling and taste is an abstraction because it abstracts everything else away. A holistic explanation is not only better than a nonholistic explanation; overall, it is better because it *is* an explanation.

Finally, Hegel's example outlines the normativity that is part and parcel of the sociological undertaking. Sociology replaces our fake moralisations and prejudices with genuine explanations. As a consequence of this knowledge it provides us with a moral, social and political responsibility. In the preceding quotation, Hegel seems to tell us that the bystanders' expressions of contempt and acts of punishment do not solve anything. Only when we understand that actions are socially conditioned can we begin to fight them effectively. Hegel's text is not a relativisation of the murder, but it draws attention to everything that happened before and contributed to the murder. It focuses on how society marginalised the person who later became a murderer. It is a reminder of the exaggerated punishment the person received and that embittered him. It might be a squire who punishes his serf way too hard for a minor negligence, and it might be the system itself and poverty that forces people to commit robbery and perhaps even murder. A sociologist knows that people never act in a vacuum.

None of the bystanders sees the murder in the same way as the sociologist (or the judge of character) does. And this is not merely a criticism of short-sightedness. It is not simply a question of scale: close up or from the outside. The overall picture is about a special form of constructivism. In order to comprehend this, it might be useful to focus on the two elements of scientific analysis: the analytical and disjunctive plus the synthesising and integrative.

The word analysis originates from Greek and in this case it means a dissolution or disintegration of something. "Ana" means "up" or "through" and "lysis" solution (that is to loosen something up). When we analyse something, we split it apart in order to understand this something as the sum of its elements. In contrast, synthesising is about putting something together. Here, the Greek origin is "syn" which means "with" and "together" and "tesis" which means "placing" or "putting". The Danish philosopher Henrik Jøker Bjerre uses a watch as illustration. The watch can be analysed by breaking it down into parts: dial, springs, glass, hands. And it can be synthesised with something else, for instance by connecting it to a bomb whereby the watch is changed into a countdown mechanism (Bjerre 2015: 9–10).

The sociological might be comprehended as consisting of a double movement, which subscribes to these two factors. First, a given matter is broken down to its constituent elements, which are then put back together in a new way. We could take a murderer and the societal condemnation of him or her as a starting position. Afterwards we could seek all the possible explanations for this action and the condemnation of the doer. Hereafter these sporadic observations can be brought together into a new overall picture and replace a prejudice with a sociologically informed understanding.

But doesn't the sociological analysis consist of something more actively creative? Isn't there always more at stake than merely splitting something into its smallest parts and putting them back together? The social is not like a box of Lego® bricks, where all the bricks are already known. And the sociological is not comparable to an assembly instruction with a predefined outcome. There is something more at stake, but this "more" is not an addition of something radically new or entirely unfamiliar. The synthesised movement, which is performed, brings forward something that is actually already there, but that we haven't been able to see or be aware of. The point is that we don't know what the individual parts sum up to in the beginning. The analysis makes us aware of something that we didn't see to begin with.

Bjerre (2015: 9–10) approaches the creative power of analysis in a discussion of an article of central importance, written by Bruno Latour

sociology as an analytic praxis

(2000), about the cause of death of the Egyptian pharaoh Ramses II. The mummy was transported to Paris in 1976 in order to determine the cause of death. It was subjected to different analyses of tissue, teeth, bones, and so on. It was discovered that Ramses had bad teeth and carried Koch's bacillus, which was considered circumstantial evidence that Ramses died of tuberculosis. However, the question was whether he actually died of tuberculosis, as Koch's bacillus was not discovered until 1882. From a contemporary perspective, he can be said to have died of tuberculosis, but back then he didn't. Today, he died of tuberculosis back then. The bacillus, the diagnosis and the entire medical discourse in which these terms and perspectives are embedded, did not exist in Ramses' time. The discovery of the bacillus and the diagnosis of tuberculosis was a break-through that actually constructed something new that did not exist in Ramses' time and that he could not die from – *back then*.

Latour's point is that physical objects and other things that are described in a scientific language also have a biography. Something comes into existence and this thing is constituted as such, that is as a thing. The conception that something already exists and is merely being named, or the conception that language constructs something that doesn't have a physical existence and materiality, are both dead ends. We will not specify the distinction between social and natural science but simply emphasise a relation that at least exists in the social world. The thematisations and appellations which we use potentially contribute to a change of the reality of that which is examined. Therefore, an analysis is also always an inter-vention of the analysing.

Bjerre (2015: 35) mentions Eisenhower's conception of "the military-industrial complex", which was introduced in his resignation speech in 1961. The point is that Eisenhower not only describes something that already exists; the term changes the social reality and offers an opportunity to act on it. Bjerre names these displacements truth effects with an ill-concealed reference to the philosopher Alain Badiou:

> [An analysis] can throw a fine-meshed net over a problem or an object and thereby contribute to seeing it in a completely different light. In this way, it sometimes produces a truth that would not otherwise be there. And through this truth the world is changed. It makes it pos-sible for us not to wish to be in a certain way (anymore) or to wish to be something new.
>
> (Bjerre 2015: 35, our translation)

Sociology at its best makes us see something that we would otherwise not discover. Of course, this new thing can originate from relatively concrete studies focused on a social phenomenon, but it can also unfold in an analysis of the overall social system. The move is as we know it – the social is parcelled out into smaller components and afterwards put together into a new conception, or better: a diagnosis. In this way, everything is reinterpreted, for instance through the category of risk, to use Ulrich Beck as an example.

One could imagine a parcelling-out of the social, which would dissolve the social into constituent elements, and where the new unity would be a thorough description of these elements and their possible relations. However, such a one-to-one description would be neither interesting nor relevant. In addition to the description being impossible – it is impossible to register and reproduce everything – the truth effect consists in the displacement of a perspective of observation. Realisation, and along with it truth, requires that we are able to see things in a new perspective. Search for the truth necessarily requires a reduction of complexity, as we will never be capable of fully understanding the truth. Sociology – especially diagnostic – has produced these new descriptions abundantly, but its extreme reduction of complexity is not without problems.

The diagnosis-of-the-time tendency in sociology

The interest in diagnosis of the time has been strong in classical and modern sociology alike. Predominant characteristics regarding the present day are knitted together in a diagnosis, which can be critical of the pathologies of the day and at the same time relate to how the present is distinguished from the past (Kristensen 2009). Diagnoses of the time are not the same as social theory, however, as not all social theories are diagnostic; just as diagnoses of the time do not always utilise theoretical concepts.

Certain "contemporary diagnosticians" actually argue that the two things are fundamentally different, as a diagnosis of the time does not merely seek to capture the tendencies of the day that are capable of "bearing history", whereas social theory analyses the actual design of society, including its structures, institutions and actors (Hammershøj 2009: 40; cf. Schmidt 1999b: 18). The question is if the difference is so clear. First, in practice it is difficult to describe and assess the tendencies that will "bear history" without rapidly approaching something tantamount to social theory and sociology. In such a process, using general concepts to capture the tendencies observed in the present is unavoidable. In other words, one inevitably moves in the direction of actual theory formation.

Second, based on this book, we argue that sociology no longer limits itself to describing the actual structures, institutions and actors observed in society. With the communicative turn in sociology, the discipline has shifted away from this type of substantial theory long ago, and now

sociology as an analytic praxis

equally addresses the question about from which perspective society is being observed. Rather, it is a gradual transition between social theory and a diagnosis of time, depending on the level of interest sociologists are taking in the unique characteristics of the day and whether or not this interest is connected to an ambition to make generalisations. Even among the sociologists who are most interested in formulating general social theory, represented here by Habermas and Luhmann, clear diagnosis-of-the-time elements can be found. For example, Habermas's analysis of the collapse of the bourgeois public sphere contains a built-in diagnosis of the pathological tendencies in a media-dominated consumer society, and his more recent criticism of the system's colonisation of the life world similarly includes a diagnosis of the legitimacy crisis of the welfare state in the 1970s and 1980s.

Similarly, Luhmann's work can be said to have diagnosis-of-the-time characteristics, even though they are not coupled to outright social criticism. For one thing, he addresses contemporary phenomena such as ecological disasters and global exclusion (Luhmann 1995; 2002); and for another, functional differentiation is a process in which contemporary social change, such as globalisation and regulatory problems, are summarised and expressed in more simple theoretical terms. Even in the heaviest of sociological theories, it is also possible to find diagnosis-of-the-time elements, which renders it difficult to distinguish completely between the two.

The sociological diagnoses of the time are not without problems, as in some circumstances they reduce and simplify a complex societal development to a single characteristic. It is not always entirely clear how representative the abstract characteristics are; and one might ask whether the diagnosis concept in itself forms the background for such misinterpretations. This calls for a more nuanced concept:

> However, it is not possible to regard diagnoses of the time as attempts at correct and carefully considered descriptions of society. The term "diagnosis" is drawn from the world of medicine, where it refers to drawing conclusions based on the symptoms of underlying illnesses. To the extent that sociological diagnosis of the time is not merely a fashionable term meant to legitimize an arbitrary description of society, it serves to identify specific and possibly unrecognized features of the state of affairs in order to provoke reflection regarding the sustainability of current views, analyses and theories.
>
> (Mortensen 2003: 52, our translation)

As emphasised here, it is not exclusively a question of whether a diagnosis of the time is correct. The tendency towards the systemic colonisation of the life world might be exceptionally clear in one place while the theory does not fit other conditions, as in other spheres of society, at another point in time or among other social groups.

Because sociological theories are so general and abstract, it becomes necessary in concrete analyses to specify how the abstract theory is applied in the analysis, including which existing literature has already made similar adjustments to the theory. At the same time, such adjustments mean that the theory is set in relation to the present in order to consider whether the diagnosis-of-the-time features still hold true. However, it is not entirely easy to determine unequivocally the extent to which a diagnosis of the time or a label for a specific "society" must hold true to be regarded as representative – or at least adequate. Any scientific observation involves a reduction of an array of details to a more simple interpretation. So the solution is not necessarily to argue for greater detail – which would also come at a price in terms of lost analytical trenchancy.

The fact that it is possible to give examples of diagnoses of the time that no longer hold true does not help clarify the validity criteria for diagnoses of the time. An important element in that clarification would otherwise be the time-related limits the diagnosis claims to have. Is the objective of the diagnosis of the time exclusively to offer a snapshot that is perfectly in line with the social conditions at a given point in time? Considering the sociological theories we have dealt with in this book, this would not appear to be the only available criterion. The theories must also be able to say something about how society changes or which mechanisms are important in the change process.

Yet another reason why social theory and diagnoses of the time are inextricably linked is that sociology is born as the science about modern society – and that this alone constitutes an important element in diagnoses of the time. Sociology was originally about the transition from traditional to modern society, but it is now clear that this transition is not an event that takes place at a specific point in time. Description of modern society is always a description of how contemporary society is distinguished from something in the past, whether this past is the Renaissance or the period immediately before the fall of the Berlin Wall. Sociology is also tied to describing modern society diagnostically, as it is fundamentally about social change – or perhaps a society in change. Snapshots are therefore insufficient; the diagnosis of the time must be used in connection with general sociological theories.

A third, more compelling argument for maintaining the contemporary diagnostic aspect in sociology is that sociologists do not have a monopoly on studying society. There is a long list of actors and systems producing general descriptions of the society in which we live, and these descriptions are utilised in politics, the mass media, art and religious institutions.

sociology as an analytic praxis

These descriptions are rarely more solid than the sociological diagnoses of the time, and for this very reason one can argue that sociology must join the fight and challenge other, possibly less advanced descriptions of contemporary society. The fact that diagnoses of the time are produced in sociology as well as in society in general means that we are presented with a cornucopia of diagnoses of the time. Are we at one and the same time living in a risk society, a late modern society, a functionally differentiated society, a control society, a world society, a society of exceptions, a postindustrial society, a neoliberal society, a global society and so forth? The question then becomes whether these descriptions are overlapping or mutually exclusive.

The ambition here is not to declare a winner among the vast number of diagnoses of the time. The high number alone ought to contribute to critical reflection regarding the durability of the respective diagnoses. Such reflection could, for example, give occasion to some descriptions being tied closer to some of society's subsystems, and others being attributed to a more fundamental shift in the structure of society. For example, it is possible to hold on to Luhmann's description of the functionally differentiated society while at the same time viewing neoliberalism as a description of the structural couplings between the political and economic subsystems. Such compromises between multiple diagnoses of the time will often limit the range of some of the descriptions; for example, if neoliberalism can suddenly no longer be used to refer to society in general. The point is that sociology must be able to deal with multiple, overlapping diagnoses of the time and one way is to differentiate between them.

Here, it is also worth considering whether it is the analytical level of sociology that creates problems, as the ambition is as a rule to describe society as a whole. Though we have also touched upon the microlevel in the examination of Goffman's sociology, sociology as represented in this book is undeniably marked by a macroperspective; for example in theories about systemic differentiation, stratification or capitalism.

In a number of other disciplines in the social sciences, the formulation of comprehensive macrotheories has become a thing of the past, as they can be hard to work with and occasionally difficult to combine. Instead, some social scientists formulate so-called mid-range theories aimed at capturing phenomena on a "mesolevel". We find institutions on this level, and examples of mesotheories include theories on how public service organisations act in negotiations or which strategies international organisations use to achieve influence in the United Nations. Mesolevel theories have the advantage of being better delineated and therefore do not overlap in the same manner as sociological macrotheories, as they only cover a limited sub-area. They are easier to couple to empirical investigations because it is only necessary to investigate whether conditions in this sub-area fit with the theory's predictions.

The disadvantage of mesotheories is the risk that they become pure ad hoc descriptions if a theoretical understanding of how the sub-element under study stands in relation to society as a whole is not produced. If the theory on service organisations builds on a set of actor assumptions and the theory on international organisations builds on an entirely different set of assumptions, how can we understand the relations between the two areas? General macrotheories can be difficult to work with, but they do ensure some consistency in the application of theoretical concepts.

Yet another consideration is whether a lower analytical level necessarily means a lower level of abstraction, such that a sociological analysis on the meso- or microlevel operates in practice with more concrete objects than a macrolevel analysis. Again, questions can be raised as to whether researchers, for example in those parts of the social sciences that are based on microeconomics-inspired notions of "homo oeconomicus", are actually working with a rather abstract and unrealistic theory concerning individual motivation. As such, the sociological descriptions of the time do not necessarily become more concrete when switching between analytical levels. The challenge is actually in the process in which different diagnoses are critically related to one another and the durability of old and new concepts alike is challenged.

Sociology should continue to relate to the diagnosis-of-the-time aspect of its legacy, but there is a need for critical reflection on how to do this. Sociological diagnoses of the time do not necessarily mean constant production of radically new descriptions of contemporary society. A sociologist can participate in a critical discussion of what characterises society by challenging the existing conceptualisations of the status of society and showing where they are mistaken.

The theories and descriptions of society presented in this book should therefore not be understood as a catalogue of all concepts sociologists use in their analytical practice. They are intended more as a review of sociological perspectives that one can challenge and correct but not easily avoid. This theoretical self-criticism makes a major difference, as it then becomes possible to challenge the all-too-simple diagnoses of the time. Even though diagnoses of the time thus involve a risk of overassessing current phenomena, we believe that this risk is worth taking for sociology while at the same time relating critically to it through critical self-reflection.

We now turn our attention to determinism and examine whether sociological attempts to explain individual behaviour under certain conditions can include a form of ethically untenable determinism.

sociology as an analytic praxis

Freedom and determinism

The core service of sociology is often seen as an illumination of social reform. Sociological knowledge is intended to contribute to reducing suffering and rendering society more effective. Criminology, which can be seen as a subdiscipline of sociology, has contributed to creating more tolerable conditions for inmates and reducing recidivism. Sociological knowledge has been used in court cases on racial segregation in schools. And, finally, the discipline has contributed to a more humane engineering of our urban spaces. Peter Berger (1963: 17–18) mentions these three examples of the virtues of sociology. Contemporary examples are the numerous reports on substance abuse, negative social inheritance and labour market barriers, and so on, which are regularly published.

Like all other good social science, sociology challenges our prejudices. We mentioned Comte in the preface, but he was merely the first in a long line of sociologists who attempted to establish empirically based (and therefore also testable) knowledge instead of religious convictions, metaphysical speculation or actual prejudice (Elias 1978: 52). On the one hand, sociology shows that the social cannot be reduced to the consciousness and will of individuals. There is, if we are using the metaphors introduced in Chapter 1, something between, over and behind the individuals, of which they are often unaware and unable to control. On the other hand, sociology reveals that society is a product of action and that change is therefore possible.

Sociological knowledge, or at least the "it's society's fault" argument, can also be used in less constructive contexts. During his trial in 1961, Adolf Eichmann – as we saw in Chapter 8 – defended himself by saying that he was only doing his duty. He was doing his best to comply with the orders he had received from his superiors, namely to organise transportation of prisoners to concentration camps. Eichmann therefore saw himself as being devoid of guilt.

As also mentioned in Chapter 8 American social psychologist Stanley Milgram conducted a number of renowned experiments to cast light on this tendency to shirk responsibility the same year Eichmann was on trial. The experiments involved three persons: a student who was supposed to remember a number of word pairings; a teacher (a randomly selected person) who was supposed to train a student to remember these word pairings; and finally an instructor who was supposed to introduce the teacher to the experiment. If the student could not put the words together properly, the teacher was supposed to administer an electric shock and increase the voltage for every wrong answer. Naturally, real shocks were not given – but the teacher did not know this.

The experiment revealed that 37 of the 40 test persons were willing to give 450-volt shocks when the instructor strongly insisted on the scientific necessity of the study. Without such encouragement, the "punishments" typically stopped earlier. The experiments also showed that the proximity between victim and instructor was important for the willingness to continue the experiment. Finally, it was decisive whether or not the experiment took place in a clinical atmosphere at a university or not. In other words, Milgram showed that all of us, not just the Nazi Eichmann, have a tendency to invest our moral will in authorities. When we commit despicable or unpleasant actions, we have a tendency to deny our agency.

As we also briefly saw in Chapter 8, German-Jewish philosopher Hannah Arendt wrote about Eichmann, arguing that his atrocities could be understood as a deliberate denial to think (Arendt 2006 [1963]). Eichmann chose not to reflect on his actions. He saw everything that was going on as external conditions for his work. He was merely one piece in a large puzzle. Arendt referred to this as the banality of evil; that is, an evil that had no fierce desire to do evil but is conditioned by an absence of thought.

Eichmann suffered from what Sartre would refer to as "bad faith" (*mauvaise foi*). Bad faith constitutes an escape from one's own agency, from one's freedom. Instead of acknowledging and accepting one's room for manoeuvre, one completely falls into a role. Berger refers to the waiter who, when at work, becomes the waiter. Or the woman who allows herself to be seduced as though she was completely at the mercy of her desire. Finally, he mentions the terrorist who explains his actions based on historical necessities, party objectives or other circumstances that absolve him of guilt. The actions are merely reactions to previous aggressions; the victims are not innocent, they could have elected a different government, and so on (Berger 1963: 164).

In Sartre's (and Berger's) words, mankind is "condemned to be free". (Berger 1963: 164ff.). Any social situation and institution can form the basis for "bad faith", but they can also have the opposite effect – as occasions for and the protection of the space for reflection and action. In other words, we have a tendency to reify social structures, forgetting that our actions contribute to their reproduction. Even though it might indeed be "society's fault", we often forget that we are also society:

> Nevertheless, today, if we are trying to think in a scientific manner we usually forget that it is possible to refer to all social structures as "mine", "his", "ours", "yours" and "theirs". Instead, we habitually speak of all such structures as if they existed not only above and beyond ourselves but even above and beyond any actual people at all. In this type of thinking, it seems self-evident that on the one hand there is an "I", or there are particular individuals, and on the other

hand there is the social structure, the "environment" which surrounds my own self and every other particular I.

(Elias 1978: 16)

One "goes with the flow" – does what "one" is supposed to do. This "one" becomes our guide in all things. Further along these lines, some accuse sociology of contributing to individuals shirking their responsibilities; to people acting in bad faith. But do sociological explanations absolve us of responsibility for our actions? Does sociology subscribe to a perception of an oversocialised individual devoid of power and ability to exercise freedom? Allow us to wrap things up with three answers to these questions: The first answer touches upon the scientific character of sociology; the second concerns our social being; and the third answer allows the subject, the self or the individual, if you will, a sliver of freedom but refuses to determine this freedom substantially.

The first, possibly slightly defensive answer is to insist that freedom cannot be described scientifically. Science is interested in regularities; and to the extent that freedom is seen as a break with these regularities, it cannot be explained scientifically. Freedom certainly exists, but it cannot be considered a social fact. It does not constitute a phenomenon that is accessible to sociology. All empirically based disciplines – at least those in the social sciences – work in relation to an understanding of phenomena being conditioned by something else. To the extent that freedom is understood as being able to define oneself, it cannot be approximated scientifically – and therefore not sociologically (Berger 1963: 142). Sociology must be kosher to have any legitimacy. If we combine a subjectivist, freedom-oriented perspective with a scientific perspective, we corrupt both.

Sociology is – and this is our second answer – far from an amoral and freedom-denying discipline. It "merely" provides a sober description of our tendency to reify social structures. Sociology is an empirically based discipline that must relate to mankind as social beings. Considering Milgram's experiment, obviously we each have a moral responsibility to object when our actions inflict unbearable pain on others. Correct, but science – here, sociology – must relate to and explain why so many are ready to deposit their conscience with a societal authority. The central sociological and empirical question therefore becomes why we choose to live our lives in bad faith.

Our third answer claims that the oversocialised individual is a caricature. We possess all abilities to reflect on our social selves. Sociology is a resource, of which we all can make use in our attempt to take control of our lives and destinies and qualify how we engage in relations and relate to one another. Let us go into this in greater detail.

234   sociology as an analytic praxis

According to social psychologist George Herbert Mead, thinking is not a monistic activity. When we think, we imagine that we are standing across from someone else. To make things easier, we sometimes think about a concrete person. In principle, however, the generalised other is an abstract person, the incarnation of specific and situation-specific roles (Mead 1977: 34). Our thought includes reflections as to how others will perceive our actions. "Will the others approve?" "Am I doing what a person in this situation ought to do?" "Would it be inappropriate to show up at the party in a tuxedo?" "Would it be inappropriate not to do so?"

We are constantly "in dialogue" with a great number of perspectives. We discuss many religious questions with a specific person and political questions with someone else; that is how our internal dialogue takes place. There are situations in which it is not entirely clear what "one" normally does. The self is necessarily complex, just as the social or societal substances are. When we are thinking, we do not fall completely into the role as the generalised other. Thinking is a form of dialogue, and as such it promotes a minimal distinction between two perspectives. Our thinking can therefore be understood as a dialogue between the "I" and the "me"; that is, between the perspective of the generalised other and how we relate to it on the basis of past experiences and incidents.

Many have claimed that the object of sociology is "the me"; that is, the expectations we encounter and our conceptions of that which we hold in common. Here, social control can be seen as "the me" pressuring "the I" (Mead 1977: 238–239). There is an obvious parallel to Sigmund Freud's writings on the superego. Societalisation, socialisation and individualisation basically refer to an understanding of the self, the individual, the person or "the I", which is the product of social forces. But this knowledge about "the me" with which sociology is contributing makes it possible for "the I" to reflect. In this sense, sociology is not the enemy of freedom but should be seen as a discipline that enables us to exercise our freedom in a genuine, qualified manner. It is only when we become aware of the existence of social structures that we are able to act in relation to them. Althusser claimed that we can only raise ourselves above ideology when we acknowledge that we are knee-deep in it. We can say the same about the social; paradoxically, not until we acknowledge that everything is social can we effectively exercise our freedom.

The challenge facing sociology is to relate critically to our tendency to reify social structures and to struggle against the consequent alienation (Adorno 2000: 3, 150). On that background, one might argue that sociology is a paradoxical discipline. Sociology states that action is societally conditioned; only with the next breath to explain that it is also possible for people – laypersons, scientists and politicians – to act in relation to this reality. As Elias writes, sociology must "make these blind uncontrolled

sociology as an analytic praxis   235

processes more accessible to human understanding"; we can add action (1978: 153–154).

Autonomy and heteronomy

This reflection on the autonomy of the individual naturally leads to a discussion of the disciplinary autonomy of sociology. If all behaviour is socially conditional, then how can sociology be anything else than a reflection of the societal reality, which is its requisite? More specifically, one could ask how sociology can guarantee an independent position vis-à-vis political and social forces. In a concluding reflection, we will discuss the autonomy (or heteronomy, i.e. lack of autonomy) of sociology compared to forces, which determine the discipline, and afterwards discuss the possibilities of sociology meeting its object, society, in an independent and prejudiced way.

Sociology is a politicising and politicised science. On the one hand, politicians want an evidence-based policy and naturally address social science as the science that is capable of providing the foundation for such a policy. Comte's ideal of sociology as a problem solver is still going strong. Apparently, it becomes problematic when politicians cherry-pick research results. If a politician disagrees with the dominant perception in a scientific field, he or she can give a special grant to a scientist who supports his or her political perspective. On this basis, science can be claimed to be dissident, and this paves the way for political prioritisation. The development of any discipline requires academic freedom in choice of method and subject. It is necessary to protect this freedom institutionally and to increasingly support innovative research.

Of course, this is only one aspect. Sociology cannot avoid intervening with the matter it describes. Whereas natural science usually responds to objects that are not affected by observation, it is completely different when it comes to social science. There is no clear line between the political and societal on the one hand and the sociological on the other. Both politicians and sociologists attempt to explain societal behaviour, and both sides suggest arrangements to make common life more tolerable. Just like other scientists, sociologists appreciate when their research makes a difference. They are players, though often weak, in what we have described as the field of power in our presentation of Bourdieu's sociology:

> The idea of a neutral science is a fiction an interested fiction which enables its authors to present a vision of the dominant representation of the social world, neutralised and euphemised into a particularly misrecognisable and symbolically, therefore, particularly effective

form, and to call it scientific. By bringing to light the social mechanisms which ensure the maintenance of the established order and owe their strictly symbolic efficacy to misrecognition of their logic or their effects, the basis of a subtly exacted recognition, social science necessarily takes sides in the political struggle.

(Bourdieu 1975: 36)

Sociology must acknowledge that it contributes to shaping the societal world and thus that its descriptions can never be neutral. Therefore, sociology ought to use its own theories on its own disciplinary practice to become aware of the symbolic violence that it exercises. Sociology should not only reflect on the way it interferes with the surrounding world; it should also respond to the way the surrounding world interferes with sociology, cf. the previous comment on political regulation of sociology. Such a reflection on the heteronomy of the discipline (which in addition to political intervention also could concern the influence of academic fashion trends) paradoxically increases the autonomy of sociology and makes it more relevant politically.

How can objectification of one's own position lead to a better and more self-critical form of sociology that is aware of its own shortages and limitations? We will discuss Bourdieu's criticism of what he describes as scholastic reason. He mentions three scholastic pitfalls. On the one hand, the purpose of mentioning these pitfalls is to point out some of the weaknesses of sociology. On the other hand, the purpose is to introduce a better form of sociology and hereby emphasise how sociology as a discipline should always contain a self-critical discussion of methods, analytical strategies and results.

The scholastics were ancient Greek philosophers who practised philosophy in a relativistic manner. Their goal was not to recommend a certain program, but to challenge everything that could be considered established knowledge. The word is known in this neutral context, but also in a more derogatory sense where the scholastic becomes a form of intervention, which does not serve a profound purpose, that is, controversy for the sake of controversy. Bourdieu's approach to the scholastic is based on these two understandings in the development of a third understanding. According to Bourdieu, the scholastic philosophers' problem was not that they practised philosophy. It was merely that they were blind to the requisites of this practice. Skholè means "free time", and the scholastics' practice exactly required someone else to take care of the practical necessities. In other words, scholastic reason is not aware of its own necessities, and scholasticism is in this way not only a philosophical discipline, but also a problem in the entire scientific field (Bourdieu 2000: 9ff.). We will discuss how these scholastic problems manifest themselves in the sociological field.

sociology as an analytic praxis   237

First, we will take a look at the epistemological scholasticism. A problem within scholasticism is the scientist's tendency to generalise on the basis of his or her own situation. French science historian Gaston Bachelard once expressed it in this way: "The world, which is thought within, is not necessarily the world in which we live" (quoted in Bourdieu 2000: 51). The sociologist – or any other scientist for that matter – often transfers features that are characteristic of a scientific habitus to his or her study objects. One example of this is the tendency to ascribe a very high degree of reflexivity to laymen. Sociology has shown that most of our behaviour is prereflexive. Especially survey research might have problems with this, as it often requires that respondents respond reflexively to a practice that is not reflective in concrete studies. With its high degree of reflexivity, "homo oeconomicus" might be more similar to "homo academicus" than something that is found "in society". Another example is the attempt to make respondents take over scientific categories, for example by asking them which class they think they belong to, cf. Bourdieu's reflections on classes in reality and classes on paper. As a result of the academic style of presentation and way of thinking, a third problem is portraying the nonacademic practice as more organised, coherent and linear than it actually is. Completely eradicating coincidence, contingency, hybridity (which is common when behaviour is placed in diagrams or other schematic presentations) or opacity and complexity is problematic and might say more about the search of stringency and classification of science than about societal life (Bourdieu 2000: 50–65).

If we look at ontological scholasticism, sociology is without doubt an Anglo-American discipline. The scholastic blindness appears as we consider the rest of the world to resemble Europe or USA, if we even care about the world "outside". For instance, Weber defined the state as given a legitimate monopoly on force. Does this monopoly apply everywhere, or is the term bound to a certain Western experience? Ulrich Beck (2006) has also criticised the methodological nationalism of sociology (see Chapter 7). It is necessary to overstep this perspective and develop sociology to make it match globalisation. In the same way, it is remarkable that sociology focuses on the residents. Sociologist Ferdinand Tönnies' (1855–1936) conceptions of *Gemeinschaft* and *Gesellschaft* might be opposed, but they both describe life forms of the residents. This conception – of society being the "small place" characterised by a relatively strong sense of stability – has changed very little since then. The norm is that one belongs in one place and then moves on from this place. But can this conception be considered tenable in the age of globalisation? What about the things that move? Is it possible to consider things in motion to be anomalies, or is it necessary to turn around the perspective so that what is moving and hybrid becomes the primary ontological factor?

The third and last scholastic problem is ethical scholasticism. The tendency to generalise on the basis of one's own perspective also appears in connection with the ethical register. To the extent sociology is explicitly normative one tends to forget that the ethical doctrines and conceptions offered by sociology are rooted in and enabled by a historical development. For instance, Bourdieu mentions Habermas's universal pragmatics and American political philosopher John Rawls's conception of the veil of ignorance as extrapolations of a very specific Western way of thinking about ethics. In a sociological perspective, there are two further problems in connection with universalistic ethics. First, a conception of neutrality might be a cover for an execution of symbolic violence. As we have seen, symbolic violence takes on exactly this shape. In case the alleged universality is not a true universality, it might cause legitimate claims of being heard not to be so. Second, the task of sociology is to listen to these claims and point out when social arrangements miss or require a social similarity and homogeneity that is not present. A relevant example is that political participation requires resources and a certain educational level and that politicians and media are aware that people are different and that the political language might not be as universally appealing as politicians tend to believe (Bourdieu 2000: 65–73).

In Chapter 1, it was stated that sociology is interested in that which lies between, over and behind the individuals. As such, the task of sociology is to objectify social behaviour. The sociologist must necessarily dissociate him- or herself from the description of the members of society themselves and replace it with a scientific description. However, this objectification does not stand alone; it must necessarily be followed by an objectification of sociology and of the sociologist – that is, a critical reflection on the place from which sociology speaks, on its methods and on its results. Of course, being aware of the three blind alleys mentioned by Bourdieu is a good starting point.

The three reservations can also be formulated in a positive manner. At its best, sociology is a discipline that constantly reflects critically on its own methods, challenges its own conceptions of the social, and should contribute to genuine ethical universality.

Sociology as a discipline in flux

Clearly, there is no simple answer to the question, "What is sociology?" For one thing, sociological theories provide many different answers, each accompanied by a large array of theoretical concepts. For another thing, the question does not lend itself to an easy answer, as an important part of the complexity is due to a disagreement on the very question itself, including how sociology understands its own purpose. Seen in relation to other scientific disciplines – not least the natural sciences – this comprehensive debate in the field of sociology might appear to represent a weakness. According to this understanding, sociology has yet to develop into a "normal science" (Kuhn 1973), as there is still conflict regarding its fundamental approach, methods and theoretical assumptions. Others see this conflict as a plus. We belong to the latter group.

Not only does the built-in competition force sociologists to strengthen their respective explanations and theoretical concepts, but this ability to critically relate to one's own production of knowledge constitutes genuine scientific progress. Sociological analysis is part of the society it is describing and must therefore consider its own conceptual production as a social fact.

Conversely, the continued debate in sociology raises major demands with respect to the new theoretical perspectives. They cannot merely describe an object but must rather relate to the sociological canon and whether or not others have previously tackled the same or similar issues. Regardless of how heavy this legacy might seem, the process by which one relates to the sociological tradition contributes to ensuring greater consistency and producing better science. Sociology is a discipline that has accepted that there is more than one way of describing everything; there is never only a single correct perspective, and it is therefore always necessary to challenge the existing social theories and apply new fundamental concepts or methods.

Some might have formed the impression that sociology is constantly revolving around itself and never makes any progress. This may be the case in certain situations; in most cases, however, the array of theoretical approaches and methods contribute to more complete cognition. For example, if we acknowledge that suicide can be regarded as both an individual phenomenon and a social condition, then we have already used multiple theoretical angles to form a more nuanced and complex understanding of suicide. This does not necessarily mean that we have gathered more empirical knowledge about suicide, but it becomes possible to sort the data in a different manner and to ascribe more reflected significance to them.

Reflection regarding the sociological tradition should not lead to conservatism. Relating to the sociological tradition does not necessarily mean that all new theories need to stand on the shoulders of the classic sociologists. For example, Luhmann uses his own discussion of the sociological canon as occasion to draw a line in the sand and insist on ontology and epistemology of differences as a new beginning for sociology (Luhmann 2000b). He even claims that sociology is in the midst of a theoretical crisis, as sociologists far too often merely study and recombine the classics instead of thinking in terms of theory concerning the object of sociology: society (Luhmann 2000a: 29–30).

Sociologists should not be surprised if the classic theories fall short in the analysis of society 150 years after they were developed. In many cases, sociology has had a direct impact on how society has been designed; or conversely, attempts have been made to distance oneself from the society that has been framed in the sociological tradition. In other words, there is interaction between theory and the object of investigation in the social sciences (Hacking 1999: 31). This means that we cannot merely study society without considering other theoretical perspectives that have been canonised, so to speak, through the development of society. Marx's concept of the classes, for example, has played a decisive role in the way our society has developed.

Sociology must continue to develop and refine its theoretical constructs, not because scientific development follows a beautiful, linear curve. The primary reason for continued conceptual development is simply that the object of investigation in sociology, society, is constantly changing. If an object of investigation is constantly moving, then the lens with which we attempt to capture the object must naturally follow.

The sociological analysis – seven attention points

In closing, we will give a brief, general introduction to how you as a student can get started on your own sociological analyses. We have so far reviewed renowned sociologists' analyses of phenomena such as capitalism, alienation, suicide, etc., and in this concluding chapter we have looked at what generally should be understood by an analysis – and how a good analysis lets us see things in a phenomenon that we would not otherwise see. As a student in the field of sociology you will at some point be challenged to conduct your own sociological analysis of a phenomenon. You may, for example during exams, be asked to conduct a sociological analysis of a phenomenon using a theory that has been covered in class. But how do you do that? How do you in concrete terms start the work?

Let's take a fictional case. You are handed a newspaper article about rising unemployment in France. Unemployment has increased from 8 per cent of the workforce to 10.5 per cent over a five-year period. The article is from a major national newspaper and describes the increase in unemployment in general. It also contains a description and an interview with a 55-year-old man who has previously worked in the industry in the northern part of France but has now lost his job. He explains how it was easier being a worker when he started as a young apprentice in a local industrial company 35 years ago and continues:

sociology as an analytic praxis 241

My old workplace is long gone. Now there are only a few jobs left in the industry in this area – and these jobs are taken over by cheap labour from Eastern Europe.

The article also describes how the young people – especially young women – leave the area in favour of the larger university cities. Once they leave, they never come back. Wealthy families are also fleeing the area.

How do you start the analysis of this case; what do you do? There are many ways to go about it, and you have to make many choices along the way. We therefore do not offer a ready-made guide, but list seven things to consider and to build on, when you start the analysis.

1. Read the assignment formulation and the empirical case carefully

One of the best pieces of advice is probably to read the assignment formulation and the empirical case carefully before you begin your analysis. What are you asked to do? Conduct an analysis, describe something, or something else? Structure the assignment in accordance with the assignment formulation. In addition to understanding the assignment and the article, it is important to have a critical approach to the case. For instance, ask yourself: Does the article reach plausible conclusions? If you are given a scientific article instead of a newspaper article, the conclusions may be perfectly consistent with the scientific knowledge in the area, but you should always critically examine the information. Are the figures in the article correct? Is the described rise in unemployment in fact a break with a general trend of declining unemployment? Is the increase related to particular industries? What is the situation in other countries; is it a cross-border phenomenon or exclusively a French phenomenon? Are all regions in France equally affected by the rise in unemployment?

2. Delineate the phenomenon

Phenomenon awareness is also crucial for a good analysis. Which phenomena are described in the article, and which phenomenon do you want to focus on? Most texts describe several phenomena, and it is important that you make up your mind as to which phenomenon you want to analyse – before you start your analysis. In this case, the phenomenon could be "general unemployment", "unemployment in France", "capitalism", "the development of the capitalist mode of production", "work", "globalisation" or "immigration". The article also notes that young women are more likely than men to leave the area. This phenomenon might also be worth looking into. Remember to explain your choices: How have you delineated your phenomenon, and why did you choose to look at this particular phenomenon?

3. Understand the phenomenon sociologically

As discussed in the example of Hegel's reading of the criminal man who was brought to the scaffold, a sociological analysis aims at understanding human actions in a broader social context. When the fictional article in our example describes how young people move from the area, a sociological analysis would not conclude that this only happens as a result of individual adventurousness or the urge to travel, but would emphasise that this apparently is a social trend that can be observed everywhere in Western Europe, perhaps even globally. A sociological analysis would also note that more young women than men seem to choose to go to the big cities, and only to a limited extent do they return.

4. Open the case up with social theory

The sociologists reviewed in this book all perform analyses of empirical phenomena – and do it sociologically. So what is characteristic of their way of seeing and approaching a phenomenon? Say that we have decided to analyse the phenomenon "the changing living and working conditions of industrial workers in northern France", how can we understand this phenomenon using social theory? The social theories reviewed in the book offer a set of lenses that can help us see things about the phenomenon that we would not otherwise see. Marx lets us see the phenomenon as part of a particular period in history, capitalism, where our basic necessities are produced in a certain way controlled by "capital's law of motion". With Sennett one would also be able to understand the phenomenon on the basis of capitalism, but also as part of the latest development of capitalism, which he calls "flexible capitalism". With Bauman's theory of globalisation, the phenomenon can be understood as a consequence of globalisation, which divides people across national borders into "globals" and "locals". Many other sociologists treated in the book could illuminate this phenomenon as well.

5. Be critical towards the selected theory

It is important to be aware of the strengths and weaknesses of the chosen theory in relation to the phenomenon. A good sociological analysis must reflect on the applied theory's scope and limits in

sociology as an analytic praxis   243

understanding the phenomenon. No matter which theory is used to illuminate a phenomenon there will always be something you cannot see with this theory. In other words, any theory has its blind spots. It may therefore be advantageous to combine several theories in the analysis in order to shed light on as much of the phenomenon as possible. Although Sennett can help us understand how capitalism currently places new demands on us to be flexible and adaptable, his theory of flexible capitalism says nothing about the relationship between "them" and "us" – between eastern Europeans and old industrial workers in northern France. Sennett's theory could therefore successfully be combined with other theories to give us a fuller picture of the phenomenon of "the changing living and working conditions of industrial workers in northern France".

6. Put the phenomenon at the centre of the analysis

One of the most common mistakes students make when they are asked to make their own sociological analyses is that they only use a phenomenon to illustrate a theoretical point of a sociologist. However, this is turning things upside down. The phenomenon must be at the centre of the analysis. It is the phenomenon we would like to know more about – not the theory. In our fictional case, we can therefore say that we analyse "the changing living and working conditions of industrial workers in northern France," and not Sennett's theory on flexible capitalism or Bauman's theory on the human consequences of globalisation. However, by looking at the worker from northern France through Bauman's and Sennett's theories he appears different than if we had looked at him without these theories – or through other theoretical lenses.

7. Be conscious of your strategy of analysis

Finally, how do you want to approach the analysis? Where are the cross points between the phenomenon and theories that you use? What elements do you in particular want to look for and how will you do it? In other words, what is your strategy of analysis? Use your own approach as the basis for your outline of the assignment. Remember, you are in the driver's seat – not the phenomenon or the theory you use. You decide with your perspective what is important in the theories. You do not have to explain the whole theory but can easily focus on individual concepts and use them in your analysis.

We hope that these seven points will help you get started with your own sociological and analytical work. It is challenging to make a good sociological analysis, but when successful it helps us to better understand the society we live in. But not only that, it also helps us understand what it means to be a human being in precisely this kind of society. So throw yourself into it. We wish you luck on your journey towards new discoveries!

References

Abbott, A. (1999). *Department and Discipline*: *Chicago Sociology at One Hundred*. Chicago: University of Chicago Press.

Adorno, T.W. (2000 [1968]). *Introduction to Sociology*. Cambridge, UK: Polity Press.

Althusser, L. (1969 [1965]). *For Marx*. London: Verso.

Althusser, L. (1971). *Essays on Ideology*. London: Verso.

Althusser, L. (2006). *Philosophy of the Encounter: Later Writings, 1978–1987*. London: Verso.

American College Health Association. (2014). *National College Health Assessment II: Reference Group Executive Summary, Spring 2014*. Hannover: American College Health Association.

Andersen, N. Åkerstrøm. (2003). *Borgerens kontraktliggørelse* [Contracting the Citizen]. Copenhagen: Hans Reitzels Forlag.

Andersen, N. Åkerstrøm. (2006). *Partnerskabelse* [Creating Partnerships]. Copenhagen: Hans Reitzels Forlag.

Anderson, J. (1995). Translator's introduction. In: A. Honneth (ed.), *The Struggle for Recognition: The Moral Grammar of Social Conflicts* (pp. x–xxi). Cambridge, UK: Polity.

Anderson, N. (1923). *On Hobos and Homelessness*. Chicago: University of Chicago Press.

Arendt, H. (2006 [1963]). *Eichmann in Jerusalem: A Report on the Banality of Evil*. London: Penguin Classics.

Baudrillard, J. (1982 [1978]). *À l'ombre des majorités silencieuses ou la fin du social*. Paris: Denoël/Gonthier.

Bauman, Z. (1989). *Modernity and the Holocaust*. Ithaca, NY: Cornell University Press.

Bauman, Z. (1993). *Postmodern Ethics*. Oxford: Blackwell Publishers.

Bauman, Z. (1998). *Globalization: The Human Consequences*. Cambridge, UK: Polity Press.

Bauman, Z. (2000). *Liquid Modernity*. Cambridge, UK: Polity Press.

Bauman, Z. (2001). *Community: Seeking Safety in an Unsecure World*. Cambridge, UK: Polity Press.

Bauman, Z. (2008). *The Art of Life*. Cambridge, UK: Polity Press.

Bauman, Z. and May, T. (2014). *Thinking Sociologically*. Hoboken, NJ: John Wiley & Sons.

Bech, H. (1999). *Leisure Pursuit Studies in Modernity, Masculinity, Homosexuality and Late Modernity: A Survey of Some Results.* Sociologisk Rapportserie, 3. Copenhagen: Sociologisk Institut.

Beck, U. (1991 [1989]). Überlebensfrage, sozialstruktur und ökologische aufklärung [Questions of survival, social structure and ecological awareness]. In: U. Beck (ed.), *Politik in der Risikogesellschaft* [Politics in the Risk-Society] (pp. 117–139). Frankfurt am Main: Suhrkamp.

Beck, U. (1992 [1986]). *Risk Society: Towards a New Modernity.* London: Sage.

Beck, U. (1994). The Reinvention of Politics: Towards a Theory of Reflexive Modernization. In: U. Beck, A. Giddens and S. Lash (eds.), *Reflexive Modernization: Politics, Tradition and Aesthetics in the Modern Social Order* (pp. 1–56). Cambridge, UK: Polity Press.

Beck, U. (1995). *Ecological Politics in an Age of Risk*. Cambridge, UK: Polity Press.

Beck, U. (2000). *What Is Globalization?* Cambridge, UK: Polity Press.

Beck, U. (2005). *Power in the Global Age*. Cambridge, UK: Polity Press.

Beck, U. (2006). *Cosmopolitan Vision*. Cambridge, UK: Polity Press.

Beck, U. (2009). *World at Risk*. Cambridge, UK: Polity Press.

Beck, U. and Beck-Gernsheim, E. (2002). *Individualization: Institutionalized Individualism and its Social and Political Consequences*. London: Sage.

Beck, U. and Grande, E. (2007). *Cosmopolitan Europe.* Cambridge, UK: Polity Press.

Bell, D. (1973). *The Coming of Post-Industrial Society: A Venture in Social Forecasting*. New York: Basic Books.

Berger, P. (1963). *Invitation to Sociology: A Humanist Perspective*. Middlesex: Penguin Books.

Bjerre, H.J. (2015). *Analysér* [Analyze]. Copenhagen: Forlaget Mindspace.

Bloch, C. (1998). Når arbejdet bliver vores andet hjem: om kommercialiseringen af sociale relationer [When Work Becomes Our Second Home: Regarding the Commercialization of Social Relations]. *Dansk Sociologi*, 9(2), pp. 91–96.

Blok, A. and Elgaard Jensen, T. (2011). *Bruno Latour: Hybrid Thoughts in a Hybrid World.* London: Routledge.

Boltanski, L. (1999 [1993]). *Distant Suffering: Morality, Media and Politics*. Cambridge, UK: Cambridge University Press.

Boltanski, L. and Chiapello, E. (2005 [1999]). *The New Spirit of Capitalism*. London: Verso.

Boltanski, L. and Thévenot, L. (2006 [1991]). *On Justification: Economies of Worth.* Princeton, NJ: Princeton University Press.

Bourdieu, P. (1975). The Specificity of the Scientific Field and the Social Conditions of the Progress of Reason. *Social Science Information*, 14(6), pp. 19–47.

Bourdieu, P. (1977 [1972]). *Outline of a Theory of Practice*. Cambridge: Cambridge University Press.

references   247

Bourdieu, P. (1984 [1979]). *Distinction: A Social Critique of the Judgment of Taste*. London: Routledge.

Bourdieu, P. (1986 [1983]). The forms of capital. In: J.G. Richardson (red.), *Handbook of Theory and Research for the Sociology of Education* (pp. 241–258). New York: Greenwood Press.

Bourdieu, P. (1987). What Makes a Social Class? On the Theoretical and Practical Existence of Groups. *Berkeley Journal of Sociology*, 32, pp. 1–17.

Bourdieu, P. (1990 [1980]). *The Logic of Practice*. Cambridge, UK: Polity Press.

Bourdieu, P. (1991a [1982]). *Language and Symbolic Power*. Cambridge, MA: Harvard University Press.

Bourdieu, P. (1991b [1971]). Genesis and Structure of the Religious Field. *Comparative Social Research*, 13, pp. 1–43.

Bourdieu, P. (2000 [1997]). *Méditations Pascaliennes*. Stanford: Stanford University Press.

Bourdieu, P. and Passeron, J.-C. (1977 [1970]). *Reproduction in Education, Society and Culture*. London: Sage.

Bourdieu, P. and Wacquant, L.J.D. (1996 [1992]). *An Invitation to Reflective Sociology.* Cambridge, UK: Polity Press.

Bulmer, M. (1984). The significance of the Chicago school of sociology. In: M. Bulmer (ed.), *The Chicago School of Sociology: Institutionalization, Diversity, and the Rise of Sociological Research* (pp. 1–11). Chicago: University of Chicago Press.

Butler, J. (1988). Performative Acts and Gender Constitution: An Essay in Phenomenology and Feminist Theory. *Theatre Journal*, 40(4), pp. 519–531.

Butler, J. (1993). *Bodies that Matter: On the Discursive Limits of "Sex"*. London: Routledge.

Butler, J. (1994). Gender as Performance: An Interview with Judith Butler. *Radical Philosophy*, 67, pp. 32–39.

Butler, J. (1999). *Gender Trouble: Feminism and the Subversion of Identity*. London: Routledge.

Butler, J. (with G. Olson and L. Worsham). (2004a). Changing the subject: Judith Butler's politics of radical resignification. In: S. Salih (ed.), *The Judith Butler Reader* (pp. 325–356). Oxford: Blackwell.

Butler, J. (2004b). *Undoing Gender*. London: Routledge.

Camus, A. (2016 [1942]). *The Stranger*. Falls Village: Hamilton Books.

Carleheden, M. (1998). Another Sociology – The Future of Sociology from a Critical Theoretical Perspective. *Dansk Sociologi*, 9, pp. 55–75.

Chiapello, È. (2003). Reconciling the Two Principal Meanings of the Notion of Ideology: The Example of the Concept of the 'Spirit of Capitalism'. *European Journal of Social Theory*, 6(2), pp. 155–171.

Chronicle of Higher Education. (2015). September 4, 62(1).

Coser, L.A. (1971). *Masters of Sociological Thought: Ideas in Historical and Social Context.* New York: Harcourt Brace Jovanovich.

De Beauvoir, S. (2007 [1949]). *The Second Sex.* London: Vintage.

Deleuze, G. (1995 [1990]). *Negotiations*. New York: Columbia University Press.

Durkheim, E. (1938 [1895]). *Rules of Sociological Methods*. Chicago: University of Chicago Press.

Durkheim, E. (1951 [1897]). *Suicide*. New York: Free Press.

Durkheim, E. (1964 [1898]). *The Division of Labour in Society*. New York: Free Press.

Elias, N. (1978 [1970]). *What Is Sociology?* New York: Columbia University Press.

Engels, F. (1975 [1883]). Speech at the graveside of Karl Marx. In: F. Engels (ed.), *On Marx* (pp. 16–18). Peking: Foreign Languages Press, http://www.marx2mao.com/M&E/OM77.html#s2

Engels, F. (1988 [1990–1995]). *Briefe über den Historischen Materialismus* [Letters on Historical Materialism (1890–1895), 25]. Letter of January 1894 (pp. 71–74). Berlin:Dietz Verlag.

Ewald, François. (1991 [1989]). Die Versicherungs-Gesellschaft [The Insurance Society]. In: U. Beck (ed.), *Politik in der Risikogesellschaft* [Politics in the Risk-Society] (pp. 288–301). Frankfurt am Main: Suhrkamp.

Featherstone, M. (1991). Georg Simmel: An Introduction. *Theory, Culture and Society*, 8, pp. 1–16.

Foucault, M. (1969). *L'archéologie du Savior*. Paris: Gallimard.

Foucault, M. (1973 [1963]). *The Birth of the Clinic: An Archeology of Medical Perception*. London: Vintage.

Foucault, M. (1977). *Discipline and Punish: The Birth of the Prison*. New York: Random House.

Foucault, M. (1978). *The Will to Knowledge: The History of Sexuality 1*. London: Penguin.

Foucault, M. (1984). Nietzsche, genealogy, history. In: P. Rabinow (ed.), *The Foucault Reader* (pp. 76–100). New York: Pantheon Books.

Foucault, M. (2004). *The Birth of Biopolitics: Lectures at the Collège de France 1978–1979*. Paris: Seuil/Gallimard.

Foucault, M. (2007 [1978]). *Security, Territory, Population: Lectures at the Collège de France 1977–1978*. New York: Palgrave Macmillan.

Foucault, M. (2008 [1983]). *Le gouvernement de soi et des autres Course au Collège de France 1982–1983*. Paris: Seuil/Gallimard.

Freud, S. (1999 [1942]). *Die Traumdeutung, Gesammelte Werke II/III* [The Interpretation of Dreams, Collected Works II/III]. Frankfurt am Main: Fischer Taschenbuch Verlag.

Garey, A.I. and Hansen, K.V. (2011). Introduction: An eye on emotion in the study of families and work. In: A. Garey and K.V. Hansen (eds.), *At the Heart of Work and Family: Engaging the Ideas of Arlie Hochschild* (pp. 1–16). New Brunswick, NJ: Rutgers University Press.

Giddens, A. (1984). *The Constitution of Society*. Los Angeles: University of California Press.

Giddens, A. (1990). *The Consequences of Modernity*. Cambridge, UK: Polity Press.

Giddens, A. (1991). *Modernity and Self-Identity: Self and Society in the Late Modern Age*. Cambridge, UK: Polity Press.

Goffman, E. (1959). *The Presentation of Self in Everyday Life*. New York: Anchor Books.

Goffman, E. (1961). *Asylums: Essays on the Social Situation of Mental Patients and Other Inmates*. New York: Anchor Books.

references

Goffman, E. (1963). *Stigma: Notes on the Management of Spoiled Identity*. Englewood Cliffs, NJ: Prentice-Hall.

Goffman, E. (1967). *Interaction Ritual*. Harmondsworth: Penguin.

Golombok, S. (2005). Unusual Families. *Reproductive Biomedicine Online*, 10(1), pp. 9–12.

Habermas, J. (1987 [1981]). *The Theory of Communicative Action, Volume Two: The Critique of Functionalist Reason*. Cambridge, UK: Polity Press.

Habermas, J. (1991 [1962]). *The Structural Transformation of the Public Sphere: An Inquiry into a Category of Bourgeois Society*. Cambridge, MA: MIT Press.

Habermas, J. (2008 [2005]). *Between Naturalism and Religion*. Cambridge, UK: Polity Press.

Hacking, I. (1999). *The Social Construction of What?* Cambridge, MA: Harvard University Press.

Hammershøj, L.G. (2009). Samtidsdiagnose som kritik [Diagnostics of the Contemporary as a Critique]. *Dansk Sociologi*, 19(4), pp. 33–47.

Haraway, D. (1988). Situated Knowledges: The Science Question in Feminism and the Privilege of Partial Perspective. *Feminist Studies*, 14(3), pp. 575–599.

Haraway, D. (1991 [1985]). A cyborg manifesto: Science, technology, and socialist-feminism in the late twentieth century. In: D. Haraway (ed.), *Simians, Cyborgs, and Women: The Reinvention of Nature* (pp. 149–181). London: Free Association Books.

Haraway, D. (1997). *Modest_Witness@Second_Millennium.FemaleMan_Meets_ OncoMouse: Feminism and Technoscience*. New York: Routledge.

Haraway, D. (2000). *How Like a Leaf: An Interview with Thyrza Nichols Goodeve*. New York: Routledge.

Haraway, D. (with N. Lykke, R. Markussen and F. Olesen). (2004a [2000]). Cyborgs, coyotes, and dogs: A kinship of feminist figurations and there are always more things going on than you thought! Methodologies as thinking technologies: An interview with Donna Haraway. In: D. Haraway (ed.), *The Haraway Reader* (pp. 321–343). London: Routledge.

Haraway, D. (2004b). *Crystals, Fabrics, and Fields: Metaphors that Shape Embryos*. Berkeley: North Atlantic Books.

Haraway, D. (2004c). The promises of monsters: A regenerative politics for inappropriate/d others. In: D. Haraway (ed.), *The Haraway Reader* (pp. 63–124). London: Routledge.

Haraway, D. (2008). *When Species Meet*. Minneapolis: University of Minnesota Press.

Haraway, D. and Gane, N. (2006). When We Have Never Been Human, What Is to Be Done? Interview with Donna Haraway. *Theory, Culture & Society*, 23(7–8), pp. 135–158.

Haraway, D. and Williams, J. (2010). Science Stories: An Interview with Donna Haraway. *Minnesota Review*, 73–74, pp. 133–163.

Harding, S. (1986). *The Science Question in Feminism*. Ithaca, NY, and London: Cornell University Press.

Harste, G. and Mortensen, N. (2007). Sociale samhandlingsteorier [Theories of social interaction]. In: H. Andersen and L.B. Kaspersen (eds.), *Klassisk og Moderne*

Samfundsteori [Classic and Modern Social Theory] (pp. 194–218). Copenhagen: Hans Reitzels Forlag.

Hastrup, K. (1992). *Det antropologiske projekt – om forbløffelse* [The Anthropological Project – on Amazement]. Copenhagen: Gyldendal.

Hegel, G.W.F. (2016 [1808]). "Who Thinks Abstractly?", https://www.marxists.org/reference/archive/hegel/works/se/abstract.htm

Helmer, O. and Žižek, S. (1995). Venstresiden bør lære av fundamentalisterne! [The Left Should Learn from the Fundamentalists!]. *Samtiden*, 6, pp. 14–23.

Hobbes, T. (1991 [1651]). *Leviathan*. Cambridge, UK: Cambridge University Press.

Hochschild, A.R. (1989). *The Second Shift: Working Parents and the Revolution at Home*. New York: Viking.

Hochschild, A.R. (1997). *The Time Bind: When Work Becomes Home and Home Becomes Work*. New York: Metropolitan/Holt.

Hochschild, A.R. (2005). On the Edge of the Time Bind: Time and Market Culture. *Social Research: An International Quarterly*, 72(2), pp. 339–354.

Hochschild, A.R. (2012 [1983]). *The Managed Heart: Commercialization of Human Feeling*. Berkeley: University of California Press.

Højgaard, L. (2007). Feministisk videnskabsfilosofi: Introduktion [Feminist Philosophy of Science: Introduction]. In: D.M. Søndergaard (ed.), *Feministiske Tænkere: En Tekstsamling* [Feminist Thinkers: A Text Collection] (pp. 265–273). Copenhagen: Hans Reitzels Forlag.

Højgaard, L. (2012). Judith Butler: Det performative køn og de sociale kategoriers dekonstruktion [Judith Butler: Performative gender and the deconstruction of social categories]. In: M.H. Jacobsen and A. Petersen (eds.), *Samfundsteori og Samtidsdiagnose: En Introduktion til Sytten Nyere Samfundstænkere for det Pædagogiske Felt* [Social Theory and Social Diagnosis. An Introduction to 17 Societal Thinkers within the Field of Education] (pp. 280–294). Copenhagen: Forlaget Unge Pædagoger.

Honneth, A. (1994). The Social Dynamics of Disrespect: On the Location of Critical Theory Today. *Constellations*, 1, pp. 255–269.

Honneth, A. (1995). *The Struggle for Recognition: The Moral Grammar of Social Conflicts*. Boston: MIT Press.

Honneth, A. (1996). Pathologies of the social: The past and present of social philosophy. In: D.M. Rasmussen (ed.), *Handbook of Critical Theory* (pp. 369–398). Cambridge, MA: Blackwell.

Honneth, A. (2004). Organized Self-Realization: Some Paradoxes of Individualization. *European Journal of Social Theory*, 7(4), pp. 463–478.

Honneth, A. (2010). *The Pathologies of Individual Freedom: Hegel's Social Theory*. Princeton, NJ: Princeton University Press.

Honneth, A. and Boltanski, L. (2009). Soziologie der Kritik oder kritische Theorie? Ein Gespräch mit Robin Celikates [Sociology of critique or critical sociologie? A talk with Robin Celikates]. In: J. Rahel and T. Wesche (eds.), *Was ist Kritik?* (pp. 81–114). Frankfurt am Main: Suhrkamp.

Horkheimer, M. and Adorno, T.W. (1996 [1944]). *Oplysningens dialektik: filosofiske fragmenter* [Dialectic of Enlightenment]. Copenhagen: Gyldendal.

references 251

Hyldgaard, K. (1998). *Fantasien til Afmagten: Syv kapitler om Lacan og filosofien* [Imagination to Impotence: Seven Chapters about Lacan and the Philosophy]. Copenhagen: Museum Tusculanums Forlag.

Iarovici, D. (2015). Perspectives on College Student Suicide. *Psychiatric Times*, 32(7), p. 27.

Jacobsen, M.H. (2007). En (u)passende mængde pessimisme? – om dystre sociologiske samtidsdiagnoser over arbejdslivet [An Inappropriate Amount of Scepticism? – Sombre Sociological Diagnoses about Work-Life]. *Tidsskrift for Arbejdsliv*, 9(2), pp. 1399–1442.

Jakobsen, J. (2011). Axel Honneth: Selvrealisering og samfundskritik [Axel Honneth: Self-realisation and social critique] In: A. Petersen (ed.), *Selvets Sociologiske Perspektiver* [Sociological Perspectives of the Self] (pp. 214–244). Copenhagen: Hans Reitzels Forlag.

Järvinen, M., Larsen, J.E. and Mortensen, N. (eds.) (2002). *Det magtfulde møde mellem system og klient* [The Powerful Meeting Between System and Client]. Aarhus: Aarhus Universitetsforlag.

Järvinen, M. and Mik-Meyer, N. (eds.) (2003). *At skabe en klient. Institutionelle identiteter i socialt arbejde* [Creating the Client: Institutional Identities in Social Work]. Copenhagen: Hans Reitzels Forlag.

Jensen, H. (2011). *Det faderløse samfund* [The Fatherless Society]. Copenhagen: People's Press.

Juul, S. (2013). *Solidarity in Individualized Societies: Recognition, Justice and Good Judgement*. London: Routledge.

Jørgensen, A. (2001). Robert Park: Humanøkologi og sociale balancer [Robert Park: Human ecology and social balances]. In: M.H. Jacobsen, M. Carleheden and S. Kristiansen (eds.), *Tradition og Fornyelse: En Problemorienteret Teorihistorie for Sociologien* [Tradition and Change: A Problem-Oriented History of Sociological Theory] (pp. 155–168). Aalborg: Aalborg Universitetsforlag.

Jørgensen, A. (2005). Chicagoskolen – farvel til 'bibliotekssociologien' [The Chicago school – goodbye to the 'library sociology']. In: M.H. Jacobsen, S. Kristiansen and A. Prieur (eds.), *Liv, fortælling, Tekst – Strejftog i Kvalitativ Sociologi* [Life, Narration and Text – Incursions in Qualitative Sociology] (pp. 2–5). Aalborg: Aalborg Universitetsforlag.

Jørgensen, A. and Schmidt, D. (2009). The Chicago School of Sociology: Survival in the urban jungle. In: M.H. Jacobsen (ed.), *Encountering the Everyday. An Introduction to the Sociologies of the Unnoticed* (pp. 45–68). New York: Palgrave Macmillan.

Kant, I. (2010 [1784]). An Answer to the Question: 'What Is Enlightenment?'. In: *An Answer to the Question: What Is Enlightenment* (pp. 1–11). London: Penguin.

Kristensen, J.E. (2009). Krise, kritik og samtidsdiagnostik [Crisis, Critique and Diagnostics of the Contemporary]. *Dansk Sociologi*, 19(4), pp. 5–31.

Kuhn, T.S. (1973 [1962]). *The Structure of Scientific Revolutions*. Chicago: University of Chicago Press.

Latour, B. (1987). *Science in Action*. Cambridge, MA: Harvard University Press.

Latour, B. (1988 [1985]). *The Pasteurization of France*. Cambridge, MA: Harvard University Press.

Latour, B. (1993 [1991]). *We Have Never Been Modern.* London: Longman.

Latour, B. (2000). When Things Strike Back: A Possible Contribution of 'Science Studies' to the Social Sciences. *British Journal of Sociology,* 51(1), pp. 107–123.

Latour, B. (2002). Gabriel Tarde and the End of the Social. In: P. Joyce (ed.), *The Social in Question: New Bearings in History and the Social Sciences* (pp. 11–132). London: Routledge.

Latour, B. (2005). *Resembling the Social: An Introduction to Actor-Network-Theory.* Oxford: Oxford University Press.

Latour, B. (2015). Fetish-factish. *Material Religion,* 7(1), pp. 42–49.

Latour, B. and Woolgar, S. (1979). *Laboratory Life: The Construction of Scientific Facts.* Princeton, NJ: Princeton University Press.

Levine, D.N. (1971). Introduction. In: D.N. Levine (ed.), *Georg Simmel – On Individuality and Social Forms* (pp. ix–lxv). Chicago: University of Chicago Press.

Luhmann, N. (1982). *The Differentiation of Society.* New York: Columbia University Press.

Luhmann, N. (1988). *Erkenntnis als Konstruktion.* Bern: Benteli.

Luhmann, N. (1989). *Ecological Communication.* Cambridge, UK: Polity Press.

Luhmann, N. (1992). The Concept of Society. *Thesis Eleven,* 31, pp. 67–80.

Luhmann, N. (1995 [1986]). Økologisk kommunikation: Kan det moderne menneske indstille sig på økologiske farer? [Organic communication: Can modern man adjust to organic dangers?]. In: J.C. Jacobsen (ed.), *Autopoiesis II: Udvalgte tekster af Niklas Luhmann* [Autopoiesis II: Selected Texts by Niklas Luhmann] (pp. 100–115). Copenhagen: Forlaget Politisk Revy.

Luhmann, N. (1996). *Social Systems.* Redwood City, CA: Stanford University Press.

Luhmann, N. (2000a [1984]). *Sociale systemer: Grundrids til en almen teori* [Social Systems]. Copenhagen: Hans Reitzels Forlag.

Luhmann, N. (2000b [1994]). 'Hvad er tilfældet?' og 'hvad ligger der bag?' De to sociologier og samfundsteorien. ['What Is Coincidence?' & 'What Lies Behind?'] *Distinktion,* 1, pp. 9–25.

Luhmann, N. (2002). Inklusion og eksklusion [Inclusion and Exclusion]. *Distinktion,* 4, pp. 121–139.

Lukács, G. (1991 [1918]). Georg Simmel. *Theory, Culture and Society,* 8, pp. 146–149.

Lykke, N. (2010). *Feminist Studies: A Guide to Intersectional Theory, Methodology and Writing.* New York: Routledge.

Lykkeberg, R. (2007). Vi aner ikke, hvornår vi brænder ud: Interview med Sennett [We Never Know When We Will Burn Out: Interview with Sennett], 21 April, pp. 12–13.

Lyotard, F. (1984 [1979]). *The Postmodern Condition: A Report on Knowledge.* Minneapolis: University of Minnesota Press.

Markussen, R. and Gad, C. (2007). Feministisk STS [Feminist STS]. In: C.B. Jensen, P. Lauritsen and F. Olesen (eds.), *Introduktion til STS: Science, Technology, Society* [Introduction to Science, Technology and Society] (pp. 157–181). Copenhagen: Hans Reitzels Forlag.

references   253

Marx, K. (1887 [1867]). *Capital. Volume I: A Critique of Political Economy*, S. Moore and E. Aveling (trans.), F. Engels (ed.). Moscow: Progress Publishers, https://www.marxists.org/archive/marx/works/download/pdf/Capital-Volume-I.pdf

Marx, K. (1959a [1844]). Estranged labour. In: *Economic and Philosophical Manuscripts of 1844.* Moscow: Progress Publishers, https://www.marxists.org/archive/marx/works/1844/manuscripts/labour.htm

Marx, K. (1959b [1894]). *Capital: The Process of Capitalist Production as a Whole.* Volume III, Friedrick Engels (ed.). New York: International Publishers, https://www.marxists.org/archive/marx/works/1894-c3/

Marx, K. (1969 [1845]). Theses on Feuerbach. In: *Marx/Engels Selected Works, Volume One* (pp. 13–15). Moscow: Progress Publishers, https://www.marxists.org/archive/marx/works/1845/theses/theses.htm

Marx, K. (1977 [1859]). Preface. In: *A Contribution to the Critique of Political Economy*, with some notes by R. Rojas. Moscow: Progress Publishers, https://www.marxists.org/archive/marx/works/1859/critique-pol-economy/preface.htm

Marx, K. (1990 [1867]). *Capital. Volume 1.* London: Penguin.

Marx, K. and Engels, F. (1969 [1848]). Manifesto of the communist party. In: *Marx/Engels Selected Works Volume One* (pp. 98–137). Moscow: Progress Publishers, https://www.marxists.org/archive/marx/works/1848/communist-manifesto/

Mead, G.H. (1977). *On Social Psychology.* Chicago: University of Chicago Press.

Mills, C.W. (2000 [1959]). *The Sociological Imagination.* Oxford: Oxford University Press.

Mortensen, N. (2003). *Det Paradoksale Samfund* [The Paradoxical Society]. Copenhagen: Hans Reitzels Forlag.

Nicol, B.J. (2001). As IF: Traversing the Fantasy in Žižek. *Paragraph: A Journal of Modern Critical Theory*, 24 (2): 140–155.

Nielsen, H.K. (2010). *Kritisk teori og samtidsanalyse* [Critical Theory and Analysis of the Times]. Aarhus: Aarhus Universitetsforlag.

Østerberg, D. (2002). *Durkheim og hans teorier om samfundet* [Durkheim and His Theories about Society]. Copenhagen: Hans Reitzels Forlag.

Park, R.E. (1915). The City: Suggestions for the Investigation of Human Behaviour in the City Environment. *American Journal of Sociology*, 20(5), pp. 577–612.

Park, R.E. (1928). Human Migration and the Marginal Man. *American Journal of Sociology*, 33(6), pp. 881–893.

Pedersen, A.Y. (2007). Richard Sennett – Det fleksible menneske [Richard Sennett – The Flexible Human]. 22 September, 2015, http://www.handoutnu.dk/2012/04/richard-sennett.html.

Petersen, A. and Willig, R. (2002). An Interview with Axel Honneth: The Role of Sociology in the Theory of Recognition. *European Journal of Social Theory*, 5(2), pp. 265–277.

Pierides, D. and Woodman, D. (2012). Object-Oriented Sociology and Organizing in the Face of Emergency: Bruno Latour, Gra Harman and the Material Turn. *The British Journal of Sociology*, 63(4), pp. 662–679.

Plummer, K. (1999). Introducing Chicago Sociology: The Foundations and Contributions of a Major Sociological Tradition. In: K. Plummer (ed.), *The Chicago School: Critical Assessments, Volume 1* (pp. 5–40). New York: Routledge.

Polanyi, K. (2001 [1944]). *The Great Transformation*. Boston: Beacon Press.

Powell, W.W. and Smith-Doerr, L. (1994). Networks and economic life. In: N.J. Smelser and R. Swedberg (eds.), *The Handbook of Economic Sociology* (pp. 368–401). Princeton, NJ: Princeton University Press.

Ritzer, G. and Goodman, D.J. (2003). *Sociological Theory*. 6th Edition. New York: McGraw-Hill.

Salih, S. (2002). *Judith Butler*. London: Routledge.

Salinger, J.D. (1991 [1951]). *The Catcher in the Rye*. Boston: Little Brown and Company.

Saussure, Ferdinand de (1998 [1916]). *Course in General Linguistic*. Illinois: Open Court.

Scelfo, J. (2015). Suicide on Campus and the Pressure for Perfection. *New York Times*, 2 August, p. 14.

Schmidt, L.-H. (1999a). *Diagnosis III: Pædagogiske forhold* [Diagnosis III: Pedagogical Matters]. Copenhagen: Danmarks Pædagogiske Institut.

Schmidt, L.-H. (1999b). *Diagnosis I: Filosoferende eksperimenter* [Diagnosis I: Philosophical Experiments]. Copenhagen: Danmarks Pædagogiske Institut.

Sennett, R. (1998). *The Corrosion of Character: The Personal Consequences of Work in the New Capitalism*. New York: W.W. Norton & Company.

Sennett, R. (2006). *The Culture of the New Capitalism*. New Haven: Yale University Press.

Sennett, R. (2008). *The Craftsman*. New Haven: Yale University Press.

Sennett, R. and Cobb, J. (1972). *The Hidden Injuries of Class*. New York: Knopf.

Shaw, C. (1930). *The Jack-Roller – A Delinquent Boy's Own Story*. Chicago: University of Chicago Press.

Simmel, G. (1971 [1908]). The problem of sociology. In: D.N. Levine (ed.), *Georg Simmel – on Individuality and Social Forms* (pp. 23–35). Chicago: University of Chicago Press.

Simmel, G. (1971a [1908]). The stranger. In: D.N. Levine (ed.), *Georg Simmel – on Individuality and Social Forms* (pp. 143–149). Chicago: University of Chicago Press.

Simmel, G. (1971b [1903]). The metropolis and mental life. In: D.N. Levine (ed.), *Georg Simmel – on Individuality and Social Forms* (pp. 324–339). Chicago: University of Chicago Press.

Simmel, G. (1971c [1908]). How Is Society Possible? In: D.N. Levine (ed.), *Georg Simmel – on Individuality and Social Forms* (pp. 6–22). Chicago: University of Chicago Press.

Simmel, G. (1998 [1908]). Sociologiens problem [The problem of sociology]. In: G. Simmel, (ed.), *Hvordan er samfundet muligt? Udvalgte sociologiske skrifter [How Is Society Possible? Selected Sociological Texts]* (pp.19–48). Copenhagen: Gyldendal.

Smith, A. (1937 [1776]). *An Inquiry into the Nature and Causes of the Wealth of Nations*. Volume 1 & 2. London: Everyman's Library.

references   255

Sørensen, M.P. and Christiansen, A. (2013). *Ulrich Beck: An Introduction to the Theory of Second Modernity and the Risk Society.* New York: Routledge.

Stormhøj, C. (1999). Kønnets regerende dronning: en introduktion til køn og krop i Judith Butlers forfatterskab [The Reigning Queen of Gender: An Introduction to Gender and Body in the Works of Butler]. *Kvinder, køn og forskning [Women, Gender and Research]*, 8(2), pp. 53–66.

Thatcher, M. (1987). Aids, Education and the Year 2000! (Interview). *Woman's Own*, 31/10.

Thomas, W.I. (1966 [1927]). Social disorganization and social reorganization. In: W.I. Thomas (ed.), *On Social Organization and Social Personality* (pp. 3–10). Chicago: University of Chicago Press.

Thompson, C. (2005). *Making Parents: The Ontological Choreography of Reproductive Technologies.* London: MIT Press.

Tonboe, J. (2009). Georg Simmel – det sociale livs former og typer [Georg Simmel – the forms and types of social life]. In: M. Hansen (ed.), *50 Samfundstænkere* [50 Societal Thinkers] (pp. 263–284). Copenhagen: Gyldendal.

Weber, M. (1978a). *Economy and Society.* Volume 1. Berkeley: University of California Press.

Weber, M. (1978b). *Economy and Society.* Volume 2. Berkeley: University of California Press.

Weber, M. (1978c). Politics as vocation. In: *From Max Weber: Essays in Sociology* (pp. 77–128). London: Routledge.

Weber, M. (1991 [1930]). *The Protestant Ethic and the Spirit of Capitalism.* Hammersmith: Harper-Collins.

Weber, M. (2002 [1919]). *Schriften 1894–1922* [Writings 1894–1922]. D. Kaesler (ed.), (pp. 474–511). Stuttgart: Kröner.

Weber, M. (2012). *Collected Methodological Writings.* London: Routledge.

Whyte, W. (1943). *Street Corner Society – The Social Structure of an Italian Slum.* Chicago: University of Chicago Press.

Willig, R. (2003). Indledning [Introduction]. In: R. Willig (ed.), *Axel Honneth: Behovet for anerkendelse* [Axel Honneth: The Need for Recognition] (pp. 7–23). Copenhagen: Hans Reitzels Forlag.

Wirth, L. (1938). Urbanism as a Way of Life. *American Journal of Sociology*, 44(1), pp. 1–24.

Žižek, S. (1989). *The Sublime Object of Ideology.* London: Verso.

Žižek, S. (1991a). *For They Know Not What They Do – Enjoyment as a Political Factor.* London: Verso.

Žižek, S. (1991b). *Looking Awry: An Introduction of Jacques Lacan through Popular Culture.* Cambridge, MA: MIT Press.

Žižek, S. (1992a). *Enjoy Your Symptom! Jacques Lacan in Hollywood and Out.* London: Routledge.

Žižek, S. (1992b). In his bold gaze my ruin writ large. In: S. Žižek (red.), *Everything You Always Wanted to Know about Lacan (But Were Afraid to Ask Hitchcock)* (pp. 211–272). London: Verso.

Žižek, S. (1993). *Tarrying with the Negative – Kant, Hegel, and the Critique of Ideology.* Durham: Duke University Press.

Žižek, S. (1994). The specter of ideology. In: S. Žižek (red.), *Mapping Ideology* (pp. 1–33). London: Verso.

Žižek, S. (1996). *The Indivisible Remainder – Essays on Schelling and Related Matters*. London: Verso.

Žižek, S. (1997). *The Plague of Fantasies*. London: Verso.

Žižek, S. (2000). *The Fragile Absolute: Or, Why Is the Christian Legacy Worth Fighting For?* London: Verso.

Index

Abbott, Andrew 63–4
absolutism 74
abstract thought, nature of 222–7
abstract trust 153
actants, networks and 199–203
acting, in social interactions 148–51
action: affective 26; purposive rational 25; reciprocity of 57; traditional 26; value-rational 26
actor network theory (ANT) 119, 198–203
Addams, Jane 66
Adorno, Theodor W. 7, 28, 44, 100
adventure capitalism 29–30
affective action 26
agency deficit 51–2
aleatory materialism 113–18
alienated labour: Marx's characterisation of 16; Weber's rationalisation thesis of 25–8
À l'ombre des majorités silencieuses ou la fin du social (Baudrillard) 12
Althusser, Louis 108–9, 181, 186, 235; analytical approach of 124–7; ideology as interpellation 113–18; imaginary and symbolic identification 114–18; theory of state 109–13
altruistic suicide 5, 42
ambiguity: of individuality 60–2; of urban life 70–2
American Journal of Sociology 63
American pragmatism 163

American Sociological Association 63
American Sociological Society 63
analysis, sociological: attention points for 241–5; nature of 221–7
Andersen, Hans Christian 213–15
Andersen, Niels Åkerstrøm 99
anomic suicide 5, 42
anomie 41–4, 104
anorexia 157
ANT (actor network theory) 119, 198–203
apparatus of bodily production 188
apparatuses of state 111–13
Arendt, Hannah 131, 233
army, repression of homosexuality in 216
artistic criticism 121, 125–6
assignment formulation 242
Association for the Taxation of financial Transaction and Aid to Citizens (ATTAC) 88
Asylums (Goffman) 150–1
Augustine, Saint 122
Austin, John Langshaw 185
autonomy 236–9
autopoiesis 93, 96

Bachelard, Gaston 238
back stage 149
bad faith 233–4
Badiou, Alain 226
banal cosmopolitanisation 139
banality of evil 131

index   259

Baudrillard, Jean 12
Bauman, Zygmunt 6, 12–13, 71, 127–8; analytical approach of 142–3; *Community: Seeking Safety in an Insecure World* 132–4; critique of modernity 128–9; *Globalization: The Human Consequences* 132; on modern bureaucracy 129–31; on modernity and morals 131–2; *Modernity and the Holocaust* 127–9; on new existential insecurity 132–5
Beauvoir, Simone de 181, 183, 188
Bech, Henning 10
Beck, Ulrich 71, 97, 127–8, 227, 238; analytical approach of 142–3; cosmopolitanisation concept 138–40; on radicalised individualisation 140–2; *Risk Society: Towards a New Modernity* 10, 127, 136; second modernity concept 135–6; on side effects of modernity 136–8; *What is Globalization?* 138
Becker, Howard 62
Bell, Daniel 127
Bell, Gwen 175–6
Bell, John 175–6
Bentham, Jeremy 77
Berger, Peter 232–3
Berkeley Socialist Review Collective, The 194
Bindestrich-Soziologie 7
biological determinism, gender and 182–4
biopolitics, sexuality and 78–80
Birth of the Clinic, The (Foucault) 73
Bjerre, Henrik Jøker 225
Blumer, Herbert 66
Bodies That Matter (Butler) 184
body: apparatus of bodily production 188; bodily consciousness 154; bodily stigma 151; *see also* gender
Boltanski, Luc 50, 108–9; analytical approach of 124–7; *On Justification: Economies of Worth* 122; justification regime theory 121–4; *La souffrance à distance* (Boltanski) 124; *The New Spirit of Capitalism* 122; project spirit theory 118–21
Borgius, Walther 17
Bourdieu, Pierre 72–3, 236–9; analytical approach of 88–90; habitus

concept 84–8; on symbolic violence 80–4
bourgeois society *see* capitalism; public sphere
bourgeois spirit 119
Boyles, Robert 205–7
Bretton Woods 165
bulimia 157
Bulmer, Martin 64
bureaucracy: bureaucratic spirit 119; modern bureaucracy 129–31; Weber's concept of 26–7
Burgess, Ernest W. 65
Butler, Judith 179–80, 192; analytical approach of 195–6; *Bodies That Matter* 184; challenges to established gender categories 180–4; *Gender Trouble* 180–4, 195; "Performative Acts and Gender Constitution" 184; performative construction of gender 184–7

Calvinism, capitalism and 14–15, 26–8, 31–2
Camus, Albert 43
capital: cultural 85; defined 84; economic 85; Marx's view of 21; social 85
Capital (Marx) 20–2
capitalism: accumulation in 78; adventure 29–30; alienation and 15–16; artistic criticism of 121; bourgeois spirit in 119; historical materialism and 15–20; industrial and bureaucratic spirit in 119; link to globalisation 133–5; Marx's characterisation of 20–2; new 120–1, 134; project spirit in 118–21; Protestant ethic and 14–15, 26–8, 31–2; rational 28–30; rationalisation thesis 25–8; social criticism of 121; spirit of 28–32; surplus value in 20–1; Weber's characterisation of 22–4, 28–32; *see also* flexible capitalism; work
Carlson, Jan 120
Cast Away 2
Catcher in the Rye (Salinger) 43
Catholicism: as basis for stop-and-go-luxury living 31; suicide rates and 5

character: character-based stigma 151; impact of flexible capitalism on 166–9; judges of 223

Chiapello, Ève 50, 108–9; analytical approach of 124–7; justification regime theory 121–4; *The New Spirit of Capitalism* 122; project spirit theory 118–21

Chicago School 54–5, 146; influence on later individualisation theories 70–1; sociohistorical content of 62–3; theoretical approaches of 64–6; *see also* Park, Robert Ezra; Simmel, Georg

Chinatowns 67

citizenship regime 122

"City, The" (Park) 63, 67

city life *see* urban life

On the City of God (Saint Augustine) 122

class: class struggle 19–20, 87–8, 111; effect of French Revolution on vii, 19; functional differentiation 94–9; habitus and 84–8; mobility of 87–8; power and 83; status and 33; *see also* capitalism; social differentiation

clientilisation 104

closed systems theory 93–4

cocoon, protective 155

codes, communication 98–9

collective consciousness 39

collectives 200

Coming of Post-Industrial Society (Bell) 127

commodities: commodity fetishism 212, 214–15; Marx's view of 21

communication codes 98–9

communication media 98–9

communicative action 104

communicative rationality 149

Community: Seeking Safety in an Insecure World (Bauman) 132–4

Comte, Auguste vii, 37, 197, 232

consciousness, levels of 154–5

constitution, modern 203–7

contemporary diagnosticism 8–11, 227–31

contemporary society *see* modernity

contract argument 4, 205

Contribution to the Critique of Political Economy, A (Marx) 17

Corrosion of Character, The (Sennett) 164–70

cosmopolitanisation 138–40

craftsmanship, value of 170

criminology 232

critical theory 100

criticism 124–7; artistic 121, 125–6; critical capacity of ordinary people 124–7; infrastructure of 121–4; justification regimes 121–4; social 121, 125

culture: burden of 155; as component of life world 104; cultural capital 85

Culture of the New Capitalism, The (Sennett) 164

cumulative life narrative 169–70

cyborg figuration 192–4

"Cyborg Manifesto, A" (Haraway) 193–4, 195

cynicism 214–16

delayed gratification 165

Deleuze, Gilles 120

delineation of phenomenon 242–3

depression, prevalence among American students 35–6

Derrida, Jacques 181, 185

determinate negation 210

determination in the last instance 112

determinism 232–6

deviance 150–1

Dewey, John 64

diachronic linguistics 81

diagnoses of the times, sociology as 8–11, 227–31

Dialectic of Enlightenment (Horkheimer and Adorno) 28

dictatorship of the proletariat 111

Diesel, Rudolf 202–3

diesel engine, production of 202–3

differentiation 92–4; functional 9, 94–9, 106–7; horizontal 106–7; public sphere 103–6; system and life world 103–6; systems theory 92–4; vertical 106

diffraction 190–1

disciplinary power 76–8

disciplinary society 78

disengagement, times of 134–5

(dis)organization in urban life 62–6

index   261

division of labour: contribution to Holocaust 130; *The Division of Labour in Society* (Durkheim) 37, 39, 41–2; Marx's view of 19–20, 22; *The Wealth of Nations* (Smith) 17–18

Division of Labour in Society, The (Durkheim) 37, 39, 41–2

domesticity regime 122

doxa 83–4

"Do You Know the Type?" 86

Durkheim, Émile 5–6, 36–7, 199; analytical approach of 51–2; conception of structure-agency relationship 51–2; *The Division of Labour in Society* 37, 39, 41–2; general theory of social integration 37–41; *L'Année Sociologique* 38; *Rules of Sociological Methods* 38–9; *Suicide* 42; theory of anomie 41–4; theory of solidarity 39–40

Ecological Communication (Luhmann) 99

economic capital 85

Economy and Society (Weber) 24

egalitarian ideal of marital roles 172

egoistic suicide 5, 42

Eichmann, Adolf 129–31, 232–3

Eichmann in Jerusalem (Arendt) 131

Eisenhower, Dwight 226

emerging properties of social 3

emotional abstinence 176

Emperor's New Clothes, The (Andersen) 213–15

empirical case 242

Engels, Friedrich: characterisation of capitalistic society 11; *The German Ideology* 16; historical materialism 15–16; letter to Walther Borgius 17; *Manifesto of the Communist Party* 16, 19, 163–4

enlightened false consciousness 212

Enlightenment, rationalisation process of 135

epistemological scholasticism 238

Essence of Christianity, The (Feuerbach) 16

ethical demand 128–32

ethical scholasticism 239

evil, banality of 131

Ewald, François 137

existential insecurity, modernity and 132–5

exogenous shocks 176

exploitation of workers 16, 19, 22

face of the Other 128–32

facework 148

factish 198, 206–7

false consciousness, ideology as 211–12

family life, work and 170–7

feminism: cyborg figuration and 192–4; feminist critical empiricism 189; situated knowledge and 188–92; *see also* gender

fetish: commodity fetishism 212, 214–15; defined 198; in primitive religion 207

Feuerbach, Ludwig 16

fields 82–4

figurations: cyborg 192–4; Onco-Mouse™ 192; primate 192

flexible capitalism: characteristics of 163–6; escape routes from 169–70; hidden dangers of 177–8; rationalised time in 164–5; work culture under 166–9; work-life dynamics in 170–7

Fontenelle, Bernard Le Bovier de 3

formal sociology 56

formation of society (*Vergesellschaftung*) 57

Foucault, Michel 72–3, 97, 185, 187; analytical approach of 88–90; analytics of power 73–6; on bipolitics and sexuality 78–80; *The Birth of the Clinic* 73; on disciplinary power relations 76–8; *History of Sexuality* 78; history of the present 9; *The Will to Knowledge* 78

Frankfurt School 44; *see also* Habermas, Jürgen; Honneth, Axel

freedom 18, 232–6

French Revolution vii, 19

Freud, Anna 210

Freud, Sigmund 155, 235

front stage 149

functional differentiation 9, 94–9, 106–7

function systems 96–9

gamekeeper metaphor 129

Gemeinschaft 238

gender 179–80; biological determinism and 182–4; challenges to established gender categories 180–4; as a construction 183; interdisciplinary approach to 187–8; performative construction of 184–7; situated knowledge and 188–92

Gender Trouble (Butler) 180–4, 195

German Ideology, The (Marx and Engels) 16

Gesellschaft 238

Giddens, Anthony 71; analytical approach of 159–60; reflexive modernity theory 151–4; on self in reflexive modernity 154–8; structuration concept 157–8

globalisation: cosmopolitanisation and 138–40; link to capitalism 133–5

Globalization: The Human Consequences (Bauman) 132

god trick 189

Goffman, Erving 62; on acting and territories 148–51; analytical approach of 159–60; *Asylums* 150–1; on deviance 150–1; focus on social interaction 146–7; microsociology 145–8; *Stigma* 150–1

Grande, Edgar 138

gratification, delayed 165

Greimas, Algirdas J. 199

Habermas, Jürgen 28, 44–5, 91–2, 239; diagnoses-of-the-times and 228; immanent critique 100–1, 103, 106; on system and life world 103–6; theory of the public sphere 100–3

habitus 84–8

Hanks, Tom 2

Haraway, Donna 179–80; analytical approach of 195–6; cyborg figuration 192–4; "A Cyborg Manifesto" 193–4, 195; interdisciplinary approach of 187–8; "The Promises of Monsters" 190–1; "Situated Knowledges" 188–92

Harding, Sandra 188

Hegel, Georg Wilhelm Friedrich 45, 220, 222–7

heteronomy 236–9

Heydrich, Reinhard 129

Hidden Injuries of Class (Sennett) 166

hierarchical differentiation 95

historical materialism 15–20

History of Sexuality (Foucault) 78

history of the present 9

Hitler, Adolf 129

Hobbes, Thomas 205–7; contract argument 4; *Leviathan* 122

Hochschild, Arlie 161–2, 170–1; analytical approach of 177–8; on cultural exchange of work/family life 170–1; *The Managed Heart* 171; microsociological perspectives on work/family life 171–3; *The Second Shift* 171–2; *The Time Bind* 172–7

holism: Durkheim's concept of 39; Marx's analyses and 32–5

holistic science, sociology as 222–4

Holocaust, modernity and 128–32

homo oeconomicus 75, 231, 238

homosexuality: as *avant-garde* 10; feminism and 183; historical repression of 75; repression in army 216

Honneth, Axel 36–7; analytical approach of 51–2; conception of structure-agency relationship 51–2; "Organized Self-Realization: Some Paradoxes of Individualization" 50; *Struggle for Recognition* 45–6; theory of recognition 44–9; writings on social pathologies 49–51

horizontal differentiation 106–7

Horkheimer, Max 28, 44, 100

"How Is Society Possible?" (Simmel) 57–8

Hughes, Everett 62

Hull House 66

human ecological trajectory (Chicago School) 65

human migration 69

"hyphenated" sociology 7–8

"the I" 235

ideal speech situation 45, 102–3

ideal typical method 24–5

ideas, matter and 32–4

identification: imaginary 114–16; symbolic 115–16

identity, as component of life world 104; *see also* gender

ideology: as false consciousness 211–12; function of 209; as interpellation 113–18; sublime object of 210–15

illusio 82
imaginary identification 114–16
immanent critique 44, 100–1, 103, 106
immigrants 88
impatient capital 165
impression management 147–8
impure sociology 218–19
inappropriate/d others 190, 192
"Inclusion and exclusion" (Luhmann) 95
independent subjects 210
individual behaviour 4
individualisation 37, 50; ambiguity
of individuality 60–2; autonomy
236–9; Durkheim's theory of social
integration 37–41; heteronomy
236–9; Honneth's theory of recognition 44–9; interdependence and
142–3; metropolitan individuality 60–2; "the me" versus "the I"
235; radicalised 140–2; reflexive
modernity and 154–8; see also
reflexive self
individualism 50; ambiguity of 60–2;
methodical individualism 22–3; metropolitan individuality 60–2
industrial and bureaucratic spirit 119
industrial society 137–8
industry regime 122
infrastructure of criticism 121–4
inspiration regime 122
institutionalised practice of sociology 6–8
integration 91
interaction: acting in 148–51; deviance
in 150–1; pure relationships 154;
spheres of 46–8; stigma in 150–1;
territories and 148–51; unwritten
rules of 145–8
interdependence 142–3
interpellation: gender norms and 186;
ideology as 113–18
interpersonal relationships, need for 1–2
Irigaray, Luce 181
Israeli Mossad, Eichmann captured by
130–1
Italian renaissance 101

James, William 64
judges of character 223
On Justification: Economies of Worth
(Boltanski and Thévenot) 122
justification regimes 121–4

Kant, Immanuel 9
Kantorowicz, Ernst 214
Kierkegaard, Søren 155
king's two bodies, political theology
of 214
knowledge, as power 75
Kristeva, Julia 181

labour, division of: contribution to Holocaust 130; The Division of Labour
in Society (Durkheim) 37, 39, 41–2;
Marx's view of 19–20, 22; The
Wealth of Nations (Smith) 17–18
Lacan, Jacques 115, 181, 213
La condition postmoderne (Lyotard) 128
language: diachronic linguistics 81;
as medium for intersubjective
understanding 44–5; synchronic
linguistics 81
L'Année Sociologique 38
La souffrance à distance (Boltanski) 124
late modernity x, 37, 153
Latour, Bruno 197–8, 225–6; analytical approach of 218–19; ANT (actor
network theory) 199–203; factish
concept 206–7; "modern constitution" concept 203–7; We Have Never
Been Modern 205–7
law, two sides of 215–18
Left Hegelians 16
Lenin, Vladimir 111
"lesser men" 123
Leviathan (Hobbes) 122
Levinas, Emmanuel 132
life world 103–6
linguistics: diachronic 81; intersubjective understanding and 44–5;
synchronic 81
liquid modernity 12–13, 128
Løgstrup, Knud Ejler 132
love, sphere of 47
Luhmann, Niklas 91–2, 240–1; analytical approach of 106–7; diagnoses-of-
the-time and 228; Ecological
Communication 99; functional dif-
ferentiation theory 9, 94–9, 106–7;
"Inclusion and Exclusion" 95; Social
Systems 93; systems theory 92–4
Lukács, György 55, 212
Lykke, Nina 181–2
Lyotard, Jean-François 127–8

Machiavelli, Niccolò 101
machine, state as 111–12
macrotheories 230
Managed Heart, The (Hochschild) 171
Manifesto of the Communist Party
(Marx and Engels) 11, 16, 19, 163–4
man-made disasters 137
Marcuse, Herbert 100
market regime 122
marginalisation, urban life and 66–70
"marginal man" 68–70
marital roles, cultural ideals for 171–2
market: importance of 108–9; justification regimes 121–4; project spirit of 118–21; *see also* capitalism
Marx, Karl 14; on alienated labour 16; analytical approach of 32–4; *Capital* 20–2; characterisation of capitalistic society 9, 11, 20–2; on commodity fetishism 21, 214–15; *A Contribution to the Critique of Political Economy* 16–17; dictatorship of the proletariat 111; economic critique 16–17; *The German Ideology* 16; historical materialism 15–20; *Manifesto of the Communist Party* 16, 19, 163–4; surplus value concept 20–1; symptomal reading of 110–11; "Theses on Feuerbach" 16–17
Marxism 101, 210; ideology as interpellation 113–18; scientific character of 117; sociology of the state 109–13
material-semiotic actor 188
material social facts 38
material turn 198
matter, ideas and 32–4
"the me" 235
Mead, George Herbert 45–6, 64, 235
means-ends mentalities 26–8
mechanical solidarity 39–40
media: communication 98–9; in public sphere 101–2
mesotheories 230–1
methodical individualism 22–3
methodological nationalism 140
"Metropolis and Mental Life, The" (Simmel) 55, 57–8, 60–1
metropolitan individuality 60–2
microsociological perspectives: on reflexive self 145–8; on work and family life 171–3

migration 69
Milgram, Stanley 131, 232–3
military: military-industrial complex 226; organisation model 164; repression of homosexuality in 216
Mills, Charles Wright 163
Minh-Ha, Trinh 190, 192
Mirror Stage as Formative of the I, The" (Lacan) 115
mobility, class 87–8
modern constitution 203–7
modernism 212
modernity: ambiguity of individuality in 60–2; anomie in 41–4; bureaucracy in 129–31; cosmopolitanisation 138–40; defined 135; diagnoses of the times 8–11; downsides of 51–2; functional differentiation in 94–9; Holocaust and 128–32; individualisation in 50; interdependence in 142–3; late 37, 153; liquid 12–13, 128; modern constitution 203–7; morals and 131–2; new existential insecurity in 132–5; public sphere 100–3; radicalised individualisation in 140–2; recognition theory and 44–5; reflexive 136–8, 151–8; second 128, 135–6; side effects of 136–8; social integration theory in 39–40; social pathologies in 49–51; solid 13; "the stranger" as representation of 58–60; systems theory and 100–3
Modernity and the Holocaust (Bauman) 127–9
monarch's two bodies, political theology of 214
money, as communication media 98
morals, modernity and 131–2
Mossad, Eichmann captured by 130–1

nationalism, methodological 140
Nazi Germany: modernity and 128–32; transgression in 216
Nebenfolgen 136
necessity, realm of 18
networks, actants and 199–203
new capitalism 120–1, 134; *see also* flexible capitalism
new existential insecurity 132–5
new risks 137

New Spirit of Capitalism, The (Boltanski and Chiapello) 122
New Yorker, The 131
nonconsciousness 154
nonmaterial social facts 38
North Korean solution 157

objectivity, scientific 188–92
OncoMouse™ figuration 192
ontological scholasticism 238
ontological security 154–8
open systems theory 93–4
operational closure 94
opinion regime 122
organic solidarity 39–40
"Organized Self-Realization: Some Paradoxes of Individualization" (Honneth) 50
other-reference 93
outsourcing: of domestic responsibilities 175–6; functional differentiation and 99
overdetermination 112

panopticism 77–8
Panopticon 77–8, 150
Park, Robert Ezra 62, 65; "The City" 63, 67; on urban sociology and marginality 66–70
Parsons, Talcott 98
Pasteur, Louis 201
peg-communities 135
performance 185
"Performative Acts and Gender Constitution" (Butler) 184
performativity: gender and 184–7; versus performance 185
phenomenon, sociological analysis of 241–5
Philosophy of Money, The (Simmel) 62
physical stigma 151
Peirce, Charles Sanders 64
Plague of Fantasies (Žižek) 209
Polish Peasant in Europe and America, The (Znaniecki and Znaniecki) 63, 65–6
positivist position for sociology 38
postmodernism 212
post-structuralism 199
power: biopolitics 78–80; class and 83; disciplinary 76–8; Foucault's

analytics of 73–6; knowledge as 75; panopticism and 77–8; subjection and 75; substantialist conception of 74; symbolic violence as 80–4
practical consciousness 154
pragmatism, American 163
primate figuration 192
prison structure, panopticism 77–8
private sphere 149
"Problem of Sociology, The" (Simmel) 56
project spirit 118–21
proletariat, dictatorship of 111
"Promises of Monsters, The" (Haraway) 190–1
protective cocoon 155
Protestant ethic: capitalism and 14–15, 26–8, 31–2; suicide rates and 5
Protestant Ethic and the Spirit of Capitalism, The (Weber) 27–8
psychoanalysis 198, 207, 209–10
psychophysical mechanism 67
public sphere 100–3, 149
pure relationships 154
purification work 203, 206
purposive rational action 25

queer: as feminist figuration 192; resignification of 186

radical constructivism 189
radicalised individualisation 140–2
Ramses II 226
rationalisation thesis (Weber) 25–8, 135
rationalised time 164–5
Rawls, John 239
Reagan, Ronald 193
realism 212
realm of freedom 18
realm of necessity 18
reciprocity of actions 57
recognition, Honneth's theory of 44–9
re-feudalisation of the public 102
reflexive modernity 136–8; self in 154–8; theory of 151–4
reflexive self 144–5; impact of acts and territories on 148–51; microsociology and 145–8; norm and exception 159–60; reflexive modernity and 154–8
regimes of justification 121–4

relationships, need for 1–2
religion: Calvinism 14–15, 26–8, 31–2; Catholicism 5, 31; secularisation 26; sociology of 2
resignification 186
reverse of law 215–18
rights, sphere of 47
risk society: characteristics of 137–8; cosmopolitanisation 138–40; radicalised individualisation in 140–2
Risk Society: Towards a New Modernity (Beck) 10, 127, 136
Roberts, Yvonne 134
Romania, orphanages in 1–2
Rousseau, Jean-Jacques 122
Royal Society, The 206
Rules of Sociological Methods (Durkheim) 38–9

Saint-Simon, Henri de 122
Salinger, Jerome David 43
Salk Institute for Biological Studies 201
Sartre, Jean-Paul 141, 233
Saussure, Ferdinand de 81
Scandinavian Airlines System 120
Schmidt, Lars-Henrik 10–11
scholasticism 237; epistemological 238; ethical 239; ontological 238
Science Question in Feminism, The (Harding) 188–9
scientific authority 205–6
scientific objectivity 188–92
Second Chicago School 62
second modernity 128, 135–6
Second Sex, The (Beauvoir) 183
Second Shift, The (Hochschild) 171–2
secularisation 26
security, ontological 154–8
segmentary differentiation 95
self, in reflexive modernity 154–8
self-confidence 47
self-creation 93
self-realization: Honneth's concept of 46–9; impact of social pathologies on 49–51
self-reference 93
self-reproduction 93
self-respect 47
Sennett, Richard 50, 125, 134, 161–2; analytical approach of 177–8; *The*

Corrosion of Character 164–70; *The Culture of the New Capitalism* 164; on "escape routes" of flexible capitalism 169–70; flexible capitalism concept 163–6; *The Hidden Injuries of Class* 166; on work culture 166–9
sexuality: bipolitics and 78–80; homosexuality 10, 75
shame, reflexive modernity and 156
side effects of modernity 136–8
Simmel, Georg 54–5; on ambiguity of individuality 60–2; analytical approach of 70–1; on content and forms of social interaction 55–8; "How Is Society Possible?" 57–8; influence on later individualisation theories 70–1; "The Metropolis and Mental Life" 55, 57–8, 60–1; *The Philosophy of Money* 62; "The Problem of Sociology" 56; research approach of 55–6; "The Stranger" 55; "the stranger" type 58–60
situated knowledge 188–92
Small, Albion 62–3
Smith, Adam 17–18, 122
social (dis)organization in urban life 62–6
social bond, two sides of 215–16
social capital 85
On the Social Contract (Rousseau) 122
social contracts 4, 116; *see also* capitalism
social criticism 125; *see also* immanent critique
social differentiation 37; functional differentiation 9, 94–9; horizontal 106–7; public sphere 103–6; system and life world 103–6; systems theory 92–4; vertical 106
social facts: Durkheim's concept of 38; material 38; nonmaterial 38
social integration, Durkheim's theory of 37–41
social interaction: acting in 148–51; ambiguity of individuality 60–2; ambiguity of urban life 70–2; content and forms of 55–8; deviance in 150–1; marginality and 66–70; metropolitan individuality 60–2; pure relationships 154; social (dis)organization in urban life 62–6; spheres

index   267

of 46–8; stigma in 150–1; "the stranger" type 58–60; territories and 148–51; unwritten rules of 145–8

Socialist Review, The 193–4

Socialist Review East Coast Collective, The 194

social pathologies 49–51

social psychological trajectory (Chicago School) 66

"the social question" 10–11

social space: class structure 84–8; fields 82–4; symbolic violence in 80–4

Social Systems (Luhmann) 93

social theory: empirical foundations of 8; versus "hyphenated" sociology 7

society: formation of 57; material objects in 201; sociological conception of 197–8; sociology as theory of 37–41

sociological analysis 240–1; attention points for 241–5; nature of 221–7

sociology: American versus continental approaches 7; analytic strategy of 1–6; Chicago School 146; development as field vii–viii; as diagnosis of times 8–11, 227–31; as discipline in flux 239–41; etymology of term vii; formal 56; as holistic science 222–4; "hyphenated" 7–8; impure 218–19; Latour's critiques of 200–1; mesotheories in 230–1; sociological analysis 221–7, 241–5; status as discipline 6–8; as theory of recognition 44–9; as theory of society 37–41

solidarity: as component of life world 104; Honneth's concept of 47–8; mechanical 39–40; organic 39–40

solid modernity 13

Sorel, Georges 117

sovereign state 23–4

speech act theory 185

spheres of interaction 46; sphere of love 47; sphere of rights 47; sphere of solidarity 47–8

spirit of capitalism: bourgeois spirit 119; industrial and bureaucratic spirit 119; project spirit 118–21

stalled gender revolution 172

Star, Ellen Gates 66

state: apparatuses 111–13; contract argument 4, 205; importance of 108–9; as machine 111–12; Marxist sociology of 109–13; Weber's definition of 23–4; *see also* market

Stigma (Goffman) 150–1

Stoics 139

stop-and-go-luxury living 31

Stranger, The (Camus) 43

"Stranger, The" (Simmel) 55

stratification: habitus and 84–8; stratificatory differentiation 95

structural coupling between function systems 99

structuralism 81, 199

structuration 157–8

structure-agency relationship: Durkheim's concept of 51–2; Honneth's concept of 51–2

Struggle for Recognition (Honneth) 45–6

subjection 75

sublime object of ideology 210–15

substantialist conception of power 74

suicide: altruistic 5, 42; anomic 5, 42; egoistic 5, 42; prevalence among American students 35–6; as social fact 5–6

Suicide (Durkheim) 42

superego 235

surface of law 215–18

surplus value 20–1

surveillance 76–8

symbolic identification 115–16

symbolic signs 153

symbolic violence 80–4

symptomal reading of Marx 110–11

synchronic linguistics 81

synthesis 225

systems, life world colonised by 103–6

systems theory 92–4

Tarde, Gabriel 199

territories 148–51

Thatcher, Margaret 12, 208–9

"Theses on Feuerbach" (Marx) 16–17

Thévenot, Laurent 122

thinking technologies 193

Thomas, William Isaac 62, 66, 70

time: rationalised 164–5; work-life dynamics 174

Time Bind, The (Hochschild) 172–7

times, diagnoses of 8–11, 227–31

times of disengagement 134–5
Tönnies, Ferdinand 238
total institutions 150–1
Total Quality Management (TQM) 174
traditional action 26
traditional ideal of marital roles 171–2
trajectories (Chicago School): human
ecological trajectory 65; trajectory of
social (dis)organisation 65–6
transgression 215–16
transitional ideal of marital roles 172
transitional spaces, creation of 215–18
translations 202–3
translation work 204
tribal stigma 151
trust, abstract 153
truth effects 226

uncertainty: cosmopolitanisation and
137–8; new existential insecurity
132–5; radicalised individualisation
and 137–8; risk society 137–8
unconscious, thesis of 207–10
unconsciousness 154
"Urbanism as a Way of Life" (Wirth) 65
urban life: ambiguity of 70–2; ambiguity of individuality in 60–2; cities
within cities 67; marginality and
66–70; metropolitan individuality
in 60–2; social (dis)organization in
62–6
usefulness 170

value-rational action 26
Vergesellschaftung 57
vertical differentiation 106
violence, symbolic 80–4
vitalism 199, 218

wage labour, alienating character of 16
Wannsee Conference 129
Wealth of Nations, The (Smith) 17–18
Weber, Max 14, 20–1, 119, 238;
analytical approach of 32–4; *Economy and Society* 24; ideal typical
method 24–8; methodical individualism and 22–4; *The Protestant Ethic
and the Spirit of Capitalism* 27–8;
rationalisation thesis 25–8, 135; on
relationship between Calvinism and
capitalism 14–15, 26–8, 31–2;
spirit of capitalism 28–32
We Have Never Been Modern (Latour)
205–7
What is Globalization? (Beck) 138
Will to Knowledge, The (Foucault) 78
Wirth, Louis 62, 65
Wittig, Monique 181
Wizniewski, Wladek 66
work: as analytical prism 162–3;
cumulative life narrative and 169–70;
work culture under flexible capitalism
166–9; work-life dynamics 170–7

Young Hegelians 16

Zeitdiagnose ("diagnosis of the
times") 9
Žižek, Slavoj 197–8, 214–15;
analytical approach of 218–19;
Plague of Fantasies 209; on
sublime object of ideology 210–15;
thesis of the unconscious 207–10;
on two sides of social bond
215–18
Znaniecki, Florian 63, 65–6
zombie science 140

index   269